Where Triples Go to Die

PRAISE FOR *WHERE TRIPLES GO TO DIE*

"*Where Triples Go To Die* … takes readers on an emotional ride of a lifetime, with great characters and a well-imagined and masterfully constructed plot…. The reader is submerged in the dynamics of campus politics and can't stop reading, compelled to discover what happens next…. Phil Hutcheon is a terrific writer and he knows how to surprise readers with intense and dramatic turns in the story. The writing is impeccable and the dialogues are exceptional, plunging the reader into the worlds and the inner workings of the hearts of the key characters … [while unveiling] a sporting culture … exciting to explore … and a quality of humor that is rare in books of this genre."

—*Readers' Favorite*

"[F]illed with sex and scandal alongside the much more serious topics of suicide, alcoholism, and race, the quick-paced novel never loses momentum. Hutcheon's writing style is down to earth, and he has a way of making the reader feel a connection with each of the characters and wonder what could possibly happen next…. Hutcheon also uses the book as a way to explore African Americans' role in baseball, both past and present. Readers will also be impressed with the historical references and quotes throughout the novel."

—*Manhattan Book Review*

"Love, race, academia, and baseball converge in the eminently readable *Where Triples Go To Die*. Readers will follow the story with the same anticipation and interest as die-hard baseball fans following their favorite teams, knowing there may be a rally in any inning, and that the game—or book—isn't over until every out is called."

—*Seattle Book Review*

"Hutcheon masterfully draws even the non-baseball lover into a story that explores the serious topics of race, suicide, alcoholism, abandonment, and unplanned pregnancy, while adding a healthy side of humor and sarcasm and small, interesting doses of relatable quotes and facts."

—*Tulsa Book Review*

"I finished Phil Hutcheon's new novel in a few sittings. It was a fantastic read. I cannot recommend it highly enough. If you have any interest in fiction that is funny, topical, and insightful about college sports, gender, race, class, and academic issues, *Where Triples Go To Die* is a terrific book that fits the bill."

—*Matt Wetstein, President, Cabrillo College*

"Phil Hutcheon has invented a new genre, a hilarious mix of sports, sex, and snarky dialog that just might entice a lost generation to put down their iPhones and Xboxes long enough to finish a book, with pleasure!"

—*Diane Oren, Past President,*
Academic Senate, Delta College

PRAISE FOR THE AUTHOR'S
PREVIOUS NOVELS

"Original, deftly crafted, and a truly memorable read from beginning to end, *Desperation Passes* is very highly recommended reading and establishes author Phil Hutcheon as an impressively talented novelist who will keep his thoroughly entertained readers looking eagerly toward his next book."

—*Midwest Book Review*

"You don't have to love football to get swept up in *Desperation Passes*. You probably don't even have to like football, because you'll quickly come to care deeply about Allenby and Wade, find yourself charmed by their clever repartee, and cheering them both on to come out on top."

—*Manhattan Book Review*

"Chronicling the battle against a host of life obstacles from bad grammar, drugs, and crime to paralysis-inducing political correctness, fickle lovers, and domestic violence, *Nobody Roots for Goliath* is a serious-minded, absorbing novel that reads like a true story because it draws so heavily upon harsh reality. Highly recommended."

—*Midwest Book Review*

WHERE TRIPLES GO TO DIE

PHIL HUTCHEON

Publisher: Inkwater Press | www.inkwaterpress.com

Paperback
ISBN-13 978-1-62901-514-9 | ISBN-10 1-62901-514-8

Kindle
ISBN-13 978-1-62901-515-6 | ISBN-10 1-62901-515-6

Printed in the U.S.A.

3 5 7 9 10 8 6 4 2

This book is dedicated to Joan Caroline Bailey, girl of my dreams, light of my life, who picked the right time to fall in love . . . with baseball.

A NOTE ON THE TITLE
OF THIS BOOK

I first became aware of the clause from which this book's title is taken many years ago, via a note pinned on my office door at Menlo College by my colleague John Heinbockel, quoting Joe Garagiola on a Saturday Game of the Week broadcast: "Willie Mays' glove is the place where triples go to die." Subsequent research revealed that this description had emerged in connection with earlier players, notably Tris Speaker, and may even have originated in connection with Shoeless Joe Jackson.

The triple is the most exciting play of the game. A triple is like meeting a woman who excites you, spending the evening talking and getting more excited, then taking her home. You're never sure how it's going to turn out.

—George Foster, OF, San Francisco Giants, Cincinnati Reds, New York Mets, Chicago White Sox

PART I: 2015

Whoever wants to know the heart and mind of America had better learn baseball.

—Jacques Barzun, from *God's Country and Mine*,
engraved on a plaque at the Baseball Hall of Fame
in Cooperstown, New York

We believe that [the integration of Major League Baseball] was the beginning of the modern-day Civil Rights movement in our country. When you put it all together, you have a story that is actually bigger than the game of baseball itself.

—Bob Kendricks, Negro Leagues historian

Like Major League Baseball, our colleges and universities have witnessed a serious lack of opportunity for African Americans in baseball. In both the playing ranks and the coaching ranks, the rates of participation for African Americans are very poor. The vision of Jackie Robinson that baseball would be fully representative of the American people on the playing field, in the coaching ranks, and in the front office, is far from being fulfilled.

—Richard Lapchick, Director, Institute for Diversity
and Ethics in Sport

I think it's very beneficial for young people to play in multiple sports. There was so much that I did in my training for football and basketball that ended up helping me in baseball. Those sports made me a more explosive athlete. I would urge kids to play many different sports.

—Aaron Judge, New York Yankees' outfielder
from Linden, California, quoted by Mike Klocke,
The Record

CHAPTER 1

If God himself came down to ride the natural earth, that is what He would aim to look like.

—of Thomas Sutpen in William Faulkner's
Absalom, Absalom!

Not that he was fit for teaching, but not being fit for teaching didn't prove that he was fit for anything else.

—of Ezra Gordon in Erik Tarloff's *The Man Who
Wrote the Book*

Julius "Juke" Jackson stood at the kitchen sink, in his left hand a bottle of bourbon and in his right a pistol, angled sharply upwards into his mouth. Malcolm Wade, after ringing the bell and knocking on the door of the shabby student apartment to no avail, had picked a path through swirling fast food trash and abundant dog turds to peer into the curtainless kitchen window. As he saw Jackson's index finger flex over the trigger, Wade dropped the pizza he was carrying, slammed both hands against the window, and screamed: "Nooooo!" His eyes squeezed shut to avoid the imminent spectacle of Jackson's brains splattered on the ceiling.

3

When he opened them a second later, no shot had been fired. No blood was in sight; no brains had been splattered. Wade spasmed with relief as Jackson set the bottle down on the counter, stepped toward the window, and slid it open.

"What the fuck, Doc? You scared the shit out of me."

"I scared *you*? What do you think you—"

"Oh, you mean this?" Jackson still had the pistol in his hand. He held it up to the window for closer inspection. "It's a squirt gun, Doc. Full of bourbon. Just loaded it."

Wade breathed, gulped, and swallowed. "Oh. Then you're not trying to—"

"Kill myself? Nah. I'm just gettin' drunk. I ain't ruled it out, but—"

"Amazing how authentic those things are." Wade was still staring at the plastic gun.

Jackson nodded. "Where I come from, cops shoot kids who point these at them all the time."

"I can see why."

Jackson had been born in Oakland and raised in Stockton. The local gendarmes were not exactly noted for their discretion. Still, Wade had to wonder how he would have reacted himself if someone drew a bead on him with such a convincing replica. He bent down to pick up the pizza at his feet.

Jackson leaned into the window for a closer look. "Is that from Fat's?"

Wade nodded. "The Instant Heart Attack. Extra meat, extra cheese." He lifted the box above his head to inspect the bottom and make sure he hadn't also added extra crap.

"You tryin' to kill me?"

"That's the plan. Death by cholesterol." *A consummation devoutly to be wished.*

Jackson had walked in the decisive run in yesterday's loss to eliminate his California State University team from what could have been a first-ever crack at the College World Series. Afterward when Wade had called and then emailed to check on him, Jackson had sent back a despondent message indicating that his live-in girlfriend had left him after the game—and had taken up with Johnny Dawes, the CSU shortstop drafted by the Dodgers and expecting a seven-figure signing bonus.

"You better come in," Jackson said now. "Watch out for the dog—"

"Shit!" His vision partially blocked by the pizza box, Wade had stepped directly into a moist pile. "Who the hell does your landscaping around here?"

Wade had mostly surrendered, with misgivings, the case against capital punishment, but for urban dog owners who allowed their darlings to defecate in public space without cleaning up after them, a choice between lethal injection and life imprisonment without possibility of parole seemed about right.

"Lot of pit bulls in this complex. Best take your shoes off then."

Wade came back around to the entrance and removed his soiled sneakers. Jackson met him at the door and ushered him into a clean but completely barren dwelling.

"Camellia took all the furniture. You okay on the floor?"

Wade nodded, set the pizza box on the carpet between them, plopped himself down, and considered from this fresh perspective the veritable study in contrasts the two of them formed. Six-and-a-half feet tall, a sculpted two hundred and twenty-five pounds, with aristocratic ebony features to rival a young Poitier's or Denzel's, Jackson seemed to have been drawn from a graphic artist's version of a superhero. If not quite able to leap tall buildings in a single bound, he could nevertheless jump higher and run faster than all but a handful of mortals extant or in memory. A foot shorter, balding, bespectacled, pasty-faced, pencil-necked, paunchy in the places where he wasn't scrawny, and out of breath instantly if he ran for the phone or dragged his aging ass up a staircase, Wade sprang from a different kind of cartoon heritage altogether.

"Her and her cousin come by with a truck, cleaned the place out while I was out there dyin' on the mound. Didn't even leave the fuckin' card table for me to eat off. Ain't that the sorriest dump-job you ever heard?"

"Top five, anyway," Wade said, thinking about the first time his wife Angela had broken up with him. At Manny's, no less. First burger in his life he couldn't finish. Maybe he and Jackson weren't such opposites after all. The carbohydrates before them might be a sort of litmus test. "Do you want to eat, or are you still too—"

"You good with your hands? I got no plates either. I mean, she took it *all*. You drinkin' bourbon or water?"

"Water's good. You want to talk about the girl first or the game?"

"Right now I just want to forget about 'em both. When'd you start your new career as a delivery boy?"

Wade pointed at the squirt gun. "Backup plan. My counseling job didn't seem to be panning out too well."

After years of indentured servitude as an adjunct instructor, Wade had briefly held a full-time position as a compliance officer in the CSU Athletic Department. When his friend and bene-factor Arthur Allenby had taken on the presidency, Wade had been offered a *best of both worlds* option, combining a half-time counseling role with a tenure-track position in the English Department. Short of a paying gig as JLo's personal nipple-twister, it was pretty much as close to a dream job as a man of Wade's modest talents could hope to attain. He taught four courses a year now and spent the rest of his time trying to keep student-athletes like Jackson on the tortuous path to graduation.

"You a okay counselor, Doc. I'm just a shitty pitcher. I best stick with outfield—or football."

Jackson had come to CSU instead of Alabama, Ohio State, or USC because he had been assured of the opportunity to play both football and baseball. The other schools had recruited him for football only and required him to be in spring practice rather than on the diamond. With its more flexible policy, CSU had seized upon the opportunity to land a four-sport superstar in high school, recruited by several other major universities for basketball or track as well. Academically ineligible in his first year, in his second he was the starring center fielder for CSU, but had been thrown into the closer role on the pitching staff when the relief core wore out during an unprecedented stretch of success in the conference playoffs. Even as a relative novice he had thrived on the mound until the season's regionally televised finale.

"I went back on my DVR and watched that last at-bat you pitched again," Wade said. "That plate ump was squeezing you like I've never seen."

Wade had grown up with the innocent assumption that umpires, like doctors and police, could be counted on to render routinely unassailable judgments. His own playing days had not lasted long enough to prove conclusively otherwise, but decades of fandom had enlightened him, especially in recent years with the proliferation of television cameras clearly showing the path of pitches as they crossed the plate or failed, sometimes flagrantly, to do so. Even Major League Baseball umpires regularly called strikes that were several inches outside or below the sanctioned zone, while the strike at the letters was so rarely called as to border on obsolescence. Other pitches clearly over the plate could be called balls at the slightest whim. The best you could hope for was consistent idiosyncrasy. The home plate umpire in the CSU championship game had reduced his ninth inning strike zone to the approximate size of Beyoncé's thong.

"What I thought, too."

"That ball four he called looked like it was belt high down the middle."

"I took somethin' off that motherfucker, too. Worried it was goin' over the wall, tell you the truth. Almost rather give up a slam, though, than walk that run in. What a punk-ass way to lose, end the season." Jackson took a bite, chewed. "What you gonna do about it, though?"

Wade gestured again at the toy gun. "Not blow your head off with the real thing, I hope."

Jackson took another bite and shrugged. "Finish this pizza first anyway."

"Camellia was gone when you got back?"

"Didn't even leave a fuckin' note. Neighbors saw the truck. Can't believe I was so stupid. Woman next door said she seen Dawes over here before, too. Guess Cammie think she gonna be partying with Magic Johnson and Puig and all them boys in L.A. now. But that fucker JD won't never make no MLB. Throw him a slider away, he chase it every damn time. Try to pull it every time, too. Man's a walkin' double play."

"He hit the ball pretty hard yesterday," Wade pointed out. Dawes had doubled twice and had driven in all three of the runs that CSU had added to Jackson's solo homer in their elimination loss.

"He can hit a fastball, I'll give him that. Won't see none once they find that hole in his zone, though."

Wade hadn't studied Dawes' at-bats carefully enough to be sure if this was an accurate scouting report or sour grapes, but Jackson's grasp of the game had been impressive all season.

"You seen him play shortstop, right?"

"Good hands, decent arm," Wade said. "Doesn't look like he has great range."

Jackson laughed. "That's cuz he don't never try for nothin' he ain't sure he can get. That streak he had, games with no errors, broke the conference record? How many times you seen him dive for a ball?"

Wade remembered hearing the same complaint about Steve Garvey at first base from his teammates, notably Don Sutton, whose statistics had allegedly suffered because the Gold Glover was protecting his own. The sabermetricians who saw only the fielding percentages and didn't put their eyes on the guys in the field would not get a true sense of who was stopping runs from scoring and who was not. Jackson, it was worth remembering, could have begged out of taking the mound in yesterday's crucible, after pitching in the previous four consecutive games, but when his coach had come out of the dugout with the bases loaded and waved him in from center field, he had taken the ball with the season on the line and no margin for error. There was no doubting his own competitive spirit. Wade thought back now over the games he had seen Dawes play and concluded that Jackson's assessment of his teammate was probably accurate.

His judgment about females was another matter altogether. Camellia Sanchez had flitted from one prominent jock to another in her two-plus years on academic probation at CSU, leaving already a trail of tears and litigation worthy of the Kardashians, her apparent role models.

"How long were you and Camellia together?"

"Six months, somethin' like that. She been talkin' 'bout us two gettin' married this summer."

"And you've been tryin' to slow her down?"

"She been pushin' it a while, but I was cool with it. I don't want to get no AIDS or nothin' from the skanks at the bars and parties. You married, right?"

"Right."

"I think I seen your wife with you one time. She come to one of our games with you?"

"She popped in for a few innings."

"Brought her laptop with her, right?"

"They're inseparable, I'm afraid."

"I seen her picture in your office, too. She hot."

"I know."

"She some kind of big shot around here, ain't she? Vice-president or—"

"Dean of Humanities."

"She make more money than you, then?"

"Way more."

"She smarter than you, too?"

"Way smarter."

"She try to tell you what to do?"

"We're still . . . working on that. Fortunately, there's not much I *can* do, so it hasn't been a huge issue so far. She's aware of my limitations. Emptying the trash is about the high end of my household skills." This was no exaggeration. Wade had once fractured a finger while trying to bait a trap that had proven too sensitive for mice or rats but more than ready to mangle human flesh, and a recent attempt to replace the battery in a smoke detector had resulted in a near-electrocution.

"You a bookworm, huh, Doc?"

"Born and bred." This was not strictly true. Wade's father had been a pilot, a boatman, a builder, a man at ease in the physical world, a DIY guy on the order of *Great Expectations'* Mr. Wemmick (*I am my own engineer, and my own carpenter, and own plumber, and my own gardener, and my own Jack of all Trades*); Wade's best friend growing up had spent half of his life in the bowels of a '57 Chevy. Somehow neither nature nor nurture had provided even rudimentary mechanical aptitude.

"You need any help with that shit, your toilet blows up or somethin', you give me a call, I come over, fix you up. I worked construction, done plumbing, dry wall, electric, all that shit. My uncle taught me when I lived with him. Made me some good money in the summers."

"I'll keep that in mind." So far the toilets in Wade's dwelling had been behaving themselves, but the mere thought of dealing with one of them in volcano mode was enough to make him cringe now. He admired and envied those capable of dealing with such eruptions. "You're a well-rounded man."

Jackson shrugged again and chewed more pizza. "Could use a little more bookworm in me. Sometimes them books we s'pose to read for our classes, I can't hardly keep my eyes open five minutes."

Wade nodded. "A lot of academic writing is pretty dry." What had Allenby called it? *Arcane, jargon-driven nonsense that no one would read without a blowtorch to his balls.*

"You wrote one of them books, too, right?"

Wade nodded again, reluctantly. A minimally revised version of his distant dissertation on Hemingway had been published to little notice and less acclaim a few years ago by a small press that Wade had never heard of before appearing under its imprimatur. In spite of its negligible reception, the publication had been enough to secure him a nomination for tenure among the comparably undistinguished faculty of the state's second tier university system.

"How many pages is it?"

"Four hundred, give or take." *None would have wished it longer than it is.*

"Shit. How long that take you?"

"About ten years, give or take a—"

"FUCK!"

"—month or two. My dissertation advisor was"—*a senile, sadistic lunatic*—"hard to please."

"Bet you wanted to beat some sense into that fool."

"The thought may have crossed my mind once or twice." Wade was reminded again of Theodor Streleski, the Stanford PhD candidate in math who had served a mere seven years in prison for taking a hammer to the skull of his advisor upon learning that he wouldn't be getting his degree after *nineteen* years of graduate school. If ever the punishment had fit the crime . . . .

Jackson brought Wade back from a revenge fantasy worthy of inclusion in a Tarantino flick. "What you think I ought to do about Camellia? I mean, I paid for all that shit she took."

"There's a spare room at our house you can stay in for a while if you like, until you get your bed back. I'll call my wife right now to make sure, but I know she'll be okay with it."

"No need. I can sleep on the floor here. I slept on plenty of floors before, in lots worse places than this."

"Are you sure?

"I'll keep busy. Be getting ready for football soon. Start my workouts tomorrow. Lot of shit to catch up on, you miss spring ball. I 'preciate you comin' by, though. You want to take the rest of this home with you?"

Wade shook his head regretfully. "I'd never make it through the door."

"No pizza 'llowed after you get married?"

"Not in my house. No cheeseburgers either."

"Shit, Doc, what you got to live for, then? Maybe you'd best move in with me instead."

Wade laughed and then stood to go. He was out the door and carefully reshodding after liberal application of his napkin when Jackson said softly behind him, "Camellia come back, you think I should give her another shot?"

Wade winced. *What should I do, Doc, if the cancer comes back?*

"Depend on if she bring back the furniture, I guess," Jackson answered for himself, before Wade could generate a response. Jackson looked back over his shoulder into his ransacked apartment. "Wonder if I'll ever even see her here again." He gestured at the remains of the pizza. "JD won't be takin' her out to no fancy dinner, I promise you that. He a cheap motherfucker. Borrowed fifty off me last month, never paid me back."

"Sounds like they deserve each other," Wade said. "Maybe you'd better just . . . try to move on."

How many times had people told Wade the same thing about Angela, after she'd left him to return to the abusive ex-Buffalo Bill she had crossed the continent to flee? Or about his impossible first wife Brenda, before Angela had come into his life? Even if the advice made perfect sense, even if all the evidence pointed to its inescapable truth, how did you tell your imbecile heart what to feel or not feel?

"You prob'ly right. Thanks for comin', Doc. I call up Fat's, give you a good review."

"I could use one. Last time a supervisor reviewed my work, she said I was an embarrassment to the university and an affront to the human race."

"That's the lady died when she fell out of her office window, right?"

"Fell or was pushed. The authorities never quite got to the bottom of that." Scandal-ridden CSU Athletic Director Delia

Herman had either committed suicide or received assistance in her deliverance from a pile of debts, threats of blackmail, and the specter of prosecution.

Jackson whistled and shook his head. "You didn't shove her out, did you, Doc?"

"I can't say I wasn't tempted."

Wade rinsed his hands at an outside faucet, then pulled a business card from his wallet, added his home phone number, and extended it toward Jackson. "Call me if you need to talk, okay?"

"You already emailed me your home phone, Doc. I'm good."

"Take the card, okay? Just in case. Call me anytime."

Jackson read the number and then saluted Wade with the card. "Don't worry about me, Doc. I be okay."

Wade drove home, hosed off his shoes and floor mat on his small patch of lawn, and then stepped into the house in his socks. He slipped immediately in the freshly waxed entryway and smacked down on his tailbone.

"Safe!" Angela signaled with a flourish, as she stepped in from the living room to observe the aftermath of the crash landing, crossing a book in one hand, a finger inserted lest she lose her place, and a brimming wine glass in the other, somehow spilling nary a drop.

Wade rubbed his buns and tried to smile as she set Wordsworth down and helped him up. "Maybe I should stick with that headfirst dive I picked up from Pete Rose."

She sniffed the air around him, a tad more emphatically than was necessary to make the point forthcoming. "Maybe you should call a divorce attorney: you smell like Manny's again."

"Fats," Wade corrected. "Just an emergency delivery. I only ate one piece of—"

"Bullshit, Wade. You couldn't stop at one piece of pizza if you were chained between Gandhi and Cesar Chavez in a food strike line. What the fuck happened to your shoes?"

Wade gestured toward the lawn and started to explain, but she interrupted: "Did you know that you have holes in both of your socks? You swore you were going to throw the old ones away. Even the Salvation Army won't take *those*."

Wade shrugged, declining an argument he was never going to win.

"The whole, holey collection. I'm tossing them all this weekend," Angela said. "Or maybe we'll have a bonfire. We can roast those fucking underpants of yours that look like they survived the Holocaust, too. I'll bet you're wearing one of those pairs right now, aren't you?"

Old fashions please me best. "You'll have to frisk me to see. Feel free."

She fingered the jersey he was wearing instead. "I can't believe you still wear *this*. Who's 23?"

"Tito Fuentes," Wade said. "A few other guys might have worn that number, too."

"Isn't he from another century?"

Wade nodded. "And planet."

"I'm sure he'll make a lovely flame."

The phone rang, forestalling at least for the moment further plans for the purge of Wade's wardrobe.

Angela picked up. She told Wade, "It's Juke Jackson."

Wade frowned. "I just left him. What—"

She shrugged and handed him the landline.

Wade took the phone, mock fury in his tone: "How the hell did you get this phone number?"

"Sorry to bug you again so soon, Doc, but—"

"It's no problem, Juke. What—"

"Camellia come back."

"Wow! That was fast. That's good news, I guess, as long as—"

"Not so good, Doc."

"Oh. Why—"

"She beat up. That Dawes fool punch her in the face. Think you could come back over here right now, talk to her, while I go kick his ass?"

CHAPTER 2

I want every young man in America to feel some strong peer pressure in terms of how they are supposed to behave and treat women.

—Barack Obama

This is a college campus. Some might have been on a mean street somewhere, and that isn't the case anymore. You've got to learn to adapt to your new environment.

—Bob Stoops, former Head Football Coach, University of Oklahoma

One of the first issues Arthur Allenby had tackled upon taking over the CSU presidency was to improve campus safety. The number of assaults, on women in particular, had been spiraling for years, and he was intent on changing the culture of the campus quickly. He had begun by brusquely dismissing an entrenched security director who had managed, while presiding over a legendarily dysfunctional crew, to turn his sinecure into a twenty-hour per week job with twelve weeks of vacation, at twice a full professor's pay. Allenby had next elected to bypass the collection of head-hunting firms lining up at his door to soak the university with exorbitant fees for recommending candidates cashiered for incompetence elsewhere. Instead, he had gone straight to military contacts dating back to his own service to identify recently retired veterans who might be suitable campus leaders. Cenon Aquino had quickly emerged from the pack to claim the job. Wade had served on the committee that interviewed him and had never been more impressed by an applicant or his history.

Aquino's grandfather had fought the Japanese as a guerilla in the Philippines. His father had served three tours with the 3rd Marine Division's 3rd Reconnaissance Battalion in Vietnam. There had never been a question that Cenon was going to serve in the military, too. He had left an eye, an arm, and a leg behind in Ramadi when an IED exploded under his ill-equipped Humvee. Even grievously wounded, he had managed to return fire to repel attacking insurgents and direct a call to a rescue team that saved three of his fellow soldiers before he passed out from loss of blood. Nominated for a Medal of Honor, he had been awarded a Silver Star. He had spent three years mastering the use of his prosthetic limbs and touring veterans' medical facilities to inspire other amputees to do the same. When hired by Allenby, he had hit the ground running, and already he had made significant strides in elevating Campus Security from the status of a punch line. He had begun by tapping the most obvious local talent pools: over the objections of some hardcore unionistas, trainees in the university's police academy and other administration of justice majors had been invited to serve their internship units by participating in campus patrols. Outreach to women and minorities had increased their representation on the force. Security cameras had been purchased and stationed to oversee especially vulnerable areas, such as stairwells, where many of the attacks in recent years had come. Emails and tweets now went out regularly to all students and staff, reminding them to maintain vigilance on campus and especially in the parking lots, and advising women to travel in company or to request an escort when traveling alone. The issues hadn't disappeared overnight, by any means, but data indicated that steady progress was being made on Aquino's watch. It was he to whom Wade, with an emphatic nudge from his wife, turned now.

Jackson had hung up the phone before any plea for reason or moderation could be uttered, so Wade had been faced with the need for some fast thinking—fortunately one of Angela's many gifts. At her bidding Wade quickly found Dawes' address at a campus fraternity in his computer files while Angela dialed the security office. Wade had thought about calling Dawes himself and urging him to absquatulate in order to avert a potential homicide, but Angela pointed out that Wade might then be aiding a criminal in his escape, and besides that would give Dawes the advantage if he decided to ambush Jackson instead of fleeing. Aquino was on duty, and when he came on the line, Angela handed the phone to Wade and dashed to grab her purse and change clothes. Wade briefed him. Aquino said he would alert the officer nearest Dawes' frat house immediately and would also go over there himself to head Jackson off. It was exactly the kind of personal touch that Aquino had already become known for and that Wade had been hoping for. He told Aquino he was going to Jackson's apartment to check on Camellia and gave the officer Angela's cell phone number. Aquino promised to call back soon with an update on his intervention.

Angela tossed Wade some shoes and they jumped into his Civic, still redolent of meat and cheese, among other lingering aromas, and hurried to Jackson's apartment. Camellia Sanchez cracked the door cautiously behind a chain at their knock and then pulled it open to offer a dramatic view of the damage her assailant had inflicted. She was a short, statuesque Latina with streaked blonde hair and starlet-level physiognomy, now trans-figured by a nasty, swollen bruise across one cheek and eye. Wade had seen her in her fully groomed glory in the stands at several CSU baseball games, and the contrast now was compelling. It was all he could do to stop himself from reminding Angela of when he'd seen a similar disfiguration of her own perfect features, at the hands of her erstwhile lover, Ronnie Parker. *What is it with you girls and purple?* he managed to keep to himself.

"Juke is gone," Camellia said. "I begged him not go, not to leave me, but he wouldn't listen. He's gonna kill that motherfucker."

Let's see, would that be the motherfucker that you dumped him for yesterday?

"We're trying to head that off. Can we come in? I'm Wade, and this is Angela Hardy."

"There's nothing to sit down on, but—"

And would that be because you packed up all the furniture he paid for and gave it to the motherfucker?

"—you guys can come in if you want."

She unlocked and pushed open the screen door to let them in. "I tried to call him, but he turned his cell phone off."

This was out of Wade's realm of expertise, in several ways, but was probably standard procedure, he figured, when you were on the way to an ass-kicking. No time to be distracted by a tweet from your sweetie.

Angela stepped in ahead of Wade, took Camellia by an arm, and guided her toward the bedroom for a private conversation, part of the plan concocted on the way over. Angela could prob-ably talk her into doing what needed to be done faster outside the presence of a man she had never met before. They needed to get her to the cops to make a statement and to get her exam-ined and treated as soon as possible. Angela popped back out a moment later when her cell phone rang. She handed it to Wade—giving him, not for the first time, the look that said, *when the fuck are you going to get one of your own?*—and returned to her ministrations.

"We've got Juke Jackson," Aquino said.

"I hope he didn't—"

"He didn't do anything. We intercepted him at the entrance to Dawes' frat. He realized we came to keep him out of trouble. He wants to talk to you. Here he is."

"Doc, is that you?"

"Don't be pissed off, Juke. We just wanted to keep you—"

"I know, Doc. I ain't pissed off at you. Plenty of time to settle this shit later. You with Camellia now?"

"We're going to take her to the police station."

"She okay with that?"

"My wife is talking her into it. Should we come and pick you up? Or do you want to meet us at—"

"School cop say he bring me home now. He won't leave me, 'less you with me. Have to come back, get my car later."

"Okay, we'll wait for you here, then take Camellia—"

"What about Dawes?"

Wade didn't know what to say about that. He took a shot. "I guess the cops will probably arrest him after Camellia gives her statement."

By the time Angela and Camellia emerged from the bedroom, the campus cop dispatched by Aquino had deposited Jackson. Wade opened the doors to the Civic and stationed Jackson in the front passenger seat, the women in the back.

Jackson ducked on the way in but still bumped his head on the ceiling. "Man, these little Japanese cars run forever, don't they, Doc? You bring this home from World War II or what?"

"What's that *smell* in here?" Camellia wanted to know, olfaction apparently unimpaired by the roundhouse she had taken to the face.

"Don't worry," Angela said. "He's going give this car a bath or drive it off a cliff, *tomorrow*."

It was not for nothing that Wade had named his ride Aborto. Impervious to vehicular aspersion, as to assaults on his attire or playlist, he shrugged and hit the gas. "It'll probably get us where we need to go."

Angela called ahead to the police station to try to expedite Camellia's report, but there was still a half-hour wait before an officer was made available. Angela had requested that a female officer take the report, but it was a male, Wen Chang, who eventually approached them, introduced himself, and then escorted Camellia to an interview room. After twenty minutes with her, he emerged by himself and indicated that Camellia would be transported to the nearest hospital for the medical examiner's report.

They drove to the hospital to wait for her there, parked, and were walking up to the entrance when a siren screeched. An ambulance roared by them and jerked to a stop. Three bleeding teenaged males were hustled in ahead of them, one screaming piteously.

Angela cringed. "Oh, Jesus, it looks like that kid got shot in the face."

"Gangbangers," Jackson said.

Angela looked at him accusatively. "How do you know they're gangbangers?"

Wade stifled a snort. *Maybe they're on their way to choir practice.*

Jackson said mildly, "Their clothes, their hats, their tats."

"*You've* got tattoos," Angela said. "That doesn't prove—"

"Not like that, I ain't."

Angela had a tattoo herself, although not one accessible to the public. Wade was still searching for the bet he couldn't lose to capture it for the upgrade he was planning for his screen saver.

They followed the chorus boys into the hospital and tried to get comfortable in a jammed, cacophonous waiting room. An ancient boxy television blared over a dozen animated conversations, complaints, sobs, moans, or pleas for treatment. A massive redheaded construction worker who had apparently sawed off a couple of fingers sat slumped in a chair with a bandage sagging toward his belly as he struggled to hold his hand above his heart. A tiny Asian woman in a wheelchair tried to comfort a wailing child with a pencil stuck in his eye. Wade wondered where an assault case would fall in the chain of the hospital's priorities. At least the gangbangers were being attended to; no doubt they'd soon be stitched up and back to spreading cheer in the community.

Angela, ever mindful of the value of her time, had brought along her Wordsworth, and she sat with her nose in it now as Wade and Jackson tried to figure out what to say to each other. Wade was naturally curious about what Camellia had told Jackson, but he wasn't sure how welcome any inquiries along those lines would be right now.

Jackson saw him struggling for a place to start and helped him out. "And we thought yesterday was fucked up."

Wade nodded. "Definitely puts losing a baseball game into perspective."

"I told her Dawes was a fool. Guess she had to find out for herself."

"Has he done something like this before?"

"Don't know about with another girl, but he always in the shit, lookin' for trouble. Got into fights a couple of times with guys on our own team, had to be pulled off. Mostly little guys, nobody bigger than him. Our second baseman, Tony, he drop a low throw one time, they give the error to Dawes, right call but he 'bout had a fit after the game. Scorekeeper changed the call, give the error to Tony. He only 'bout five-six, five-seven, you seen him, but he don't take shit from nobody. Coaches had to break it up when them two went at it."

Coaches were also supposed to report such incidents to Wade, in his role as compliance officer, but this was the first he had heard of it.

"He way out of control. Likes to party, drink, smoke"—Jackson mimed a toke—"with his boys at the frat."

Angela marked her book with her finger, looked over. "Camellia told me he was drunk when he attacked her."

Jackson nodded. "They both drunk, I guess. She got sick, threw up or somethin', wanted to lay down by herself, I guess, but he wanted to . . . you know. Wouldn't take *no* for a answer."

Angela nodded. "That's more or less what she told me, too."

Wade wondered what *more or less* meant.

Jackson looked at Wade. "Dodgers ain't gonna be too thrilled when they read the police report."

"Fuck the Dodgers," Angela said hotly. Though this was a sentiment with which Wade had never before imagined finding occasion to take issue, he could see trouble coming now. "There's a woman in there"—she jerked her head toward the examining rooms—"who has been viciously assaulted, and—"

"Don't have to tell me," Jackson said. "I was on my way to—"

"We know what you were on your way to do, Juke," Wade said, glancing between them anxiously. "We're glad you didn't make the situation worse by getting yourself in trouble. We'll let the cops handle it."

"Speak for yourself," Angela said to Wade, before turning to Jackson. "I wish you had given the fucker a taste of his own medicine."

Jackson shrugged. "Maybe still time to get to that. What's that book you readin'?"

Angela, taken aback, held it up. "Probably not exactly your cup of—"

"Wordsworth. He a poet, right?"

"Right."

"He alive today, he probably be a rapper." Jackson looked at Wade for confirmation.

Wade glanced at Angela and considered his choices, imminent divorce again prominent among them. He turned back to Jackson and played it safe: "You think?"

"Only way to make any bank off poetry these days. How 'bout readin' us off one of his pieces?"

Angela blinked, recoiled from a sudden new shriek from the lad with the Number 2 lead in his eye, and then nodded. She glanced needlessly at her page, looked up, and began:

It is a beauteous evening, calm and free;
The holy time is quiet as a nun
Breathless with adoration.

She stopped and met Jackson's eyes: "We good?"

Jackson smiled. Wade looked around, soaking in the ambience for WW's hip-hop debut. "Lil Wayne couldn't have said it better himself."

An hour later, her face bandaged, Camellia emerged, accompanied by a harried nurse who looked like she was on the eleventh hour of her third twelve. "She needs to come back tomorrow for some more tests. There's a possibility of a concussion."

In light of the furniture shortage chez Jackson, Wade had conferred with Angela about offering their guest room to the reunited pair, but she had suggested giving them a couple hundred bucks for a motel room and a meal instead, arguing that they might prefer the privacy thus afforded. In an era when coaches made millions and student-athletes could be busted for accepting a free T-shirt, Wade wasn't one hundred percent sure he could do this without jeopardizing Jackson's eligibility, especially if Camellia got wind of it, since discretion was hardly her hallmark, but he decided under the circumstances to risk it. He had borrowed the bills from Angela, and while she accompanied Camellia back into the apartment, he drove Jackson to pick up his car, followed him home, then took him aside in the parking lot, showed him an envelope, told him it was a loan with no urgent repayment date, and asked him to keep the transaction to himself.

It couldn't have been the first time an athlete of Jackson's talents had been offered financial assistance, but the frown on his face now took Wade by surprise.

"I got money, Doc. Saved up from all them summer jobs I told you 'bout. Besides, she can sleep on the floor, same as me. Won't kill nobody. She the one moved the bed out of there. I already owe you for a pizza. You take that fine wife of yours out to dinner with your cash."

Wade stuffed the envelope back into his pocket.

"I 'preciate your help, hers too. I didn't really know how to talk to Cam about it, and you probably kept me out of jail tonight, maybe worse, if I'd caught up with that motherfucker. That officer with the fake leg and the fake arm, one eye, I'll bet he seen some crazy shit in the Army, huh?

Wade recalled that Jackson's mother had been in the Army, too, and had died in Iraq when he was a child. He wondered if the memory of her service had influenced Jackson's acquiescence to Aquino. "He surely paid his dues," Wade said. "Maybe yours and mine, too. I'm glad you listened to him."

Jackson nodded. "He 'bout half my size, didn't back down from me one bit." He looked away for a moment and then met Wade's gaze again. "You think they can put JD away for what he done?"

It was a good question. The record of convictions in domestic violence cases involving athletes with the potential to earn money for their universities or professional teams had so far been unimpressive, to put it mildly. A stern warning and a two-game suspension seemed to be the prevailing trend in punishment for the virile heroes who had punched, kicked, or sexually violated their wives, girlfriends, or escorts. Meanwhile, Tom Brady got kicked out of *four* games for (allegedly) letting the air out of a football.

"I guess it depends on the physical evidence they were able to find and on what she told the cops," Wade said.

Angela came out of the apartment with her cell phone to her ear and then handed it to Wade with the *when the fuck* look again.

"Dawes already has a lawyer. They've been invited to report to the police station tomorrow," Aquino said. "I've been asked to wait until the cops have a chance to interrogate him before I conduct my own interview, which I'll do as soon as possible afterward. And we need to make damn sure Julius Jackson stays away from Dawes' fraternity. If he shows up there again, we may not be able to keep him out of grief."

"You want to tell him yourself?"

"Put him on."

Jackson took the phone, listened solemnly for a minute, then said, "Yes, sir," and handed it back to Wade, who thanked Aquino and returned the indispensable item to its owner.

"Little man say he kick my ass hisself if I show up over there again."

Wade nodded. "Just let the cops do their job."

"Like they did in Stephenson, Missouri?" Angela, ever helpful, wanted to know, as she stowed her phone in her purse.

Jackson thanked them again and then headed inside to work out the bedless sleeping arrangements.

Wade and Angela had a late supper at a favorite restaurant, Wade choking down steamed salmon to offset his earlier splurge. He joined her in a cocktail before and wine during but, in deference to his driving duties, demurred when she ordered a cordial afterward. She put her arm around him when they reached his car in the parking lot.

"I'm glad you helped your friend. He seems like a good guy."

"He *is* a good guy. That girl, on the other—"

She leaned in to interrupt him with a liquid kiss. "You're a good guy, too."

He opened the door for her, closed it behind her, then got into the driver's seat and, having put the bill on a credit card, handed her the envelope with her cash. "So, the night is still young. Plenty of time yet for more good deeds. You want to go back and visit the Boy Scouts at the hospital, or—"

"Shut up and take me home, Wade." She swatted him with the envelope and then kissed him again, punctuating the smooch with a strategic squeeze. "If someone doesn't run his mouth too much on the way, he might get lucky when we get there."

CHAPTER 3

I have, all my life, been lying till noon; yet I tell all young
men, and tell them sincerely, that nobody who does not
rise early will ever do any good.

—Samuel Johnson, qtd. by James Boswell,
The Journal of a Tour to the Hebrides

English was what people who didn't know what to major
in majored in.

—Jeffrey Eugenides, *The Marriage Plot*

There were people Wade knew, his wife chief among them, who
bounced out of bed at daybreak, bright-eyed, bushy-tailed, and
ready to write a book before breakfast. Fuck Hemingway and
his five hundred words a day: Angela could blast out a thousand
before squeezing her orange juice. Wade was not like that. He
slept fitfully, often miserably, usually getting off soundly only an
hour or two before time to rise and . . . pine for a return to the
dear sweet pillow he was forced to forsake. It took hours for him
to become fully wakeful. In years past when he had endured the
indignity of eight o'clock classes, he had often wondered how his
students even pretended to understand the garbled nonsense that

passed his lips. (Of course, half of them were usually stuporous, too, recuperating from the revels of the night before, the other half AWOL, sensibly sleeping in at home.) Weekend mornings he had always prized for the opportunity to at least try to catch up on the z's he was missing, and he forced himself reluctantly upright now at nine o'clock when Angela poked her head in to tell him to pick up the bedside phone for the university president.

"I need to see you tomorrow morning," Arthur Allenby said after a brief exchange of greetings. "I want to make sure we stay on top of this business with Juke Jackson. I've got another research project for you, too."

Wade mumbled assent, set down the phone, rubbed his eyes, and started to swing his legs out of bed. Angela came back into the bedroom, took a healthy swig from the Bloody Mary she was toting, and handed it to him.

"Up before noon on a Sunday? This can't be good news."

Wade took a sip, popped his eyes at the dosage, and handed the firewater back to her.

She perched next to him on the bed, short-shorts rising provocatively, and ran a lacquered fingernail across his stubble. "How about breakfast in bed and I'll shave you after? You always miss this spot right under your nose."

Add barbering to the list of his deficiencies second marriage had made Wade aware of. Of course, he was usually so bleary-eyed when he tried, he could hardly be held accountable for the consequences. You couldn't hit what you couldn't see.

"Breakfast in bed, huh? What's on the menu?"

She unbuttoned her blouse, leaned in, braless, nipples at full alert, and reached for the front of his briefs. "Anything you want, mister. *A hard man is good to find.*"

"Thanks, Mae, but—"

"An ancient Chinese proverb says"—now she was leaning down to fertile ground—"man who wakes up with hard-on is . . ."

In urgent need of a pee. Wade managed not to kill the mood as the rest of Angela's sentence disappeared into his shorts. A full bladder was reported to improve the intensity of the male orgasm anyway, he remembered reading somewhere. Worth a try.

After the protracted delights of the previous night, epic from Wade's perspective, a fallow period had seemed likely, but apparently his wife's appetite had merely been whetted. Marriage was nothing if not a perpetual series of adjustments. Wade had suffered most of his life from the typical male twinned afflictions of a hyperactive imagination and chronic, acute sexual deprivation, his fantasy inventing for himself far more voluminous and varied satisfactions than he had managed in reality to procure. He understood completely the men who turned to pornography or paid for company when their brides doubled in size and decided that shopping for clothes to adorn their bloated forms was more fulfilling than sex. The prevailing view of the wives seemed to be that your dick was a youthful toy to be set aside when maturity and its attendant obligations arrived. He sometimes wondered what he might have accomplished in his life had he not squandered so many of his waking and half-sleeping hours hopelessly plotting interludes with the endless chorus line of women who caught his eye.

Wade had come of age in an era when skirts rose, seemingly overnight, from the middle of the calf to the middle of the thigh, from "See you in church" to "You can fuck me if you try." Breasts, in his boyhood rarely on full display outside the pages of *Playboy* or *Penthouse*, had still aroused within their padded bras, but with nothing like the impact of today's tit parade. It was not unusual now for a well-endowed and barely covered coed to plop herself down in the front row of his classroom, a few feet from his face, tantalizing him with vistas of twin peaks while he stood at the podium and tried his best to keep his eyes off the forbidden topography or the occasional panties-free beaver view below. These temptations he had always managed to resist, while maintaining faint hope of finding an appropriate channel for his passion. To have wooed and won at this late stage a woman whose desires equaled or even exceeded his own, after so many lost years of bottling up his lust, Wade counted among the least expected and most gratifying curves in his life's path—even if he was at times like these challenged to rise to the level of his bedmate's libido.

Afterward, having reciprocated, with interest, he complimented his purring partner on her efforts.

"Just remember what you miss when you start the day in the middle of the fucking afternoon."

"I suppose you tore off another chapter this morning before you came in here and had your way with me?"

Angela stretched luxuriantly, licked a finger, raised it, and made a check mark in the air. "Just warming up for you, tiger. Fuck the shave: go cook me some eggs. Easy on the cheese. And try not to burn the house down this time. Make some more Bloody Marys, too."

Wade assembled ingredients while Angela showered. After many years of reliance upon fast or frozen food, Wade's cooking was finally improving. He had picked up a few tips from Allenby, who excelled in the kitchen as everywhere else, and Angela's supervision had extended his range. He now sauteed onions and red peppers in olive oil, added eggs to the scramble, grated in some parmesan, lightly fried some sweet potatoes, and sliced some fresh strawberries. They lingered over the meal, Angela having also prevailed upon him to slow down the pace of his consumption so that the product of an hour's preparation was not wolfed down in five minutes.

"Not bad, Wade," she said, as she declined his offer to refill her coffee cup and reached instead for the vodka bottle. "There may be a spot for you as a sous chef at McDonald's if this tenure thing doesn't pan out at CSU."

"I just hope the dean remembers my extracurricular activities when I go in for my evaluation."

"Church and state, Wade. Don't forget: we have to keep them separate." A salacious waggle of her busy tongue accentuated the admonition and left him in confusion, as usual.

At the same time that Wade's hybrid position in English and Counseling had been created, Angela had been recruited away from the University of Connecticut to return to CSU as Dean of Humanities, thus becoming his boss for half of his assignment—and the portion that would determine his fate in the tenure wars to come. She had replaced a longtime incumbent, Simon Dedalus—inevitably, *Dean Deadass* to anyone who worked with or for him or viewed him from any of his many unpropitious angles. This worthy had never learned Wade's name in the seven years Wade had worked as a part-time instructor under his putative supervision. Along with his chief succubus, Gordon Brooks, Chairman of the English Department and the dullest man not hailing from Texas and never twice-elected President (*not only dull himself but the cause of dullness in others*), Dedalus had soon after Allenby's inauguration been relieved of his neglected duties and obliged to begin drawing his obscenely padded pension. (Wade had volunteered to save the state a packet by serving on a firing squad.)

Angela carried her Bloody Mary back to her computer now to tend to deandom's drudgery while Wade assessed the debris accruing from his culinary efforts. It appeared that he had once again grossly violated the single-digit limit Angela had imposed on his use of pots and pans. He rolled up his sleeves and plunged in, banged away cheerfully, and, as he made gradual inroads in the vast stacks of his tasks, even found himself humming. Sunday at home with someone you loved beat the hell out of Sunday anywhere else by yourself.

Angela came back into the kitchen to freshen her drink half an hour later and caught him in the act.

"Should we call in FEMA, or are you just about finished in here? What's that you're gargling?"

Wade's hum turned to words: *"I've Got You Under My—"*

"Sinatra." She no longer accompanied the ID with a question mark.

Cole Porter had written it, but, as with so many of his signature songs, FS had made this one his alone. Wade felt comfortable with the position that any other man who tried to record it should be garroted on the spot. He shuddered over the recollection of a brief recent exposure to Rod Stewart's croaking version on the radio. Better to listen to your dog licking his balls. Now even Dylan had joined the ranks of the *tribute artists* attempting the impossible task of measuring up to the master.

Angela saw an opening, Wade's arms raised to dry a frying pan, and goosed him.

"You should get some new tunes, dude—to go with your new moves." She licked her lips, winked, and faked a grab at his groin with her free hand.

"Wu Tang Clan, coming up," Wade promised. "Just give me another thousand years or so to get—"

"Hard again?" She followed the feint with the real deal, to small avail.

"—up to speed. Those eggs must have really agreed with you."

"Don't let it go to your head, bozo."

"Want to walk them off?"

"Let me know when you're ready."

She kissed him lightly on the lips and carried her drink back to her computer while Wade finished drying, then put on a sweat suit and did his stretching and calisthenics. Angela, firmly seconded by Allenby, had got him started on a workout routine. He was now regularly beginning his days, just as those distant, reviled high school gym teachers had preached, with a set of push-ups and sit-ups, exertions that a short time ago would have seemed likely to invite the summoning of a paramedic, if not a priest. Often on school days, instead of thrusting himself into the mortal combat required to secure a parking spot on campus—luminaries like Angela parked up front in their reserved spaces, leaving the peon faculty to war with students over anything within a day's march of the classrooms—Wade walked in to work, assured of burning more calories before his labors even began than many of his sedentary colleagues would expend all day. He sometimes even took an extra spin at noon with Erica Wiley, the new department chair, who was determined not to let her ascension to the ruling class interfere with her own admirable fitness regimen. Type-A Angela, naturally, went to a gym three times a week for a more intensive workout, under professional supervision, and ran five miles on the off-days. Wade wasn't crazy enough to try to keep up with that (*they stumble that run fast*), but on the weekends they usually went together for a walk, if not exactly leisurely, at least at a pace he could sustain if he kept his concentration on the rewards awaiting those who kept their equipment in proper working order.

After an hour's ramble, Angela poured another drink and went straight back to her computer. Wade showered, clipped his toenails, dug the lint out of his navel, reviewed in the newspaper the daily litany of atrocities across the globe, and found a dozen other excuses to delay heading for his. The belated publication of his first book had brought with it a contract for a second, and he was finally attempting to fulfill the destiny he had long ago staked out for himself. Trying to produce a new tome under the same roof with Superwoman was proving daunting, to say the least.

Like millions of other American boys before and after him, Wade had been forced to abandon the fantasy of becoming a professional baseball player when he failed to survive the first cut in junior high school. With this dream *nipped in the butt*, as one of his subsequent students would put it, two years later, he had discovered Hemingway, and, again in the company of deluded millions, decided to become a writer. An early and avid reader, he had formed many previous infatuations (Freddy the Pig, Bronc Burnett, Will Henry, Samuel Shellabarger), but it was *For Whom the Bell Tolls* that had made him feel that this was what he was meant to do with his life. After settling on this career path, with teaching as a *fallback plan*, Wade had found himself a long way down the pike with a shitload of quizzes, tests, and term papers on his odometer but very little writing of his own. Whenever he sat down to try to compose something, he remembered Hemingway's line in a letter to Charles Scribner: *That is why I like it at war. Every day and every night there is a strong possibility that you will get killed and not have to write.* Wade had never been to war; he had gone instead to class, where you were unlikely, at least so far, to be shot, bayoneted, or blown to bits, although there was a good chance on any given day you could be ignored, scorned, humiliated, or bored to death. At least it was easier than writing, and if you showed up (or logged on or phoned in), you got paid.

The very modest success of his book, its publication arranged through Allenby's contacts, had led to the proposal for his current project, and the publisher had surprisingly, if less than delightedly, accepted his proposal for the baseball book in lieu of literary criticism, Wade's purported area of expertise. The truth was that literary criticism had never much interested him. He found unreadable whole vast tracts of America's sacred literary heritage, and in measuring its merits he sided with Hemingway: *All modern American literature comes from one book by Mark Twain called Huckleberry Finn. There was nothing before.* You could take all the awful stolid volumes churned out by Cooper and Hawthorne and their ilk, toss them into a sack, and dump it into the East River or the Cuyahoga or any of those other flammable waterways that came in so handy for disposition of America's detritus, with no significant loss to the nation's literary stockpile. Wade had a certain awed admiration for readers who could plow through that muck, as he did for illiterate laborers who could stitch garments sixteen hours a day in dimly lit sweatshops; he imagined that the impact on personality development of the two endeavors was pretty much the same. At Berkeley he'd endured a seminar from a Melvillean whose idea of student-centered learning was to have his charges sit in a circle and read aloud their twenty-page essays, mostly composed on speed or No Doz between the preceding midnight and dawn, Wade *never so bethump'd with words* before or since. As if trying to get through *Omoo* and *Mardi* on your own without going into a coma wasn't horrible enough, listening to other students, who hadn't read any more of the crap than you'd pretended to, trying to fake their way through their *analyses* was enough to make you pine for a round of Russian roulette or death by a thousand cuts. The professor himself, of course, was blissfully unperturbed, having nodded off to oblivion five minutes into the first disquisition of the day, secure in the impenetrable fortress of rank and tenure. Looking back, Wade often wondered (liberal doses of marijuana notwithstanding) how he had survived more than ten years of this and other comparable nonsense to earn the dubious distinction of a doctorate in English, emerging with his devalued degree at the very moment that full-time employment in the profession of college teaching appeared to be on the brink of extinction (publications notwithstanding).

He was working now on a chapter about race relations on Cincinnati's Big Red Machine teams of the 1970s. Wade had followed the Reds during the bitter years after the Giants had, unforgivably, traded Willie Mays and before they had hired Frank Robinson to manage. Pete Rose had credited Robinson and another black Cincinnati teammate, Vada Pinson, for accepting his *Charlie Hustle* attitude and helping him to become a better player. Joe Morgan, in turn, had credited Rose with passing their lessons on to him when he joined the Reds. Though he was as dismayed as anyone else by the depravities of the all-time hit leader's post-playing days, Wade still had a soft spot in his heart for the man of whom Morgan had said, *He was the only guy I ever played with who played every game like it was the seventh game of the World Series*, the man who at age 45 had knocked out a five-for-five in one of his last games against San Francisco. Wade could still call up from memory the opening line of *The Chronicle's* Bruce Jenkins' elegiac game story: *Today the Giants looked into the face of a legend, and the legend laughed back.* However tarnished the legend had become, it was hard to be proud of living in a country where a gambler who evaded taxes went to prison and a casino owner who went bankrupt to avoid them ran for President.

The 1975-76 Reds remained among Wade's all-time favorite teams, with a batting order so potent that, even without elite pitching, they had become the first National League team to win back-to-back World Series in seventy years, and no NL team had matched the feat in the four decades since. It was Rose who had volunteered to move to third base, a switch not many Gold Glove, All-Star outfielders would have embraced (it wasn't called The Hot Corner for nothing) in order to get George Foster's bat into the lineup, which Wade could still easily rattle off: Rose, Griffey, Morgan, Bench, Foster, Perez, Concepcion, Geronimo, and whoever was lucky enough to be on the mound with those stalwarts behind them in the field and chasing runs across the plate at a record pace. It had been the last great flourish of an old-time franchise, a team compared for sheer dominance with the 1927 Yankees (or, as Allenby preferred, to the 1930's Pittsburgh Crawfords, featuring perhaps the three greatest players of their era, Satchel Paige, Josh Gibson, and Cool Papa Bell, among other Hall of Famers), before free-agency had turned baseball's world upside down. Then Steinbrenner's next generation Yankees had bought the Reds' one premium starter, Don Gullett, along with Catfish Hunter from the A's. Add Reggie Jackson to stir the mix, and the best team that money could buy had ended the Reds' brief era of supremacy. Wade still smoldered at the inequity, and he had a plan to eliminate at once and forever the ongoing lack of competitive balance in MLB. The Yankees would be demoted to the Pioneer League and relocated to North Dakota, where they could keep exclusive rights to their precious radio and television income. The Dodgers would be deported to Yemen.

The last time Angela had quizzed him on his progress, Wade's reveries had led to a discussion of Rose's forty-four game hitting streak in 1978. Wade held with the heretics who considered the achievement, in an era of integrated competition, night games, relief specialists, scrutinized scorekeepers, and media frenzy, to be even greater than Joe DiMaggio's record-setting streak in 1941. Rose had been known to her only as a pariah and Joe D. chiefly as the rinse-cycle husband of Marilyn Monroe before Angela had hooked up with Wade. A few hours somehow disappeared now, with very little to show for them on his screen, before she came into his study, cupping her hand under a spoon.

"I need you to taste this to see if it's too spicy for your white-bread guts." She leaned over his shoulder to kibitz. "Making any more . . . headway? Still stuck in Cincinnati, I see. Why are you writing a book about baseball anyway? No one's going to read it."

He tasted her pomodoro sauce and made a face. "Maybe instead of umpires I'll put in vampires."

"They already slaughtered that cash cow. It's all serial killers, mommy porn, and LGBT these days. You're wasting your time."

"Wasting my time is what I do best," Wade said. "You should know that better than anyone. Besides, what about Chad Harbach?"

"*The Art of Fielding*, you mean?"

"Didn't he make the best-seller list?"

"Yeah, but in order to do it, he had to put a gay black poet on the bench and then into bed with a bisexual university president three times his age."

"You don't have to be so high and mighty about it. How many people read *your* last book anyway? A kinky little interracial May-December ballpark homo romance might have been just the ticket to get you a movie deal." *Or at least a second printing.*

Angela was a bona fide scholar who had actually read and claimed to make sense of *Finnegans Wake*. The best Wade could say about his own history with that storied volume was that he had once owned a copy and had set foot upon it a few times to inspect the top of his refrigerator to see if he could put off cleaning there for another year or two; it beat the hell out of trying to get a boost from *Four Quartets* or *The Great Gatsby*. Angela's recent book, her third, had been an analysis of Shakespeare's influence on Joyce and Faulkner. Atop her earlier scholarship, it had earned her offers of full professorships from several high-end universities, far from the dusty hinterlands of California's Central

Valley, seeking to lure her back to the classroom and conference circuit. She had talked from time to time of tossing in her two cents worth, in her next book, on the question of the authorship of the plays credited to WS. She was convinced that no one outside of the aristocracy could have acquired or demonstrated the universality of knowledge and sophistication of language marking the quartos and folios as the greatest literary achievement on record. Wade was skeptical. He viewed the controversy much as he did the conspiracy theories seeking to attribute JFK's assassination to Castro, Sam Giancana, or Boris Badenov. At bottom, for him, it was a matter of ego: he simply could not persuade himself that someone who had written something so transcendent, so much better than anything anyone else had ever put on paper or papyrus, could possibly keep his authorship a secret—just as the trigger man for the crime of the century couldn't have resisted taking credit. It didn't seem humanly possible to abstain from claiming that sort of fame—or to watch another man claim it. When Angela warmed to the subject, Wade sometimes found it necessary after a certain term to distract her with a topic from his own purview. To forestall her now, he left the glorious Queen City and rolled out the conjectures about Babe Ruth's ethnicity.

"One of his nicknames was *Niggerlips*, you know."

"I thought he was *The Sultan of Swat*."

"That too. How many lily-white sultans can you name?"

"Do you think it's true?"

Wade shrugged. "It's one theory to explain the degree of his superiority over his contemporaries. I'm just suggesting that tracing his genealogy might be more productive than trying to fill in gaps about what we don't know from four centuries ago."

"So what are you saying? Your research on baseball is more valuable than mine on—"

"Equally valueless, in all likelihood. Maybe a tad more feasible."

"Face it, Wade. Most people think baseball is boring."

Angela had been in this benighted camp herself until recent years. Her emergence from it Wade ranked among the foremost wonders of her return to his life; nevertheless, this was the sort of nattering that demanded preemptive response.

"Most people think Shakespeare is boring, too."

He ducked as she swatted at him. Swing and a miss. "Are you comparing the greatest genius who ever lived with a bunch of lugs who spit tobacco juice all over themselves and blow snotwads on national TV?"

"Most of the players have switched to gum or seeds, and fans seem to get past the flying boogers. Seventy-five million people attended Major League Baseball games last year. Forty million or so watched the World Series on TV. Hell, more than three hundred thousand went to the *College* World Series. And they had to go to fucking Omaha to do it. How many folks do you suppose saw a Shakespeare play in Omaha last year?"

Wade was playing devil's advocate here: he couldn't cite act and scene from *Timon of Athens* as Angela could, but he revered The Bard almost as much as she did. He was prepared, however, to deliver on a moment's notice his list of things she liked that *were* boring to him: opera, symphony, ballet, dance of any kind not involving a pole, museums, modern paintings (*any* paintings that didn't feature portraits, landscapes, or naked women), sculpture, architecture, furniture—the list was endless. His cultural indifference was nearly all encompassing. If it wasn't about sports, sex, food, booze, movies, or books, he really didn't give a shit. Pretending that he did was sometimes harder work than he had signed up for.

"Why don't you write a love story instead?" Angela said.

He looked up from his screen in surprise. "You mean like … *our* story?"

"You could do worse."

"Who would believe a beautiful, sophisticated girl like you would fall for a guy like me? I still can't quite believe it my—"

"I can't either. Are you going to be able to handle this sauce, or—"

"Unless you want me to call Manny's, and—"

She brandished the spoon as if to smite him.

"Better make it a tad milder then."

"Wimp."

"*Wimps get all the snatch.*" Wade pointed a finger at her to signal game on.

"You're too easy: *American Graffiti.* Curt. Richard Dreyfuss in his adorable nerd-next-door phase, before he went bald and got pudgy, like you. Did you remember to record the Giants' game?"

Wade wasn't the only one who could play devil's advocate. Having ruled out football as too barbaric and basketball as the province of genetic freaks, Angela had decided a few seasons ago, after first connecting with him, to make an effort with baseball. It just so happened that she had chosen the magical campaign of 2010 to take an interest in the Giants and had gone right to the World Series with them in her rookie year. Then, after missing the compound misery of Buster Posey's fractured leg and the dismal 2011 season while she and Wade were separated, she had come back to California just in time to revel in the repeated glory of a second championship in 2012. Two seasons later, with a lineup featuring the redoubtable Juan Perez in left field and Gregor Blanco in center, the Giants had somehow won their third title in five years, a stretch of fandom for Angela so preposterous that Wade was hard-pressed to explain to her the scale of cosmic injustice involved.

He had told her more than once about sitting beside his father, facing his first cancer surgery, in his hospital bed to watch the World Series in 2002, when a steroid-powered superstar had lifted the Giants back into prominence for the first time since the disastrous earthquake series against the similarly enhanced A's in 1989, and only the third time in San Francisco's history. The Giants had taken a lead of three games to two, one win away from a historic victory, Wade and his father savoring every second together after the decades of frustration since Mays had led the Giants west in 1958 and then had died on second base, the potential winning run, when McCovey had lined out to end game seven in 1962 against Mantle's Yankees. Forty years later, leading in game six, manager Dusty Baker pulled his starting pitcher in the late innings and, in full view of the disbelieving nation, as the spent starter was leaving the mound, handed him the ball, as if it were a trophy, game over, an act of hubris so egregious that the gods, however remote, disengaged, or indifferent, simply could not let it pass. Wade remembered startling a nurse by blurting, *What the fuck is he doing?* His father, a gentleman of milder idiom and mien, merely shook his head in fatal resignation. Sure enough, the Angels had rallied against the Giants' exhausted bullpen and won, then won again the next day to send San Francisco and its desperate fans to yet another soul-sucking Series defeat. Angela had skipped all that—a half-century of purgatory—and gone straight to multiple orgasms at the pearly gates.

Calamities (beanballs, busted thumbs, torn hams, twisted limbs, something new called a *high ankle sprain* that sounded suspiciously like something old called a *sprained ankle*) had returned in more customary plague-like numbers during the current season, and Angela, like Wade, had struggled to maintain interest as an SF squad with neither power nor speed struggled to get even one or two runs across the plate in support of a beleaguered pitching staff. In response to Angela's question Wade nodded now in the direction of the DVR, the priceless device that made it possible to speed through three hours of torment in fifteen minutes or go back at leisure to revel in more felicitous moments.

"Okay, later, then," Angela said. "I'll leave you to decide what—"

"Not to write next?"

"Exactly."

"*Procrastination, thy name is Wade.* Maybe my meatballs will inspire you."

Wade did the cleanup again after dinner. He found he actually enjoyed washing dishes. There was something soothing about the mindless monotony of the project, and there was even a measurable outcome that you could immediately assess. From the vagaries of teaching or counseling—or the torture of trying to turn a blank screen into words that didn't make you want to put your fist through it or hang yourself afterward—this was a welcome escape. Whether he would have derived the same satisfaction from doing it eight hours a day for a minimum wage was another matter, but in the meantime he patted himself on the back a bit for allowing himself to take pleasure in the quotidian.

When he finished, he started back toward his computer, then remembered the game and made a detour, promising himself to get back to work in half an hour. With the mute on to spare himself the inanities of the announcing crew, who routinely flubbed the names of the players, lost track of the outs in the inning, and spent more time drooling over corndogs in the crowd shots than paying attention to the action on the field, he began now to zip through the recording at warp speed.

"How can you even tell what's happening when you go that fast?" Angela asked, a familiar complaint, when she came in to join him for a few minutes.

"Trust me, it's nothing you want to see," Wade said. Tim Lincecum swung away on a 2-0 pitch with one out and the bases loaded: can of corn double play, Angel Pagan twisting futilely in the on deck circle. An ad for urinary leakage products came briefly onscreen.

"You're missing the journey, Wade."

"I'm missing the commercials."

The phone rang during the next half inning, sparing Wade and Angela the sight of the double Cy Young winner's trudge to the dugout as a dead-armed reliever came on to contend with the runners the once invincible ace had walked aboard. Angela went back to work, while Wade picked up the phone. The caller was Johnny Dawes. Wade turned the television off.

"You're the counselor who helps the ballplayers, right?"

Wade cleared his throat, bought himself some time. *And the one who sends thugs who hit women to prison where they belong.* "Right."

"I need your help."

"I understand you're going to be talking to the police and that you have a lawyer to—"

"Shit, yeah, I have a lawyer. That's not what I need your help with."

"Okay, what—"

"I need you to keep Juke Jackson the fuck away from me. People tell me he was here last night lookin' for me. Did you hear what he did to Camellia Sanchez?"

Wade was stunned by the brazenness of the ass-backwards spin. "That's not quite the way I heard the story."

"Oh, yeah? What did you—"

"I heard he just went over to visit his furniture, make sure some careless shortstop didn't scratch the polish on—"

"Do you think I want that nigger shit in my house?" Wade winced, as always, at the slur. He recalled Jackson's telling him that Dawes' father was half-black, his mother white. Dawes was light-complexioned and disdainful of his African heritage. "I told Cammie to get rid of it."

"I see. Is that what caused your altercation?"

"What fucking altercation? We had a little . . . issue over here, that's all, then she ran back to his place, and I guess he beat the crap out of her."

"Again, not quite the way I heard the story before. What sort of *little issue* did you have, Mr. Dawes? Camellia told my wife that you—"

"The bitch was drunk off her ass. Stoned, too. She doesn't have a clue what went on here before she went back to that—"

Wade tried again. "She told my wife that you punched her in the face."

"I never touched her. There were some guys here, friends of a friend, frat guys I don't really know that well, and one or two of them might've got a little . . . real with her, but—"

"Are you rehearsing for the cops? Do you really expect me to believe—"

"I don't give a shit what you believe. Just keep that motherfucker away from me. Remind him about what he saw in my locker."

Your Bible, you mean?

"I see him around here again, I'll blow his fucking head off."

CHAPTER 4

It's because of giants like Willie that someone like me could even think about running for President.

—Barack Obama, on presenting to Willie Mays
The Presidential Medal of Freedom

On a bet ($5), I tried out for the baseball team and made it. I really wanted to get out of spring football, and my dad wanted me to play baseball.

—Reggie Jackson, by his own account the first black baseball player at Arizona State University

"We're going backwards," Arthur Allenby said, as he stood in his office to greet Wade. The CSU president waved a sheaf of papers in his left hand, apparently plucked from an imposing collection on his desk, as he gestured toward a chair with his right. "Have you seen this report from Lapchick at Central Florida? Look at this: percentage of African American baseball players in Division I universities—2.6. Percentage of head coaches—0.9. Not even one fucking percent. In the sport of Jackie Robinson and Willie Mays!"

On a corner of Allenby's desk, dwarfed by the paper-work towering over it, was a framed photo, posed in front of a venerable team bus, of the 1949 Birmingham Black Barons. Unmistakable among the veterans surrounding him was the teenager who would go on to become the greatest center fielder ever to play the game.

Allenby had grown up in Harlem in the early 1950s before moving in adolescence with his family to L.A. He had attended games at the Polo Grounds and Ebbets Field and had witnessed the hallowed early years of baseball's integration and its impact on America. Wade, who had only read of these wonders, nodded, took a seat, and resisted the temptation to remind his harried friend who it was that had found and forwarded the report in his hand. Allenby was up to his ass in reports. The first black varsi-ty athlete to graduate from CSU—before earning a law degree from Stanford—he'd recently stepped down as CEO of the soft-ware corporation he had built from the ground up to tackle the much less lucrative and so far largely thankless job of guiding his alma mater. Trying to straighten out the mess left by his indicted predecessor was testing even Allenby's formidable reserves of patience and positive thinking.

"And Bud Selig said *it's getting better,*" Allenby grumbled now after reclaiming his chair, naming the faineant former Commissioner of Major League Baseball.

Wade shrugged. "At least he retired before they had to have him stuffed."

"Did you know the rate of American-born black players in the big leagues has dropped to 8%?"

Wade did know this; he had known it even before he'd read Lapchick's report. He knew, too, that in the generation after Mays and Henry Aaron and Frank Robinson, along with Mickey Mantle the greatest combinations of power and speed the game had seen, the rate of African Americans in Major League Baseball had peaked at 27%. Now there were whole teams that had none, a grand total of one on two teams in Chicago. Wade's beloved Giants had won three World Series without a significant contribution from an African American player—and with none even on the roster of the most recent championship squad, nor of the St. Louis team they had defeated to win the pennant.

"We are 13% of the population," Allenby continued. "It's great that the Latinos are thriving in the game, and many of them are great players. No one questions that they've earned their place, but how have we let our own black athletes fall so far to the wayside of our supposed national pastime? What the hell happened to the example that Jackie and Willie set?"

This was in fact the topic of the book Wade was trying to write. What *had* happened to black participation in baseball, the sport that had played such a seminal role in the expansion of opportunities for people of color in the U.S.? Michael Jordan had slam-dunked it, of course, for one thing. Everybody knew that. Black kids—and white and brown kids, too—wanted to fly like Mike. It was no small irony that Jordan had loved baseball so much himself that he had tried to switch to it after winning three titles and three MVPs. Long before he came along, or Magic Johnson before him, to elevate the NBA, the NFL had taken over much of the spotlight from baseball, and black athletes had increasingly gravitated to the gridiron. When Jim Brown was racking up his thousand-yard seasons in Wade's distant youth, there had been only a few black players on each NFL team, all starters, mostly stars. Now there were whole defenses that were black. Except for offensive linemen, kickers, and quarterbacks (where the gap was closing fast, now that the opportunity was available), it had become the black man's game, almost as much as basketball.

Wade had recently turned his attention to the rates of participation by black athletes on high school teams. Whole towns converged on Friday nights for football or packed the gyms for basketball, but how many people, besides family members and a few friends of the players, regularly sat in the stands to watch high school baseball? Dee Gordon, the electrifying young second baseman the Dodgers had unaccountably swapped to the Marlins, son of a major leaguer himself, had no doubt spoken for many others: *High school basketball games, the girls were there. Football games, the girls were there. But ain't no girls at the baseball game. Why should I play baseball?* Kansas City's superb center fielder Lorenzo Cain had left the girls implied but otherwise made the same point: *If I would have made the basketball team in high school, there's no chance I would have played baseball. There's no chance.*

Another factor Wade kept running into was the prevalence of travel teams and the edge that expert coaching and extra experience gave to their participants. Many of the kids on the high school baseball squads played on summer or even year-round teams now, and often the expenses for travel and equipment were beyond the budgets of black families. Wade had heard this from students in his classes when he had asked about their experiences in high school athletics. In many cases, they reported, all the slots on the school teams were sewn up before the *try-outs* even started. A black assistant coach on the CSU football team had told Wade that he'd been cut from his high school freshman baseball team, deemed not good enough for the last spot on the roster, even though he'd gone on to All-League status in football and track.

Increasingly, Wade's research was leading him to the role of fathers. There was a consensus that basketball and football depended on explosive athletic talent, which blacks possessed in a higher percentage than whites or others, an ironic legacy of survival of the fittest. The genes that had enabled the select few to survive the conditions of slavery, however diluted over the intervening generations, were still superior to those of the general population. Black kids could run faster and jump higher, and they used those skills to get to the forefront of the football and basketball teams quickly. But baseball, at the higher levels at least, required extraordinary dedication to details in order to complement and enhance natural ability. With nearly three-fourths of black children born out of wedlock, many fathers were simply missing in action when it came to supplying the kind of encouragement and support required, on practice fields and in batting cages, to achieve distinction amid a throng of privileged competitors.

"Or even something as simple as going out to the backyard to play catch," Allenby said now, as Wade brought him up to date on his latest findings. Wade could recall children in his own neighborhood envying him the father who took the time to do this. Thrice-divorced himself, Allenby was no great defender of the sanctity of marriage, but he had shared fondly with Wade memories of his own father's role in his development as an athlete. Chester Allenby had returned from his service as a mechanic for the Red Ball Express during World War II, started a family in New York, and then followed the American dream to L.A., where he had somehow found the time to coach the teams his kids played on while working two full-time jobs for twenty years to give them a life of more opportunity than his own. A chain smoker, like so many of his generation, he had died at forty-six. He had lived long enough to see his first-born son reject his advice and follow him into the service of his country in time of war but had been denied the satisfaction of the spectacular successes that followed.

"Too many black fathers today are simply not in the picture to push their sons," Allenby continued. "I'm not saying black kids don't work hard: they'll put in the time in the weight room or in the gym to get stronger, get better, but the kind of dedication that baseball requires is a different level."

"Right," Wade said. "You could argue that the single hardest thing to do in any of the major sports is to throw a pitch at ninety-plus miles per hour, with movement, into a tiny zone sixty-feet-six-inches away. The average asshole who can barely bend over to tie his shoe has no clue how difficult that is to do."

"True," Allenby said. "And the second hardest thing to do is to hit it."

"Not that easy to catch it either, especially in the infield, if someone smokes it at you," Wade added. Stationed once, unforgettably, at third base in a Little League game, he had made three errors in one inning. The experience remained his archetypal nightmare. He drew small comfort from the fact that the same thing had once happened to Brooks Robinson, perhaps the greatest defensive third baseman in history, in a game against the A's. The Giants' Bob Brenly (not among history's elite defenders) had one-upped both of them with *four* errors in a single frame before redeeming himself with a game-winning home run. Wade had never hit a home run, even in batting practice.

Allenby went on: "Put *the average asshole*, to quote a well-known sage, on a football field, have him run or stumble twenty yards down the field and throw him a pass, not Elway-velocity, just normal NFL, there's a chance he might catch it. Or put him on the three-point line in basketball and let him shoot an uncontested shot, which we all know there are plenty of even in the NBA until the playoffs start, there's a chance he might make it. But put the same guy in the batter's box against a major league pitcher, and—"

"He'd be lucky to get a swing off before the ball hit the catcher's mitt," Wade finished for him.

Allenby nodded. "The one thing I regret the most about my time in sports is giving up pitching. I quit football in college when they wouldn't let me play quarterback, but there's a good chance I'd have wrecked a knee or been knocked goofy with concussions in that game, so no real regrets over the shift to basketball then. But I wish I'd figured out a way to keep pitching in high school. There was a real bias against letting the black kids pitch—or catch—back then. Any position that involved thinking was out. You remember that crap the Dodgers' executive said: *Black people lack the necessities.* The Dodgers, the team not just of Jackie Robinson but of Don Newcombe and Roy Campanella, for Christ's sake. We were supposed to roam the outfield, run down the balls out there, leave the brainwaves to the white boys. I was a good fielder, a decent hitter, but I could really bust that sucker in there from the mound. I could hit a target, and I could make the ball move a bit. I was foolin' around with a screwball one day, and I beaned the coach's kid, a dumb fuck who forgot to duck, and that was it: I was banished to the outfield for good. I never got another chance to pitch."

"I'm not sure it's much different today," Wade said. "There are only a handful of African American pitchers in the majors now."

Allenby nodded again. "Which brings us to our man Jackson."

If absent fathers and elitist high schools had dropped the ball, the report Allenby clutched now made it clear that colleges and universities nationwide hadn't exactly been rushing to pick it up. He was determined to do things differently on his watch. Faced shortly after taking over the presidency with a vote in the faculty senate recommending elimination of several varsity athletic programs, including baseball, he had come up with the plan by which Juke Jackson and other premier multi-sport athletes had been recruited to CSU. Wade had been present at the conception of the stratagem. He had been hosting Allenby's visit at his condo, the two of them watching the Seattle Seahawks humiliate Wade's 49ers on television. As Russell Wilson's inspired improvisations turned the 49ers' defense into Keystone Kops, Allenby commented on how impressed he had been when the quarterback, then still in college, had responded to the attempt by his head football coach to deny him the opportunity to play baseball as well. Instead of capitulating to the ultimatum, Wilson had transferred to another school, where he'd set multiple passing records—and played minor league baseball in the summer as well. He'd hit only .230 in Double-A, a little farther above the Mendoza Line than Michael Jordan had managed in Single-A—another testimony to baseball's degree of difficulty—but it was the independence he'd shown that had intrigued Allenby and led him to wonder how many two-sport athletes were currently competing in the NCAA. Specifically, he had wanted to know how many athletes who might have a shot at a career in baseball were limited to football or basketball by an arbitrary coach.

A little research by Wade had revealed that many other martinets at major universities were also restricting their athletes to a single sport. There had been only ten student-athletes in the whole country who played both major college football and baseball in the year preceding Juke Jackson's matriculation. By establishing a more flexible policy, CSU under Allenby had nearly matched the figure for the rest of the country singlehandedly, in the process establishing a chance to recruit the kind of athletes who could quickly turn around its athletic programs, especially baseball, and also bring a level of national attention to the university while broadening opportunities for student-athletes.

Wade had initially been skeptical about the plan, in no small part because he feared he would find himself in the middle of a tug-of-war between the CSU coaches. It was hard enough keeping kids eligible for one college sport. Some of the football players spoke of putting fifty hours a week into practice, weight room sessions, and playbook study; the baseball team played fifty games in four months, half of them on the road. There were dozens of players on both teams who barely qualified to play each semester, and Wade couldn't imagine recruiting to CSU the kind of student-athletes who could handle the demands of two sports and any semblance of a legitimate academic load.

There was a reason, though, that Wade was working on his first hundred-thousand-dollar contract while Allenby had banked a billion or two. The new president had reached out to friends he'd kept at Stanford since earning his law degree. He had managed to tap into a pool of talent and eventually to establish a pipeline of two-sport high school athletes initially recruited there but deemed a bit below the intellectual threshold necessary for success at the West Coast's most prestigious institution. Again, Wade had been at first flabbergasted at the notion that anyone at Stanford would want to help a rival university's athletic programs, but Allenby had quite pragmatically pointed out that it was a way to keep some studs from lining up against the Cardinal for Oregon or UCLA.

Allenby had arranged with CSU's head football coach, Sherman Slate, his first hire, to allow a few of his recruits to play baseball as well, reasoning that some of them would rather spend the semester cavorting on the basepaths than getting flogged into shape in spring football practice, as long as they knew they wouldn't lose their spots on the depth chart. Slate had expressed some initial concerns but ultimately had embraced Allenby's point that this was a way to attract premier talents to his program. Allenby had then made the same arrangement with the new CSU basketball coach, Charles Cody, like Slate, the first African American to serve as head coach in his sport at CSU. Although the seasons overlapped and the potential for roster sharing was smaller with basketball, a point guard/short-stop and two forwards who were also pitchers had joined the baseball squad when the basketball season ended. The baseball coach, Lawrence *Sharky* Sheehan, on the job for many moribund seasons, had put up a token protest about interference with his roster, but he had piped down when he got a look at Jackson, whose decision to attend CSU had triggered several of the others'. Of the eight combo athletes who had signed on in the first two years of the experiment, five were African Americans—on a baseball team that had previously had only one—and four more black multi-sport recruits had committed to CSU for the coming fall. Three starting position players and two starting pitchers had emerged from the group who had come in together as freshmen or transfers to transform the program. Even with little depth behind them and most of the new starters talented but raw, this season the team had won more than half of its games for the first time in decades, and then, with a late boost from the pitchers from the basketball contingent, had made an unexpected splash in the post-season tournament before Jackson's ninth inning walk had sealed the loss in the conference championship game.

"So how is our prodigy faring today?"

Keeping Jackson out of more negative headlines and on track to compete in the fall football season was going to be crucial to the fate of the whole two-sport gambit. He was the poster boy for the program, and if he flamed out, others would likely follow suit or turn their attention elsewhere.

Wade filled Allenby in on the phone call from Dawes. Then he added, "Other than death threats from his teammates, my real concern is keeping Juke eligible for football in the fall. He's really struggling with the academics."

"Even with all those cake classes and the tutors you lined up for him?"

"Cake for you and me, maybe, but not for him. He's bright, but his reading level is about where a high school freshman's should be. He goes to his classes, meets with his tutors, but it's still a struggle. He's a hands-on guy. Books have never really interested him. You don't just flip a switch and—"

"What would you think about signing him up for African American History this summer?"

Wade saw where this was going and hesitated for a moment before replying. "With Carlotta Baynes, you mean?"

"She's the one who's teaching it."

Wade nodded. He had never met this colleague but was well acquainted with her reputation. "The athletes do really well with her."

"I've heard that," Allenby said. "I'd like to find out what's going on there. If she's legit, then maybe she's got a model we can use to help other instructors with athletes in their classes. If anything phony is going on, I need to know about that, too—and soon. We've got an accreditation team that will be crawling all over us in a few months. We can't afford to get caught with our pants down and our dicks out like North Carolina."

The Tarheels' once sacrosanct basketball program had finally been busted by whistleblowers. Among the revelations: athletes received a free pass from the campus's African American Studies Department, getting credits for classes they rarely attended, while a team of tutors wrote their papers for them. One NBA prospect had even made the Dean's List with straight A's in four classes he had never set foot in.

"You want Jackson to be a guinea pig?"

"Doesn't have to be him, but I know you're tracking his progress closely, so I figured it would make sense to see how he does.

It might even be a subject he could take an interest in. I took that class myself, you know. It was a good course when I was here. The prof was from Harvard, one of the first black PhDs in his field. He'd published several books and was well-known around the country. Taught a real tough class: kicked ass and didn't bother to take names. Used to lock the door at 8:00, and if you arrived at 8:01, don't bother trying to whine your way in with some *CP time* bullshit."

Wade nodded in somewhat disingenuous approbation. He had been raised by a man who would rather be two hours early than two seconds late. The life or death of a flight crew had been in his father's hands for three years, and he had carried his reverence for punctuality from World War II into civilian life, including occasional airport runs for which his son was roused from raptures with Stella Stevens and/or Nancy Wilson an hour or more before strictly necessary. Wade was rarely late himself but had been known to scramble to avoid it, sometimes in his teaching days arriving at the podium in a state of risible dishabille: half-shaven, mismatched, untucked, and unzipped.

"After I graduated," Allenby continued, "I heard the Harvard guy got an offer to go to Spelman, an endowed chair that Cosby might've forked out for in between slipping mickeys. Unfortunately, they hired a series of jokers to replace him here, one screw-up after another. One guy claimed he used to be a Panther and best buds with Huey Newton."

"I think I met him once," Wade said. "He's the one who got canned for smoking crack with his students, wasn't he?"

"No one gets canned around here," Allenby reminded him. "They paid him to go away. I think Compton College picked him up, so he probably got paid twice for a while. Anyway, Ms. Baynes is the one who seems to be—"

"Carrying the torch?"

"So to speak. See what you can find out, okay?"

"That's the new research project you were telling me about?"

"Correct."

Wade nodded and stood to depart.

Allenby stood up, too, tapping the pages he'd quoted earlier. "You're the one who sent me this shit from Lapchick, aren't you."

Wade nodded again.

"Just didn't want you to think I'd gone completely senile in here." Allenby studied the stacks of paper on his desk. Little of it seemed likely to contain good news, and certainly there were no bursting profit reports or buy-out offers to crow over.

Wade smiled. "The old corporate life starting to look pretty good in the afterglow?"

Allenby shrugged. "Been there, done that. I'll get the hang of this pretty soon."

"You've already accomplished a—"

"Just getting started, my friend," Allenby cut him off. "Save the raves for when we've actually gotten something worthwhile done around here. In the meantime, keep me posted on Jackson—and on Baynes."

Wade paused at the door. "If she's passing out grades like Halloween candy, are you sure you want to know?"

"She might be the least of my problems. That journalist who wrote in the newspaper about my military service is persisting in examining my time in Vietnam. She's contacted the accrediting team and is pushing them to investigate further before their visit."

Wade was puzzled now. "You haven't made any secret of your service."

"That's true, but I also haven't disclosed publicly every detail— or as much detail as I have with you."

Like most of the combat veterans Wade had met, Allenby did not like to talk about what he had done in war or what war had done to him. After more than a few drinks one night, when the topic of inane media comparisons between football and war had arisen, he had shut the subject down quickly by telling Wade the grisly details of his time in hell. Entering villages suspected to be sympathetic to the Viet Cong, his battalion had been given the command to obliterate all traces of life and had followed it to the letter.

Then, as now, Wade felt the humbling, utter ignorance of the non-combatant in the presence of someone who had faced and dealt death. Like Wade's father, Allenby had followed orders to kill. He had also seen friends blown to bits right beside him; he had peeled their burning flesh from his own. Nothing in Wade's experience, or even in his imagination, could remotely begin to compare with the carnage that Allenby had participated in and survived. The pundits who continually urged judgment of those who did the fighting—how many of *them* had faced what Allenby had faced? How many of them could credibly claim that they would have risked court martial to disobey an order?

"I think the journo who's on my case is getting a push from one of the candidates who didn't get this job when I applied," Allenby explained.

"Probably a guy who spent the Vietnam War on the beach in Waikiki, AWOL from the Lifeguard Squad," Wade said. "Or on a Search and Enjoy mission to Paris with Brother Romney." Wade, who had spent the war in the library at San Francisco State (*but for these vile guns/He would himself have been a soldier*), was somehow more outraged than Allenby by the chickenhawk politicos eager to consign a new generation to battlefields they had never bled upon themselves. "Seems like there are enough real problems to solve around here today without worrying about what you did or didn't do almost fifty years ago."

Allenby shrugged again. The phone on his desk rang, and a moment later Cenon Aquino knocked and entered. Wade started to move past him on the way out, but Aquino stopped him.

"You'll want to stay to hear this."

Allenby nodded for Wade to stay and Aquino to proceed.

"Camellia Sanchez has dropped the charges against Johnny Dawes, and she's refusing to testify against him."

"Christ! How in the world did—"

"There's more, Dr. Wade. She's—"

"Oh, no. Don't tell me she's—"

"—changed her story."

"You can't be serious," Allenby said.

"Couldn't be *more* serious, I'm afraid."

Wade closed his eyes; he saw the head-on coming before he heard it.

"Now she says it was Julius Jackson who—"

"Christ, don't tell me she says *he's* the one who—"

"—beat her up, and—"

"Oh, my God!"

"—raped her."

CHAPTER 5

Is it possible for white America to really understand blacks' distrust of the legal system, their fears of racial profiling and the police, without understanding how cheap a black life was for so long a time in our nation's history?

—Philip Dray, *At the Hands of Persons Unknown: The Lynching of Black America*

We have other targets. We don't just shoot at black males.

—Major Kathy Katerman, North Miami Beach Police Department, qtd. in *San Francisco Chronicle*, January 19, 2015

Juke Jackson had complicated the case against him considerably by reporting to the local police station without benefit of an attorney. After taking his statement, the police had decided to arrest him.

"The kid is just naïve," Aquino said to Wade as they waited in the station, hoping to procure Jackson's release into their custody. "He knew he hadn't done anything wrong, so he figured he had nothing to hide. He didn't count on the cops playing games with him when they interrogated him."

Wade shook his head. "I can't believe they locked him up." He remembered, though, that cops had handcuffed and arrested Joe Morgan at LAX after two World Series titles and two MVPs, mistaking maybe the greatest second baseman in history for a drug dealer because he *fit the profile.* "What did Dawes say when you interviewed him?"

"His lawyer wouldn't let him talk to me at all. Said there's no legal requirement for him to do so. Dawes has already filed a petition to withdraw from school. We can't touch him."

"And Camellia has retracted her accusations against him?"

"Her new version is that she and Dawes argued but he never struck her."

"In the meantime she's still got a smashed face to show for it."

"It happens a lot," Aquino said. "A woman gets decked by a jock with some money, then the next day, or the next week, the charges suddenly disappear when she realizes she won't have access to all of that cash if she sticks with her story."

Wade nodded. "Mrs. Ray Rice. Mrs. Warren Moon."

"Right. She won't be that person any more, live that life. So she gives the guy another chance—and drops the charges."

"Or blames somebody else?"

"That's a new twist for me," Aquino said. "I haven't seen anyone accuse someone else quite as blatantly as this before, especially in view of what Ms. Sanchez told your wife. If we run into complications now, we may have to get the dean down here to clarify what Sanchez told her. Once they hear that, they'll back off fast, I imagine."

"How could they take anything she said against Juke seriously after what she reported before?"

"It's possible there were some differences between what Sanchez told your wife and what she said to Officer Chang in the original interview. But Dawes—or more to the point his attorney—knows there's no way they'll make any charges against Jackson stick. They just wanted Sanchez to tell that story so that her charges against Dawes would be tossed out. She's totally compromised her own credibility."

"I wonder what the payoff was. I'll bet that was a pretty expensive punch."

A tall, buff cop emerged, shook hands with Aquino, and nodded to Wade, who read the ID on his shirt: Officer White. *Perfect.* "You two are getting to be regulars down here."

"Is Officer Chang available?" Wade asked. "He's familiar with this case."

"He's off duty now. We reviewed his report on the interrogation of Camellia Sanchez."

"And still arrested Juke Jackson?"

Aquino motioned to Wade to back off.

White sighed. "Look, it's probably not our finest hour, but we're getting beat with both ends of the stick here. Whenever there's an allegation of campus rape, we're taking the charge very seriously, and—"

"Arresting a guy with no previous criminal history who—"

"Who told you he had no history?"

Oh shit. Wade gulped. "There's a background check for all the student-athletes. We didn't find anything on—"

"He was booked twice on shoplifting charges as a juvenile. Both cases were dropped before they went to trial, but—"

"Shoplifting? What did he take?"

"Does that really matter?"

"I guess you'd have to tell me."

"These kids are not angels, Dr. Wade. Your guy was ready to go beat the shit out of his teammate over this girl."

"What would *you* want to do to a guy who did that to your wife?" Knowing the divorce rate among cops, Wade wasn't sure what the odds were that there was a Mrs. White, but the question still seemed relevant. "But that's not why he was arrested, was it?"

"Ms. Sanchez has accused him of sexual assault and battery."

"After she accused Jonathan Dawes of the same," Aquino added quietly as Wade fumed.

"Chang's notes don't show a sexual assault allegation. And it's not clear from what she reported then whether she knew who had caused the damage to her face."

Wade almost jumped out of his chair. Aquino restrained him with his prosthetic arm. White looked up from Chang's report. "Maybe she told a different story to your wife."

"That's exactly why we wanted a female officer to take the report."

"Chang knows the drill. Don't be putting this off on him."

"The girl is obviously confused," Aquino said.

"And beat up," Wade added. "Are you telling me you believe her story about Jackson but don't believe what she said about Dawes?"

"I'm not telling you anything of the kind. We thought there was enough likelihood of guilt to hold Jackson here."

"Of course, if he had come with an attorney, like Dawes did, that never would have happened," Wade said.

"It's not our fault if the kid is too cocky to get counsel. Maybe he'll learn a lesson from this."

Wade was ready to punch Officer White in the face. *Maybe you'll* learn a lesson from *this. POW.* Wade bunched his mighty academic fist, briefly pictured it arcing through the fetid constabulary air—then saw the burly cop catch it nonchalantly in his own massive paw, twist it into a pretzel, effortlessly turn him upside down and bounce him off the concrete floor, *BOINGO, SPLAT,* then knee him in the groin, spray some MACE in his face, and Tase him before handcuffing him to the leg of the chair he was now perching in. Wade decided not to throw the punch after all.

Maybe let Aquino give the cop a whack instead with that bionic arm of his, knock him right through the wall into the cell behind it with a creep who peed in public.

Aquino, not privy to Wade's deliberations and evidently not able to divine them, said to White, still quietly, "Are you ready to release the student in our custody, or do we need to get an attorney down here now?"

"We're going to turn the kid over to you. Just make sure to get him back down here right away if we need to talk to him again."

White obviously had some respect for the campus cop. Wade wondered if White had served abroad, too. He reminded himself not to be so quick to dismiss him as a complete asshole. This might be another guy who had been searching house-to-house in 120 degrees in Fallujah while Wade was sitting in his den with the AC cranked up, a beer in one hand, remote control in the other, and mute button at the ready to quash any annoyance as unseemly as an overloud advertisement or a sound-bite from a war-mongering congressman with multiple deferments who wondered why it was taking our *boots on the ground* so damn long to stamp out radical Islam.

Jackson was released, and Aquino offered to drive him home. Wade shook off the call.

"You've had a long day. I'll take him."

"Straight home, right?"

Wade shrugged, then flexed and pointed at a largely notional biceps. "I thought we might drop by Dawes' frat first and see if we can beat some sense into him."

"He's already moved out." Aquino smiled thinly and looked at Jackson. "Don't let this guy get you into any more trouble than you can handle."

"'Nuff trouble for one day." Jackson looked exhausted. Wade had never seen him this distraught before, even full of squirt-gun bourbon, missing his furniture, and mourning his treacherous ex. "Let's go home, Doc."

On the way to the apartment, Wade asked Jackson about the issue of a prior police record.

"I was twelve, but I was already real tall, probably looked like fifteen, sixteen. I was in a Safeway. I picked up a apple, smelled it to see if it was ripe. They thought I was trying to eat it without paying for it, so they called the manager, he called the cops, and they arrested me. No shit. For a fuckin' apple that I didn't even take a bite of."

"White said there were two arrests. What was the other case?"

"Couple years later. I was in a clothes store, Ross's. Cheap shit, you know the one. Friend was with me. He owed me some money, said he'd pay for a stupid cap I picked up. I said okay, went to look at some other stuff. He told me he paid for the cap, so I put it on and walked out. Security guard grab me up five feet out the door. My friend laughin' his ass off, thought it was a big joke. Then they busted his ass, too. He in prison now, for passin' bad checks, later on."

"Doesn't seem like the kind of guy you'd hang with."

Jackson shrugged. "I grew up with the motherfucker. We was like brothers—till then anyway. I didn't do nothin' with him after that, won't when he get out neither."

They reached the apartment complex, inviting as ever. A young mother with purple hair and multiple piercings sat at the doorstep of the unit next to Jackson's, smoking a cigarette while screaming at one toddler and changing the diaper of another, with more demands evidently on the way: it looked like she was pregnant with number three. Hand on the passenger's door handle, about to step out, Jackson paused, then looked back over at Wade. "There was one other time I didn't tell you about."

Wade frowned. "Another arrest?"

Jackson shook his head. "Could've been that, could've been worse. Didn't happen. Right after I got my license, I ran through a stop sign. You know, how we all do it, California stop, slid up to the sign, took a look, didn't see nobody comin', sure as *hell* didn't see the cop hidin' behind a parked van on his chopper. He pull me over, see me up close, call in backup, then tell me to get out of the car. I ask him why I got to get out, and he pull the door open, pull me out. He push me up against the car—and I pushed him back. Dumbest thing I ever did, just a reflex though. I mean, the fool could've shot me right then. I'd been just one more dead nigger. No tellin' what story he would've told: maybe I reached for his gun or somethin'. But lucky for me, the backup car arrive, another cop jump out, calm him down. First cop try to say I hit him, but the other cop back him down, and he admit I just push him a little bit. They run my plates, check my driver's license, didn't find nothin', write me a big fuckin' ticket, let me go. End of story. But I know it could've turned out different if that other cop didn't show up so fast or if he was a crazyass cracker like the first one." Jackson sighed, looked at Wade, and smiled. "After that, cops pull me over, I just smile like this and do what they say. Nice as pie."

"How often does that happen?"

Jackson shrugged. "I don't keep track no more. Maybe eight, ten times the last year or two."

Wade had been driving more than twice as long as Jackson had been alive. He'd been pulled over four times in his life.

"For what?"

"Stupid shit. You know, like one time that little light bulb out on my tail end burned out. Not the brake light, nothin' important, just the little light that s'posed to shine over your license plate so they can read it."

"If you've had all this trouble with cops before, how come you went down to the police station without a lawyer? How come you didn't at least call me?"

Jackson sighed again and shook his head, ruing the easy hindsight. "When they called me, I thought they just wanted me to back up Cammie's story about Dawes. Didn't have no idea she was gonna back out. *Never* 'curred to me she would flip on it and 'cuse me. Then, while they was interviewin' me, I guess I just fell into a trap. They started askin' if I ever touch her rough or push her around at the apartment, and I said only time might've been when I was going after Dawes after he hit her. She was blockin' the door, tryin' to keep me inside, so I gave her a little shove, just enough to get her out of the way so I could go. Didn't knock her down or nothin'. She maybe bumped her face on the door, same spot she already banged up. I guess they took that and turned it into some big thing they thought they could press charges on."

Wade tried to remember if in frustration or haste he had ever pushed Angela or Brenda out of his own path. Budging Brenda was unlikely, as it would have required a backhoe; Angela, a black belt, probably would have dropped him in his tracks. But the assault charge was the least of Jackson's worries, as Wade reminded him now.

"When they match the lab reports, will they find your semen inside her?"

"We was together the night before the game, like lots of other nights. But I always used a rubber. Besides, they'd find yours inside your wife, right? Don't mean you raped her."

"You don't have to convince me," Wade said. "I just hope they'll see it that way, too."

Jackson shook his head again. "You're right: I never should've talked to them cops."

"They're not all out to get you," Wade reminded him. "Aquino is obviously in your corner, and—"

"He just a campus cop, though."

"I'm sure there are other straight-up guys like him—and like the backup cop on your traffic stop—on the city force. But anyway, I want you to promise that you'll call me first before you talk to any cops again."

"That's a deal, Doc. Thanks again for helpin' me out. Be my turn to do somethin' for you one of these days. You want me to tune up this old car or something for you? Sounds like she's runnin' a little rough. Don't smell too great neither." He sniffed. "You burnin' cat-piss instead of gas in there, or—"

"I can't get the cat to piss into the tank anymore," Wade said. "Good trick while it—"

"You should lemme take a look some time. Your ride break down 'round here, you liable to get shot or cut to nothin'."

A hoodied black youth passed them on the sidewalk, clutching his pants far below his ass with one hand and barely restraining with the other what appeared to be a cross between a pit bull and an assault vehicle. He shot a glare through the windshield at Wade and a WTF at Jackson as he yanked on the leash. Purpletop screamed something at him, but he did not look back.

"I hope that fucker didn't take a dump in my doorway," Jackson muttered, as he stepped out of the car.

I hope his dog didn't do any business there either. Wade studied their progress in his rearview mirror. "Think I should offer to give them a lift?"

Jackson laughed. "You a crazy motherfucker, Doc. You pull up next to them two, I never see you in one piece again. You keep clear—and I'll keep clear of the cops. Deal?"

"Deal."

As he turned his car around to head home, Wade couldn't help glancing again at the menacing pair. Even though there was no indication of criminal activity here—parading a vicious attack animal, bred and trained to maul and maim, was perfectly legal on the streets of this city, as on most others across the state and nation—Wade was reminded of Allenby's recent Scotch-inspired plan for inner city intervention. He proposed to round up all the wannabe badasses with their stalking companions and airdrop the whole gang (parachutes optional) over Iraq or Afghanistan. Let them prove how tough they were by showing their tattoos and their pooper-scoopers to ISIS and Al-Qaeda.

Still covertly peeking as he pulled even, Wade was stirred to recall the days when stopping to give a ride to strangers was the norm rather than an invitation to dismemberment. He had done it often when he first started driving, and he had benefited a few times from others doing it for him. One year when the brakes on his first beater car were especially whimsical, he had taken a long bus ride to Eureka in pursuit of a community college teaching job. He had miscalculated how long it would take him to walk from the bus station. A kid in a pickup had seen him jogging on the sidewalk in his monkey suit for the interview and had pulled over, picked him up, and driven two miles out of his way to drop Wade off on campus, with about ten minutes to spare; no way he would have made it in time without the lift. Farcically overqualified, he had fucked up the interview anyway and blown the job, as usual, but at least he hadn't ridden eight hours on a bus without getting his shot, thanks to the Samaritan. It seemed deplorable to him now that almost no one considered it safe to offer this simple service to a fellow traveler—or to take the risk of accepting an offer.

He remembered the terror he had seen in the eyes of a middle-aged Latina trudging up the hill he had grown up on, as she struggled to carry two stuffed bags of groceries, during one of his last visits home before his mother died, when he had pulled over to offer a ride. It was only the saintly smile his mother offered up from the passenger seat that had persuaded the señora to pile her groceries into the back seat and climb in. A few minutes later, when they dropped her off, she had looked as if she wanted to scurry immediately into her house, perhaps fearing that Mom was just a front after all for the organ thief at the wheel. But she had lingered instead to thank them so profusely that Wade had been moved nearly to tears. His mother's *raison d'être* had been planned and random acts of kindness; the latter were getting much harder to execute now that no one trusted or even knew their neighbors.

There were good reasons to be cautious, of course, for both pedestrian and motorist. A do-gooder had made front pages when he stopped to offer assistance to an apparently stranded soul on the Golden Gate Bridge. The beneficiary of the act of kindness had repaid the favor by knifing the driver, castrating him, and tossing his balls into the bay. Also by stealing his car, Wade recalled, the definitive addition of insult to injury.

Wade blanched at the memory, touched himself for luck, left footling boy and beast in his rearview, and drove home, testicles intact, to his wife, whom he found awaiting him in a peignoir and with a baseball question. Talk about the best of both worlds.

"So it's DiMaggio who still holds the record for the streak then, right?" she said, as she turned down the spread on his side of the bed.

"That's right. Fifty-six in a row."

"That doesn't sound so hard to beat."

"Hard? *Impossible* is more like it. What the hell are you talking a—"

"Hop in and find out, slugger."

CHAPTER 6

You ever been in love with two women at the same time?

—Ernest Hemingway to A.E. Hotchner, qtd.
in *Hemingway in Love*

We don't really need baseball, but baseball needs *us* [. . . .]
Maybe if baseball gets a little hipper, a little cooler, just a
little more black, the future can change.

—Chris Rock

Facing in the wake of the latest scandal a renewed call by the
faculty senate to sanction or shut down the baseball program,
Allenby asked Wade to forestall the pleasures of parsing more
student prose and to return full-time, temporarily, to his counseling role in Athletics. Wade scheduled a meeting with his
English chair, Erica Wiley, to let her know about the likelihood
of the switch, so she could arrange to replace him in the lineup
for the fall semester. Erica was one of Wade's favorite people at
CSU—or anywhere. An expert on the Harlem Renaissance and
a distinguished full professor before her recent promotion, she
had always gone out of her way to be cordial to anyone who
crossed her path, even the lowly adjunct instructor, Wade's caste

until recently. Some full profs wouldn't even meet the gaze of underlings so far beneath their station, let alone speak to them or, God forbid, give them any encouragement or support. From his first few days at the campus, Erica had treated Wade as a valued colleague, generously sharing her expertise and offering advice when it was sought. When he had mentioned, after giving up on getting Brenda to address her health issues, a desire to improve his own well-being amid a hectic, piecemeal teaching schedule, Erica had invited him to join her for the midday constitutionals that kept her own physique in splendid shape. Their walks together had served not only to prepare him for the subsequent challenges of keeping pace with Angela but also to extend the range and depth of their own friendship. Single for some years after two failed marriages, she was as striking as she was stylish, and before reconnecting with Angela, Wade had often wished for the nerve to approach her about a different kind of relationship. Perceiving himself as unworthy, instead he had fixed her up with Allenby, a liaison they had agreed to suspend when the presidency beckoned.

When Wade went to meet Erica now at her office, he was immediately reminded of another major change at the English Department: Clara Shelby, for many decades officially the department's secretary but in truth its absolute despot, had abruptly retired, in her seventies, after Erica had been appointed chair. Her temporary replacement was out to lunch when Wade arrived. Erica emerged from her office to find Wade staring nostalgically at the desk of his old friend and occasional benefactor, now bereft of her many incriminating photos and other memorabilia. Clara, who could be a bitch on a stick with faculty she didn't care for, had for some reason taken a liking to Wade during his first semester at CSU. She had helped him more than once in the years since to secure an extra section at the last minute or to extricate himself from a mess brought on by an undermedicated student or an overconstipated administrator.

"My first failure in office," Erica said, with a nod at the empty desk. "I thought we were friends, but I guess she just couldn't work for a black woman."

Wade felt the sudden sickening in the pit of his stomach that always came when he heard that someone he liked had said or done something awful to someone else he cared about. He remembered that Clara had been born and raised in Alabama and had never completely left it behind. "That must have been really hard for you."

Erica shrugged. "For her, too, I guess. I thought she'd at least give it a try."

"It was probably getting to be time for her to think about retiring anyway."

"Who are you kidding, Wade? We both know she was still running the show."

"Doesn't she have great-grandchildren, or something, she wanted to indoctrinate?"

"You don't have to try to soften it for me, Wade. I know I gave it my best shot. I took her out to lunch and asked her to show me the ropes, let her know I'd be counting on her to call the shots around here just like she always has. Her mind was made up before we even sat down to eat. I guess I'm mildly surprised that she even let me pay for her meal."

Wade shook his head. "I'm really sorry. I just never saw that coming. After years of working for a twat like Gordon Brooks, I figured she'd be elated to have a boss like you. Do you think it was more gender than race? Some women have a hard time working for—"

"Enough. I've let it go. Come in and see what I've done with Gordo's digs."

One step into the inner sanctum was enough to savor the transformation. Just getting rid of the fusty unread volumes and ponderous piles of paper that her predecessor had accumulated and stacked haphazardly in all directions had opened up the room considerably. You could actually see out the windows now. The fragrance upgrade was unquantifiable. Wade filled his lungs instead of holding his nose.

"Smells good in here. Life in league with the devil must agree with you."

"I understand it's you I have to thank—or curse—for the dean's bringing me over to the dark side."

"I'm sure Angela would have thought of you on her own."

"That's not a very convincing denial. How come you didn't take the job yourself?"

Angela, upon becoming dean, had offered to negotiate the chairmanship for Wade on the strength of his Berkeley pedigree and his Hemingway book. Whether the appointment would have come to pass in spite of his otherwise spectacularly undistinguished background was hard to say, although Allenby's backing might have made it possible, had Wade been interested. He hadn't been.

"My dad," he said now. "I couldn't get it out of my head how he—no personal reflection intended—ruined his life when he accepted a promotion from teaching to go into administration. Ten years later he couldn't wait to retire, get out from under all that paperwork, all those meetings. He gave up the fun and freedom of teaching to make more money for our family as a bureaucrat—and killed his own spirit in the process."

Erica gestured now at the room around her. "Coming up here after all those years in the classroom wasn't a no-brainer for me either. You're right, of course, that there's a lot of autonomy in teaching you give up when you take on oversight of other teachers. I knew that going in, but I was getting a little burned out at the rostrum myself, starting to trot out the old notes a little more often than was probably best. I thought it could be good to try something new. But it's just amazing the nonsense you find out that other teachers get away with—or try to. Some of them haven't been to a conference or updated their research for years."

Wade was ambivalent about the conference end of this. Most of the professional meetings he had attended had consisted of the presenter's throwing up a Powerpoint slide, leaving it in view ten times longer than necessary, and spending the session bloviating about the wonderfulness of himself/herself, while the audience snoozed, drooled, thumbed cell phones, or prayed for the blessed relief of an earthquake or a jihadist bombing. Often the topic of the presentation was *interactiveness.* Almost inevitably the content was some repackaging of a bad or trite idea that had made the rounds of composition theory thirty years ago. There was no silver bullet for improving literacy. Maybe literature sessions were more uplifting, but, recalling those deadly read-arounds at Berkeley, Wade had his doubts. There was no doubt, however, about the complacency of the CSU full-time faculty.

Erica continued: "What's really distressing is how high and mighty they become when they get caught red-handed and confronted with their dereliction of duty. After working with some of these people for years as a colleague, never having a cross word with most of them, honestly, it's a little tough to have to be the one to tell them to get their act together or put in for their pension."

Wade nodded and moved toward firmer ground. "Get it together as in show up on time and don't dismiss your class after ten minutes, you mean?"

"Right. And don't arm-wrestle a student to get his cell phone away from him or tell a Latina that she isn't college material because she spelled your name wrong on the first paper or a black kid that he's a disgrace to his race because he doesn't know where jazz originated. That's not even counting the professor who takes a taxi to campus on the first day of classes because he's too drunk to drive, and then keeps nipping from a bottle in full view of his students for the rest of the day. I mean, we've all come to class hungover or a little . . . potted from time to time—"

Wade nodded again and held up his forefinger, *mea culpa*.

"—but this guy was way over the line. I had six students come in separately to complain about him—*on the first day*! Do you have any idea how many grievances are filed against English faculty every semester around here?"

Wade toted up, gave it a shot: "Probably about half as many as there should be. We're a pretty grievous lot."

"Be that as it may, there are more than enough to ensure that I won't be winning any popularity contests around here."

"Good thing you can still win the beauty contest hands down, then."

"You may need to be remanded for another go at the sexual harassment seminar if you keep that up, young man."

Wade smiled. "Feel free to report me to the dean."

She smiled back. "But thank you. If I see any stress lines developing, trust me, I'll know it's time to retire."

"Were you thinking about it before?"

"Not seriously. I've been seeing a gentleman who recently retired, and he's been encouraging me to consider it. Have you ever spent any time around couples who tried to retire together?"

"My dad again—and his second wife. Started drinking at four p.m. and were at each other's throats by five. They drove each other fucking nuts. When I told Angela about what it was like to visit them, she said it sounded like going on a picnic with Netanyahu and Hamas. I think Dad would have strangled her if he hadn't got sick himself and died first."

"Exactly. My gent wants us to travel, but how much of your life can you spend doing that without wanting to wring each other's necks?"

Wade cited the ultimate togetherness couple he had read about who pulled stunts like crossing the ocean in a rowboat, together 24/7 for six weeks.

"Romantic inspiration *would* seem to be inhibited by peeing over the bow in full view of your partner," Erica said. "Not even to mention the other business."

"Let's not," Wade agreed, although he knew the unmentionable would be hard to forget.

"Privacy is a precious commodity. I never did find a man who understood that I could be perfectly content without him for hours, even days or weeks, at a time. The notion of living with one who is home with me all day, without a job to go to, no one else to talk to, tell what to do, wow, that's really scary. As you know, I taught in Japan for a few years before I came to CSU, and I still have some friends there. One of them was telling me in an email that there's even a term for this problem now in that country. It's called RHS: Retired Husband Syndrome. The husband retires from work, stays home all day in an environment that the wife was used to having to herself, having control over, and now all of a sudden he's underfoot all the time and, knowing Japanese men as I do, undoubtedly giving her instructions all day long: how to cook dinner, how to clean the house—the same house she's been cleaning without benefit of his supervision for years. I'll bet she's ready to commit *hara-kiri*, or murder—*satsujin*—in a week. Too much time together does not a happy marriage make."

TMTT: a new acronym was born in Wade's imagination.

Erica shifted gears. "How's the book coming along?" Author of three books and numerous articles herself, she had been foremost among those encouraging Wade's overdue entry into the publishing arena, although she had expressed a preference for another focus on literature in his follow-up effort. "Finding any progress in getting blacks back into baseball?"

"The opposite, actually. Angela says no one is going to read my book, anyway—she says people who read think baseball is boring."

"She may have something there. Have you considered the possibility that baseball *is* boring, and that black people simply figured this out before everybody else?" She smiled again. "We're always at the cutting edge of culture, you know."

Wade recalled the sagging dog-walker he had spotted but resisted a cheap shot. Erica was as appalled as he was by the asscracks and grundies everywhere on display.

"Seriously, Wade, when was the last time you saw anyone on a baseball field do anything half as thrilling as what Steph Curry does every time he takes the court?"

He thought immediately of Jarrod Dyson's balls-out steal of third against the A's in the bottom of the ninth in the 2014 play-in game—the boldest stroke he had seen in a lifetime's obsession with the sport—with the Royals two outs from elimination, before crossing the plate on a tying sacrifice fly. (*That's what speed do,* Dyson explained later.) But there was no point in attempting a conversion. It was like arguing about religion: you either felt the holy spirit or you didn't. Erica enjoyed basketball and tolerated football but had no use for baseball, and, unlike Angela, did not seem destined to evolve.

Wade remembered his current purpose and turned the conversation to Allenby's proposition, resisting the temptation to ask Erica how her own relationship with the boss was unfolding. After Wade's foray into matchmaking, she and Allenby had dated briefly the year before while he was estranged from his then wife, from whom he had since been divorced after a last-gasp attempt at reconciliation fell through. The third Mrs. Allenby had apparently balked at the notion of recalibrating her lifestyle to become First Lady at CSU after years in a mansion in Beverly Hills, a beach pad in Malibu, and summers and winters on the Riviera or in the Alps. Wade decided it was a topic more suited for their next afternoon walk than for today's agenda, so he focused on the altering of his own role and the long-sought literature elective he would be letting go.

"I hope you can hold the spot for me for next fall."

"Let's try for next semester," she suggested. "I don't want to give this class to some burn-out. You've been waiting a long time to teach Hemingway. Maybe you'll have the damage in the Athletic Department under control by the end of the year."

"I hope so," Wade said, without much hope. "How much trouble do you think we're in for with this accreditation visit, though?"

"It's all politics, isn't it? I've been teaching here for almost thirty years, and I've been through seven full or partial accreditations. In all those years I've never once had an official connected with the accrediting team visit my classroom, nor have I ever had a colleague tell me that his or her class was visited. Wouldn't you think someone charged with evaluating the efficacy of an educational institution would spend some time in actual classes to find out what was going on in them?"

"Deadass used to bomb us with memos telling us to be on our toes, lest the Gestapo pop in and catch us in the middle of a vocabulary quiz," Wade remembered.

Erica nodded. "I recall the first accreditation visit after I was hired here. Even Dedalus was relatively new on the job back then, and he and the other managers made a huge production out of it, warning us to be on full nuclear alert, told us to make sure we were giving a real, formal lecture with all the trimmings, not giving a test or showing a movie. I think everyone, or at least all the recent hires, of whom there were many in those golden days, ratcheted up their lecture prep, set aside anything potentially more dynamic that might actually have worked in the classroom, and got ready to orate for the inspection. When no one showed up to notice, it sort of took the starch out of similar warnings in subsequent years. No teacher I know has paid any attention to that stuff in years."

"Did you ever get drafted to work on the reports?" Wade was still wondering how much of his own time he would need to devote to his assigned portion of the Athletic Department's.

"Oh, of course. You learn to give them what that they want to hear. Just recycle the boilerplate from the syllabi and the course information sheets, pop in some stats from the data bank, and make sure you get the trendy buzzwords right. This year's magic phrase is *student success*. God only knows what fate will befall any academic program that fails to repeat this mantra fifty times in its report or substitutes something totally inappropriate like *results* for *assessment outcomes*. One year I was strong-armed to attend a postmortem to review the team's report on our composition program. The accrediting team member chairing the meeting spent the whole hour, or God, now that I think of it, maybe it was *two* hours, talking about his sabbatical in England and bragging about the comp program on his own campus, supposedly based on the Oxbridge model."

"CSU Oxford/Cambridge," Wade said. "Nice ring to it. I hope you brought him up to speed on the Bakersfield model."

"He never even asked what we were trying to do here. Dedalus spent the whole meeting genuflecting—"

Wade pictured the deposed dean, eating shit with a spoon and shoveling it in with a gratified grin.

"—as if *the best minds of their generation* had finally convened. I think at one point he may even have patted Oxbridge on the back. Gordon Brooks fell asleep and woke up only when he broke up the meeting with his favorite party trick. No way we could continue in there after that detonation. Garlic-infused, if I remember correctly."

"I don't see how you could forget." Wade, a fellow survivor of his former chairman's gas attacks, literal and figurative, nodded in sympathy. "You're lucky you're alive."

"I imagine I'll be getting a summons this time around to talk up the minority hiring rate." She pointed at herself. "Exhibit B, after our prez. But have you seen the list of the other new faculty hires on this campus from the last few years? Almost all white women."

"I guess they're still next in line," Wade said. "I think Allenby will—"

"And have you checked out the *diversity reports* coming out of Silicon Valley? Even white women are having a hard time getting hired there. It's all white and Asian males."

"He can't do much about the dotcoms, but I think Allenby will improve things around here—if the accreditation team doesn't shut the campus down and turn it into a parking lot for the for-profits. He's hired the first black football coach and the first black basketball coach on this campus, and . . ." *promoted you*, Wade didn't need to remind her. He hesitated, then decided to venture into potentially more controversial territory. "Carlotta Baynes is up for tenure this year. What's your take on her?"

He had a hard time gauging the reaction to his question. Her disdain for incompetents notwithstanding, Erica was not normally one to dish the dirt, and if not quite the *if you can't say something nice, don't say anything* type, still closer to that side of the fence.

"I can't really say too much. She's nominally under my supervision now, as you may or may not know."

"I didn't know that."

"African American Studies, here as in lots of other places, has been a bit of a maverick department. Had its own dean for a while. Arthur asked me to take a look at the course offerings and see if there is some . . . fat we can trim. I guess maybe he thought it would be easier for me to tackle that than for Angela. For a while, faculty over there were just throwing anything they wanted together and getting it approved. Some of the courses appear to . . . overlap."

This Wade already knew. "Some of the athletes take three or four courses that seem to cover the same content."

Erica smiled. "I'm sure that's good for their GPAs. I'm not so sure it's a curricular model that we want to promulgate."

"Allenby will be hanged in effigy around here if he tries to cut back on that program. Are you going to stand on the scaffold with him?"

She shrugged. "What about you?"

"He wants me to meet with Carlotta next week about the student-athletes in her classes. I did a little preliminary research. She has the highest grade distribution, by far, of any full-time faculty member on this campus."

Erica smiled thinly, and, Wade guessed, a bit warily, or perhaps just wearily. "She's a very popular teacher."

Wade sensed that his friend had more to say on this subject but was not ready to say it, so he started to get up to leave, but Erica held up a hand to stop him. "There's something else I want to talk to you about." If wary or weary before, she now suddenly looked genuinely uncomfortable.

What the hell was *this* about? Wade sank back into his chair, his mind suddenly exploding with possibilities: was it conceivable, just his luck, now that he was married and out of play, that she was going to confess? All these years they had been friends, and he'd nurtured a huge crush on her, had she been wanting him to make a move? Had she been crushing on him, too? *This gorgeous creature wants my body! Who would've thunk it? Maybe we can figure out a way to—*

"It's about you and Angela."

There was the solution: A two-on-one! Wade's fevered brain sped immediately to the archetypal male fantasy, never mind that he had his hands—and other parts—full satisfying the needs of one avid woman. *If only she'd told me years ago, instead of—*

"More about Angela, really."

"Oh." *Shit.* Wade's dream team abruptly disintegrated. *Christ, don't tell me* she's *the one you've got a crush on. God, what if it's reciprocal and Angela's crushing on you, too? My wife's a lesbian. She's leaving me for another woman. I knew this marriage was too good to—*

"At the reception for the new faculty hires, I noticed she was hitting the cocktails pretty hard. She got a little . . . loopy. I was just concerned about her. I'm pretty sure Arthur noticed it, too—and others there couldn't have helped noticing as well. I think I've told you my second husband was a drinker. He was really close to his mother, and when we lost her, he just disappeared into the bottle. I don't know if I could have saved him, but I know I waited too long to try. I'm not saying Angela's there. I'm not sure *where* she is or what you can do, or even if you need to do anything now, but I just wanted to let you know it's . . . something to keep an eye on."

Wade sat back farther and tried to digest the news. He wasn't stunned by the revelation, he realized, and he'd certainly been noticing himself how often Angela had a drink in hand around the house and how seldom she settled for a single serving.

I've driven my wife to drink.

"You look like you've seen a ghost, Wade. I'm sorry if I—"

"You didn't do anything wrong," he assured her. "I just need to pay more attention to what's going on with her." *A minute ago she was a lesbian; now she's an alcoholic.*

"It's not an easy thing to talk with someone about."

"I know," Wade said. "I tried to talk to my dad about it. He let alcohol control his life at the end."

"There's still time with Angela," Erica said gently. "Maybe I'm overreacting, but—"

"You're not overreacting," Wade said. "If anything, I *under-reacted*. I need to find out what the problem is. Maybe this dean job is more pressure for her than she lets on."

Erica shrugged again. "It's possible. But I suspect she can handle anything CSU can throw at her. How are things on the home front?"

"I thought we were doing great," Wade said. "But maybe I was only looking at it from my side: it's been pretty great for me. I'll . . . talk to her tonight. Thank you for telling me."

He started to get up to go, but she motioned for him to stay in his seat. "There's one more thing you need to know about Carlotta Baynes." So she was going to open up after all. Perhaps she had been encouraged by his not shooting the messenger for the news about his wife. "I didn't want to prejudice your investigation, but—"

"Yes?"

"The first time I met her, at a meet and greet for the African American employees, she made a pass at me." Erica reported this with the calm nonchalance of a classic beauty who had undoubtedly been fending off since puberty unwelcome advances from all points on the gender spectrum, men, women, and everything in between.

"Christ! Is she—"

"Omnivorous, I'd say, considering the eye she was also giving Sherman Slate and a couple of the other coaches. I just thought you should know, in case she—"

"Swell. Well, maybe she draws the line at short white dorks."

Wade stood up again to go, a bit dizzied by the latest news-flash, atop the prior. Erica didn't stop him this time, but came out from behind her desk, stood next to him, and whisked a stray thread from his collar.

"You're not that short, Wade."

Some elements of destiny were beyond your control. Shoes you could put lifts in. White flesh you could bronze in the sun, or if the prospect of melanoma didn't faze you, at the tanning salon. Dorkhood, on the other hand, on the scale it had been visited upon Wade, was immutable. He tingled now at Erica's fleeting touch, a nanosecond of ecstasy, wondering again where *she* drew the line and if he had missed his chance when he married Angela—another beauty by all rights far beyond his reach. *What the hell is wrong with me?* He flashed for some reason to the ancient history of Lance Rentzel, golden receiver for America's Team, busted for consorting with prostitutes when he had Joey Heatherton waiting for him at home. *Wise men know well enough what monsters you make of . . .* us.

"Watch yourself there, okay? I have a hunch Carlotta could turn into a problem."

"Thanks for the heads-up. *Ups*, I mean."

"If I can help in any way with Angela, just let me know." Erica walked him to the door. As he put his hand on the knob, she leaned in for a light hug and a lighter kiss on the cheek. "Think about Hemingway in the spring, okay?"

Wade nodded, thinking instead about Hemingway in the summer, when he'd stuck a shotgun in his mouth. He closed the door behind his cherished friend/boss, stepped out into the dazing Central Valley sunlight, and pondered whether to track down his frisky colleague first or go straight home to brace his bibulous bride. What a choice. Scylla and Charybdis came to mind.

CHAPTER 7

When you come to a fork in the road, take it.

—Yogi Berra

There's a real mother talking.

—George, of Martha, in Edward Albee's *Who's Afraid of Virginia Woolf?*

"I want a baby, Wade," Angela said, after her apparently conclusive climax, graciously waiting until its quietus to make her announcement, thereby averting the stillbirth of Wade's own singular ejaculation, an event so subtle of late that there were times when he wasn't completely certain it had actually occurred.

So much for twin demons: *And then there were three.* Wade spasmed meagerly, cursed under his breath, and then said, "We talked about that, and . . ."

Angela was forty, Wade twenty years older, and the medical risks of reproduction had seemed (to him at least) transparently repellent: he pictured now, as every time the prospect arose, a hairless, hare-lipped mongoloid tearing around the domicile in diapers at age fourteen, communicating in a porcine squeal because he'd never learned to speak or feed himself or use the toilet.

". . . I thought we decided—"

"I changed my mind. Is that allowed?"

"I don't know. Are you allowed to change *my* mind, too?"

"Relax, asshole. I didn't say I wanted to have *your* baby."

"Oh." *Now I feel better.* Wade couldn't avoid yet another vision of Angela's recoupling with Ronnie Parker. If it was *that* asshole's kid she wanted him to raise, she could go take a flying—

"I know what you're thinking. Ronnie makes beautiful babies, but—"

Fuck. The woman was positively psychic.

"—he's already got enough of them scattered around here and there."

"It's good to know that his needs are being met. Who else did you have in mind?"

"I don't want to get fat. I thought we'd adopt."

"Oh." Calmed for only a moment, Wade's imagination quickly went into overdrive again, calling up in swift succession a litany of the horror stories he had heard or read over the years about adoptions gone not just wrong but cataclysmic: enraged former orphans who had come back to hearth and home from boarding or reform school or prison and rewarded their benefactors by burning them to death in the very beds they had once welcomed the ungrateful little bastards and their teddy bears into when they wet their own and couldn't get to sleep alone. "That sounds like a good idea."

"Don't bullshit me, Wade. You're shitting your pants right now."

"Actually, I'm not wearing any pants right now."

"Good point. Thanks for reminding me." She reached a hand down to stroke his recently hyperactive member. It shriveled under her touch. "I guess you don't find this baby-talk arousing."

"I suppose you could try rubbing harder."

She laid hands upon him again, to small avail. "Feels like we might be done here for a while."

"Sorry about that. I guess we won't be going for double figures after all tonight."

Wade had stopped counting after her seventh climax. The ease and frequency with which in the right mood she could reach orgasm never failed to amaze him. When he had been with Brenda, an Act of Congress had been required to get her into bed and an Act of God to get her to come. Angela, in the proper frame of mind, could get off as soon as he put his fingers inside her or applied the tip of his tongue to her hot spot. He offered to go there now.

"Let's finish this conversation first."

"Oh, good. Then we can go straight down to the pound instead and pick out a—"

"That's not happening," she said. "You hate dogs anyway."

"Only the ones that poop."

"I can hardly wait to see you at the changing station."

"What are the options here? If you insist on intraspecies, Miley Cyrus could use some parenting."

"Forget it, Humbert. You're *not* going all Woody Allen on me. I said a BABY."

"Who's going to take care of it? Are you going to quit your job?"

"Come out of the Dark Ages, Wade. Women don't quit their jobs any more when they have babies. Some women go back to work the next week."

Now there was progress. "Why not just dump the bundle on the desk at work the same day and not burn *any* leave?"

"Your sister keeps saying she's ready to retire. She'll have an empty nest when your niece goes off to college next year. I thought we could invite her to come live with us and take care of the baby while we're at school."

Wade scratched his head, furrowed his brow. "Let me get this straight: you want to have a baby, but you don't want to carry or give birth to it, and you don't want to take care of it. What exactly is your contribution going to be?"

"*Our* contribution, *stronzo,* is going to be raising the most gifted child in the history of the universe."

"I don't know," Wade said. "It just seems like so much work." *Even if my sister is doing most of it.* "Plus, what if he turns out to be a—"

"Who said we're getting a *he*?"

"—serial killer. Or *she* turns out to—?"

"Well, then you can write a book about him/her. It'll beat the hell out of that baseball crap you're wasting your time on."

Back to his repository of horrors: "Usually they torture and kill their adoptive family first, don't they, before they go on the rest of the spree?"

"See, problem solved: you've got your plotline down right there. This'll be a breeze. You're halfway to the best-seller list already."

"We talked about all this before," Wade reminded her again. "Is this why you've been drinking so much?" He had broached the subject of her consumption gingerly after dinner when she had poured her third large glass of wine.

"We talked about it at a party when *you* were drunk. Do you remember the description you came up with for a hypothetical personals ad when we were playing that stupid shots game?"

Wade closed his eyes and dredged it from foggy memory banks. "I was pretty wasted, but I think it was something like this: *Hot, fit, smart, sensible about money, loves sports, doesn't want kids.*"

"That's a pretty small demographic you've pinned yourself into there, pigman."

He nodded. "Especially for a short, balding—"

"Slow-witted," she threw in.

"—definitely slow-witted guy, who—"

"Who drives a fucking Civic."

"I thought that's what drew you to me in the first place. What are you *doing* down there?"

Angela had shifted to some kind of a tricky new two-handed stroke.

"Just relax. I'm choking up a little more than usual. Seems like it would be pretty much impossible to find a girl who fits *all* of your criteria."

"Evidently."

"I've tried pretty damn hard to put up with your Giants."

"God bless you for that. Can you imagine how many innings we'd have to miss if we were taking care of a baby?"

"So you'll miss a few ball games on TV. Can you honestly say that you'd rather devote your attention every day to a bunch of people you don't even know and will never meet instead of nurturing someone who will love you for the rest of your life, hang onto your every word, and take care of you in your old age—which, by the way, in your case isn't that far off?"

Wade took a moment to measure the pros and cons. The assumption, often voiced across the years by his students receiving multiple forms of public assistance, that adults childless by choice were *selfish* had always struck him as supremely ironic. Who was really the selfish one? The childless adult who took responsibility for his or her own economic impact on the world and contributed to others' welfare through taxes, or the fecund one dependent on those same tax dollars to feed, house, clothe, and provide cell phones for multiple offspring? Given the failure rate of parents in the population Wade had observed, he felt safe in the position that a great many reproducers could have better served the world with a more *selfish* choice. It was true that the baseball end of the argument was a lot harder to make when your team was eight games out before the All-Star break than when they were winning three World Series, but when you added football and basketball, especially the gloriously resurgent Warriors, into the equation, the answer quickly became clear.

"Yes, I think I can honestly say that. It's a *choice* to pay attention to a ball game. If you lose interest, you can turn it off. There's no choice if you have a kid. You *can't* lose interest. You *have* to have pay attention—forever. There's no off button. You turn your back on the fucker for fifteen seconds and he could skip out to play on the freeway and get run over by a half-track, or just disappear. You never see his face again except on a milk carton, and you spend the rest of your life wondering if he wound up in a sex trafficking ring or getting sliced and diced by a child molester. Or maybe *he* becomes the freak, and twenty years later when some dickhead judge lets him out on parole, he turns up on your doorstep with a hacksaw, because he blames you for everything you did to fuck him up when he was a kid."

"You worry too much, Wade."

"Thank you for the diagnosis."

"Want to hear the cure?"

"Let me guess: just say—"

"Yes!" Angela moistened her lips theatrically and nodded toward the relevant region. "You sure you couldn't . . . come along again?"

"Not a fucking chance in hell, Angie. Let's sleep on it, and—"

"Okay." She released him, turned onto her side, and was snoring almost instantly, her ability to nod off at will nearly matching her alacrity in reaching satisfaction.

Wade, as usual, couldn't get to sleep. He got up to worry some more instead. He didn't want a baby. The only thing he didn't want more than he didn't want a baby was to be without Angela again. *Being Without Angela* had been the hardest chapter of his life, even harder than losing his beloved parents, and he didn't know how he would survive going through that deprivation again. How many men, he wondered, had faced the same terrifying choice? How many reluctant fathers had been conscripted by the threat of abandonment? How many men actually *wanted* to be fathers rather than merely consenting to it to hang onto the woman that they loved? The old biological argument about males' drive to spread their seed seemed ludicrously antiquated now, with 7.5 billion crowding the planet; most of the men he knew, those with any education anyway, strove to delay, minimize, or avoid altogether the mantle of fatherhood.

It was just the next, staggering step into the series of sinkholes that life led you into. First, you looked around at the fucked up marriages of all the other people in your life, including your own parents, for Christ's sake, and you swore you would never do *that* to yourself. Marriage was a stupid, senseless, obsolete institution, riddled with hypocrisy and impossible constraints, a trapdoor leading straight to the hottest hole in hell, and nobody you knew who got married was happy about it by the time a few years had passed. Half of the couples you knew or had known didn't even talk to each other anymore, except to issue complaints, insults, accusations, or injunctions; the other half were already divorced. The ones who stayed married did it for financial reasons, or *for the sake of the children* they were fucking up for the next round of fiascos, and never had sex any more to speak of. Oh, maybe there was a token handjob or a pity fuck once every other month or so if the guy was lucky and obedient and his wife could spare five minutes from shopping for crap there was no room for in her closets or cupboards—you knew that because all of your friends, many guys you despised, and some you barely knew insisted on sharing with you the pathetic details, and you vowed to take a lesson from their miseries. Then an irresistible Angela came along and said *I'm leaving you unless . . .*, and so you bought the ring and put it around her finger and through your nose and swore that at least you would never have kids. That way when you got a divorce like everybody else there would be one less mess to clean up and no child support payments following you from here to Ouagadougou. But then when the next ultimatum was issued, you caved on that one, too, had the kid, the little son-of-a-bitch, and of course nobody wants to let you raise an only child, so you caved again and had another, and then maybe one or two more, and before you knew it, before you had even stopped to take a deep breath and figure out what the fuck was happening to your life, you found yourself responsible for five other people and their fucking cell phones instead of just yourself. All your plans to suck pleasure from the planet, to HAVE FUN, disappeared forever into the abyss of PROVIDING FOR OTHERS. Such was fatherhood. Wade thought again how his dad had wrecked his own life, and now here he was, poised on the brink of reenacting the catastrophe, at sixty no less. Do we learn *nothing* from the sins of the fathers?

On that comforting note, Wade finally fell asleep. He woke two hours later to find Angela awake ahead of him, watching him. Maybe she had even wakened him. This was getting serious.

"How come you're awake? You never—"

"I'm sure you'll be pleased to know that I drank too much wine. I had to pee."

"See?"

"See *what*? I've seen you put away a six-pack during a night game and then spend the rest of the night getting up and down to get rid of it."

"That was the World Series," Wade protested. "Game seven. I required anesthesia."

"Don't you think life is meaningless unless we pass something of ourselves on to the next generation?"

"Nice transition." Bombarded with existentialist literature from childhood SRAs through the completion of his PhD, Wade had long ago embraced as a core principle the futility of human endeavor. "As opposed to the fulfilling lives that the folks who begat Lee Harvey Oswald, Ted Bundy, and Timothy McVeigh led, you mean?"

"You realize, of course, that your paradigm is both racist and sexist in its exclusionary nature?"

"Must be because someone just woke me up. Okay, throw in the proud parents of Pol Pot, Lizzie Borden, and Joseph Kony."

"Homophobic, too. You miss almost all the bases, don't you?"

"Sorry, I don't have any gay serial killers on the tip of my tongue, unless you count Alexander the Great, whose whole goal in life, as I understand it, was to make his dead papa proud by slaughtering or enslaving the rest of the human race. See what crazy ideas parents put into their kids' heads?"

"You're leaving out all the good stuff."

"Look, Angie, the most important decision anyone makes in life is to bring another human being into this world. More important than where you live or what work you do or who you marry: you can move or quit your job or divorce your spouse, or—"

"Or, in some cultures, send her back to her parents, or set her on fire."

"Thanks for reminding me of the options on the table. The point is—"

"The point is you're a chicken, Wade. A big fat fucking chicken. You're afraid to take a chance to do something that could change your life, something that could be really—"

"Hard." *Also terrifying, humiliating, awful, and—*

—"great."

"Who says I need to change my life, anyway? Other than cleaning my car and burning my clothes, I mean. What if I *like* easy? What if I'm perfectly happy the way—"

"*Perfectly* isn't even in the conversation, Wade. Nobody gets that. But I'm saying *we* could be happi*er* if we . . . I just think a baby is what we need to get us out of the doldrums."

"I didn't know we were in them. Tell me again: Is *this* why you've been drinking so much?"

"I was afraid to tell you. I knew you'd freak out. I drank to—"

"Get your courage up?"

"—distract myself from—"

Ruining our lives?

"—telling you and . . . screwing things up between us."

"I thought we'd been pretty happy."

"*You've* been happy, Wade. You're married to a gorgeous woman who makes a ton of money and is dynamite in bed. Why wouldn't you be?"

"You don't have to be so modest about it. Is this what you were like in your interview for dean? Allenby said you were cocky as hell in there."

"I think it kind of turned him on."

Wade lay back. He imagined Angela gloating next to him in the dark. "Great. Are you sure you don't want to have *his* baby?"

"Billionaire genes are hard to come by," she acknowledged. "But you haven't been paying attention. Even though I'm still gorgeous, I'm too old to be sure of a healthy baby, and besides, I told you, I'm not putting forty extra pounds on this body."

Wade thought of Elizabeth Taylor, at the acme of her career, by acclamation the most beautiful woman in the world, packing on forty for the role of a lifetime onscreen opposite her equally celebrated sometime spouse—and then struggling to keep the excess off for the rest of her life in the real world. "Afraid you couldn't take it off again?"

"I'm not afraid, Wade. What are *you* so afraid of?"

"Nothing." *Everything.* It was the question he knew he had been evading for most of his adult life. When he had been married to Brenda, there had been the eminently logical excuse that no rational human being would choose to reproduce a version of her. But with Angela, there was no such easy out. He turned toward her to meet her eyes, aglow in the night, and was struck all over again by her beauty. What the fuck was a schmuck like him doing in bed with this impossibly perfect woman? He sighed and then took a shot at a real answer to her question.

"I think I knew from the time I was a little kid that I didn't want kids of my own. I just watched my dad . . . give up so much. This was a guy who could've done *anything*, climbed mountains, sailed to Byzantium, flown around the world—but he gave it all up to watch me pop up with the bases loaded in Little League."

"But you were there for him when he got sick, Wade. You held his hand when he took his dying breath."

Wade's stepmother had left to him the task of caring for his father in his final days. She had been on a golf course in a foursome with her next victim when the end had finally come.

"I did what I could," Wade said, "just like my sister did for my mom later, but it wasn't nearly enough. It was *nothing* compared to the sacrifices they made for us. It just doesn't ever even out."

"I doubt if they saw it that way."

"It's not just the ending that matters; it's the whole stretch of life you go through with—or without—them to get there." Wade's father had left his mother the week after Wade's sister had graduated from high school. Like a lot of men of his generation, *liberated* by the 1960s, he had come to see parenthood as a job that was done when your last kid crossed that particular finish line—never mind the thirty or forty years of fractured family life to come. "After the divorce, I spent the rest of their lives bouncing between them on the holidays. Thanksgiving and Christmas never felt right again. When I was with one, I was worried about the other, always missing someone I loved. I *hated* that. You must have, too."

Angela's father had been married three times, her mother four. Wade had met both of them (her father just once, at the wedding) and found them attractive, warm, charming—and the perfect complements to each other. He had even seen them flirting with each other at the reception, right under the noses of their third and fourth spouses, respectively. Two months ago, when her father had suffered a heart attack, Angela had raced to the airport to fly to his side—and had found her mother there ahead of her. What the hell had gone wrong for those two?

Once upon a time they had been the proverbial *perfect couple*, Angela had told him, with golden jobs at Johns Hopkins. Then her father got the hots for a graduate student, couldn't keep his hands off her, and the whole thing went to hell. The graduate student became wife number two, lasted for a few years, and then the cycle had repeated itself. In the meantime, Angela's mother tried out three more husbands—and carried on with Angela's father intermittently between the subsequent unions.

"Just because our parents fucked up doesn't mean we have to." Angela went undercover and put her hands upon him again, with a notably improved result. "A little rest seems to have done wonders for little Wade."

"Imagine what he could do if you let him sleep through the night."

"Just getting you . . . *up* for those four o'clock feedings you'll be signing on for."

"Can we talk about this"—*at the mortuary, when you take me in for a measuring*—"some other time?"

"We can talk about it anytime you want to, Wade. As long as we talk about it soon."

"Speaking of soon . . . better slow down now unless you want me to—"

"I knew you'd come along eventually."

He broke free of her grip and slipped inside her.

"We'll talk about the baby tomorrow, right?"

"Are you going to try to cut down on the drinking in the meantime?"

"I can't believe you asked me that with your dick inside me."

"I can't believe it's inside you again either. Two hours ago I was thinking of trying to get on the list for a transplant."

"If you go that route, see if you can upgrade to a larger—"

"Thanks for the vote of—"

"Did you just—"

"I think so."

"Better see if you can get a package deal."

CHAPTER 8

Why should we have to go to class if we came here to play FOOTBALL, we ain't come to play SCHOOL.

> —tweet by Cardale Jones, QB, Ohio State

The real losers here are black male student-athletes—we exploit their bodies while neglecting their minds.

> —Michele Siqueiros, Campaign for College
> Opportunity, and Ryan Smith, Education
> Trust-West

A comely coed had once asked Wade his choice for the most beautiful word in the English language. *Fellatio* had sprung quickly to mind but seemed impolitic in context; he had settled upon *summer* instead. Sitting in his office now in late-June, he recalled Joseph Heller's description of the summers of our youth *that lasted a hundred thousand years and still ended too soon*, the glorious, carefree, sun-filled days lined up seemingly forever, full of ball games and bike rides, swimming in pools, ponds, rivers, and lakes, building forts and climbing trees, outwitting lizards and frogs, staying up late and sleeping in later, playing hide-and-seek in the moonlit streets and begging your parents to let you stay out for just ten minutes more that inevitably turned into almost an hour before full darkness finally fell and you had to come inside to watch other people's adventures on TV until it was time for more of your own tomorrow. Of course he knew that it had been a magical kingdom he'd grown up in, made possible by the sacrifices and accomplishments of parents who had known nary a trace of the freedom from want and worry that they had bestowed upon him and his sister.

One of the central ironies of Wade's professional life was that he had settled on his *fallback* career largely because of the universally established pattern of summers off. Few, if any, other attainable professions provided such a generous vacation schedule. So many other people worked nearly year-round, it seemed, taking two measly weeks off, if they were lucky. Increasingly, Wade had read, Americans weren't even taking that much time off, fearful of losing their jobs if they fell behind at their desks. Working seemed to have replaced living for many of them. By contrast, teaching had seemed to promise paradisiacal periods of freedom from the grind of routine. In reality, however, for Wade as for many others, *summers off* had turned into *summer school* (a term Wade might have nominated for his *least* favorite in the lexicon, or down there at the bottom anyway with *concentration camp* and *prostate cancer*). The bills didn't stop coming when the semesters ended. For the favored few who had secured full-time teaching jobs early in their careers and could spread their salary comfortably over twelve months, this was not a concern; many of these fortunate souls were still out the door and off to Sandpoint or Aruba the day after commencement. However, across academia the percentage of full-time faculty had been steadily dwindling for years, and by now most college teachers, like Wade, had spent a good portion of their careers patching together subsistence income from any teaching jobs they could get—including in June, July, and August. Marriage to Angela had technically freed Wade from the economic necessity to work during these months, but since her job compelled her to work then, a sense of doing his fair share had kicked in. At least in the Athletic Department he was getting a break from grading papers, after too many splendid seasons squandered in the fluorescence of the classroom or the dust of his study.

With Angela off to a conference (devoted to recruiting out-of-state students, who could be billed at higher tuition rates, to replace local applicants, one of the ways California's university systems rewarded the taxpayers who funded them) Wade had been left to ponder for a few more days the baby ultimatum, if that's what it was. As usual, he put the problem off. He decided to tackle instead the presumably less consequential task of assessing the integrity of Carlotta Baynes' classes.

He had begun by exploring her Web site and making a few phone calls to her references before trying to schedule an interview with her a few days before the summer session started. She hadn't responded to any of his emails or phone messages, nor to the note he had left on her office door after stopping by during an hour when she was scheduled to be available on the first day of the session. In the meantime he hadn't acquired much in the way of useful background information. Several of her colleagues from the three previous universities that had employed her declined to speak with him at all; two others were so curt and guarded in their responses that Wade wondered whether she had not merely burned her bridges but bombed them. In a litigation-happy society, of course, you had to be careful, but Wade had never before encountered such taciturnity in conducting routine reference checks. Usually faculty you phoned were laying it on with a trowel, trying to help someone they knew to get a job or a promotion so they could pat themselves on the back for being so important, or building up points to be redeemed later when they tried for a better job themselves. Networking in academia worked much the same as everywhere else in the world, and to much the same effect, freezing out talented newcomers or candidates from unconventional backgrounds in favor of an endless parade of cheerleaders, toadies, backslappers, and bootlickers. Wade was genuinely surprised that no one seemed to want to tell him what a fabulous teacher Carlotta Baynes was.

She had been hired at CSU a few years before Allenby took over, and her impact had been immediate. She had doubled enrollment in the existing African American history courses and in record time had rammed five new courses through a curriculum committee notorious for its entropy. No one seemed to be able to say no to her or even to slow her down. The classes she taught had not only the highest grade distribution but also the longest waiting lists of any on campus. Students raved about her on ratemyprofessors.com, and athletes were always first in line to sign up for her offerings. Wade had been forced to inform several of them that they could not substitute multiple courses in her discipline for prerequisites in the kinesiology or computer science majors they had, sometimes delusionally, declared.

Wade knew that teaching effectively and being popular with the clientele were not necessarily mutually exclusive, but he also was well aware of the standard correlation between grades and student evaluation. Students, after all, were only human, even if sometimes just barely, and they had the same foibles as everyone else: they loved to be praised, no matter how lazy and incompetent they were, and they loved teachers who gave them what they wanted without making them work for it. Students busy with math and science courses liked having a class to coast in. Students who couldn't hack it in math and science were looking for something warm and fuzzy in which they could earn a degree. Carlotta Baynes was making a lot of them happy.

Juke Jackson turned out not to be one of them. At Allenby's urging, Wade had enrolled him in one of her summer courses, but the experiment lasted for only two class meetings before Jackson showed up at Wade's office with a request for a change to another class. According to his report, on the first day of class the instructor had spent the entire period talking about herself. On the second day she had invited students to bring in rap CDs and talk about why they liked them.

"I already know how to listen to CDs. I don't need a class for that."

Meeting students at CSU regularly reminded Wade that many youngsters did not enjoy the kind of privileges his own childhood had provided. Jackson's disrupted upbringing, while not normative, was not all that unusual either, and there were quite a few students who, like him, had gone to work early in life and continued now the struggle of balancing jobs with school and/or sports. They didn't appreciate having their time wasted.

Jackson's GPA could benefit from the class even if he couldn't, so Wade proceeded cautiously. "Maybe she was just trying to build a bond with the students, show you that she's open to your interests so that you'll be more open to hers."

"She real hard on some of the girls in there. They give her any attitude, she right in their face. But the dudes, they can do whatever they want. Couple brothers from the basketball team, they sit up in the back of the room, talkin', laughin', eatin' shit, while we supposed to be listenin' to her."

Wade had heard this about quite a few classes at CSU, especially the large lecture sections. Apparently many teachers had stopped enforcing civility in the classroom. He waxed nostalgic for a moment over Allenby's vaunted curmudgeon who had padlocked the door at 8:00 a.m.

"She talkin' a lot of smack in there, too. You think Abe Lincoln was gay?"

"I guess a few historians think it's possible." If not exactly scandalized by the question, Wade was at least mildly taken aback. He had grown up at a time when homosexuality was still categorized in textbooks under Abnormal Psychology, and a random game of dodge ball at recess on the schoolyard could easily morph into *Smear the Queer*. Even if he worried not a whit about what consenting adults got up to in their bedrooms, hot tubs, or closets, and even if his years in the classroom had pushed him steadily toward an egalitarian posture, it was still hard to let go entirely of certain ingrained irrational biases, and at times he couldn't help wondering if the LGBTQ contingent didn't protest a bit too much or too flamboyantly, while turning a blind eye to injustices faced by others. *When the niggers was burning down Watts, you motherfuckers was doin' what you wanted to do on Hollywood Boulevard. You didn't give a shit about the riot*, his favorite social commentator had famously said forty years ago to a largely gay audience at an AIDS fundraiser, and for Wade the rebuke still held some truth. Angela, a generation younger, was constantly pushing him toward a more contemporary view. She was in his ear now as he steered for the high ground. "Does it matter? The man issued The Emancipation Proclamation."

"Miz Baynes say he tight with his butler, black man name of Jackson—maybe one of *my* people."

"Johnson," Wade corrected, remembering from a PBS documentary and wondering if Jackson had mixed up the names or if Baynes had made the error in lecture. "William Henry Johnson. Lincoln buried him after Johnson caught smallpox taking care of the President when he caught it, coming home from giving the Gettysburg Address."

"Smallpox, huh? That like herpes, back in the day?"

"More like HIV back in that day, I imagine. Lincoln was lucky to survive." *To get shot two years later. Some guys had all the luck.* Wade wondered how pious types parsed Lincoln's assassination. Maybe God was punishing him for holding hands on a train with his valet. "I don't know that there's any evidence they slept together, though."

"What I'm saying. Seems like there's more important stuff to learn."

Wade found another class for Jackson and then decided to take another chance on catching his colleague at her posted office hour. Twenty minutes after her scheduled appearance, he was debating whether to leave another love note or hire a process server when she arrived with a pair of muscular myrmidons in tow, each bearing a portion of what was apparently her classroom paraphernalia. She appeared to be about forty, a bit heavy but attractive, with curly brown hair and a very light complexion. Seeing her on the street, Wade would not have assumed that she was black. The photo on her home page had seemed substantially darker. She opened the door for her minions. They deposited her books and stacks of paper, and then she shooed them away, winking and blowing a kiss, impossible to miss, at the more ripped of the pair before turning a smile on Wade, surprising him with imperfect teeth not altogether unlike his own serviceable but chopworn remnants.

"Sorry to keep you waiting. Busy day today! Are you here to buy some books?" She looked past Wade as she spoke, plainly admiring the rearview of the air-kiss recipient.

"I sent you a few emails and left a couple of voice mails. I'm Malcolm Wade, and—"

"Of course you are! Come the hell in, Malcolm Wade, and make yourself comfortable. I've been hoping we'd run into each other."

Of course you have. That must be why you spit on all my messages.

Wade entered a world apart from his own spartan work space. By CSU standards the office was huge, and he wondered if Carlotta had somehow managed to have the walls knocked out of two or three adjoining stations in order to create her own. He reminded himself to check the adjacent room numbers when he left, although CSU's schematic had been known to mystify even the most ardent of charters and explorers. Inside, every surface was crammed with African or African American photographs and artifacts.

"This is me," she said, swinging an arm wide to take it all in. "This is my life. What you see is—"

Oh, fuck. Is she really going to say—

"—what you get."

Wade heard Popeye: *I am what I am, and—*

"And you can *get* it if you try."

Did she really say that?

The lascivious wink again, this time straight at Wade. He eyed the doorway he had just passed through, debating the merits of a quick dash back through it.

"Now sit yourself down and tell me all about Malcolm Wade."

She cleared a chair, patted him into it, and then, before he could frame a syllable, launched into a high-speed recitation that obviated any need or chance for him to respond to her request for his own bio. He listened for perhaps ten minutes as she rattled off a laundry list of personal history, current projects, and connections to prominent types, local, national, and global. Obama's name, and his wife's, came up several times, in a blur of references, several of them borderline pornographic. Wade couldn't quite tell if he was meant to believe that she knew the President, knew the First Lady, or knew and had been to bed with both of them. She grinned at his apparent bewilderment when she finally paused to draw a breath.

Wade took a deep breath, too. He tried to figure out how he had gotten himself into this conversation and how the hell he was going to get out of it. *Allenby can do his own dirty work next time*, he promised himself.

"Allenby sent you over here to check me out, didn't he?"

Jesus. Why can women always read my mind?

"I like him, he a fine lookin' old dude, got some nice threads, too, but he really ought to come see me hisself, 'stead of sendin' his porch nigger."

Wade winced at the word, as usual. "Thank you," he said. "No one's ever called me that before."

She laughed. "I bet somebody somewhere called you that, maybe not to your face, but after you give him a D or a F on a paper he copied off the Internet and turned in like it was his own sweet epiphany."

Wondering if this was her attempt at an anticipatory deflection, Wade nevertheless saw an opening and took a shot. "I understand there has been an issue with that sort of behavior in some of the African American history classes."

"Now we gettin' to it, ain't we? You here to bust me for givin' up some grades to the boys on the team?"

"Teams," Wade said. "It appears that almost all of the athletes on the football, basketball, and track teams have taken your classes—and, far from getting D's and F's, have done remarkably well."

"Well, I'm a remarkable teacher. Couldn't it be just as simple as that?"

Wade sighed, pulled out his notes, and got down to business. "There were three hundred students in one of your lecture classes in the spring. You gave A's to—"

"That's confidential information. You a spy from the FBI or somethin'?"

"CIA," Wade said, trying for a smile that she didn't supply. "Actually, all this information is available faculty-wide on a Web site in the counseling office." This was true. Wade even knew of advisors on the CSU campus who scheduled their students' classes purely on the basis of instructors' grading patterns. He continued, "You gave A's to two hundred and eighty of them. Every male athlete in the class got an A."

She didn't run from it. "That's possible."

"The other twenty got B's."

"Everyone has room for improvement."

"Don't you think that grade distribution is a little . . . generous? How long do you think CSU would keep its accreditation if every teacher graded like that?"

"But every teacher *doesn't* grade like that. That's the whole point. You need some balance around here. You need someone like *me*, who *wants* students to be successful, to balance out the tight-asses who flunk eighty percent of their students and brag about it to all their equally fucked up elitist friends. You a teacher here, too, right? What do you teach?"

"English," Wade said. "But right now I'm—"

"What I thought. You look like the type of tight-ass motherfucker who flunks a student if he puts a comma in the wrong damn place."

"That sounds more like a D to me. Usually it takes *two* botched commas to get to—"

"In my classes it's the *ideas* that matter. When a student writes a paper, I grade on the content, not the little grammar errors they make."

Wade wondered if she even read the papers that she put the A's and (once in a great while) B's on. "You mean the little grammar errors like running three sentences together as one, or writing whole paragraphs that don't make any sense?" He didn't bother inquiring again about the *content* her students probably cribbed liberally from Wikipedia.

"Hey, that's in your classes, not mine. Don't be judgin' the work my students do when you ain't even seen it."

Wade had in fact seen plenty of essays drafted by his students for other classes. He had reached the inescapable conclusion that students who couldn't craft coherent sentences in an essay for an English class had the same problem in every other subject they tackled. Many teachers had solved the problem by giving up on assigning essays and substituting multiple choice or short answer testing; others simply delegated the paperwork to their readers, often employing in this role students who were barely literate themselves to rubber stamp the atrocities submitted by the masses of undergraduates now entering the university with the literacy skills of seventh-graders.

Wade guessed that the argument was pointless in present company but persisted with it nonetheless. "I don't see how your students could be so much different from mine. It seems to me that—"

"Seems to *me* like someone got a serious problem with his love life. Maybe I can help you out there. Let's put all this grading bullshit away and talk about somethin' *real*."

Wade blinked.

She laughed in his face. "Here you are five feet away from a gorgeous, sexy woman that you want to fuck so bad you can barely keep your pants on, am I right?"

Wade blinked again and forced himself not to gape.

"I thought so." She obviously took his silence for assent rather than confoundment. "You look like you eat pussy. That right, too?"

Wade stood up, blushing and squirming under the heat of her steady gaze. He considered the practice just referred to, however startling the context, pretty much *de rigeur* in this *day in age*, as his students were wont to proclaim it; nevertheless, as he eyed the open door again, knowing very well that he should just run through it and never look back, he couldn't resist asking, "What makes you say that?"

She shrugged. "White dude like you, middle-old, short, average appearance at best, and let's face it, I'm bein' kind there, no meat on your bones, probably got a dick like a thimble, I figure what other choice you got? You want to get yourself took care of, you got to munch some muff. Simple as that. You probably a expert in that department."

Wade swallowed. "I see. Interesting theory."

Wade was no expert. It was true that he had studied the matter at hand extensively, read books, watched film, came to the game prepared to give his all, attacked from every angle, stuck with it like a good soldier, and lasted as long as he could muster a trickle of saliva, but the results he could report were mixed at best. Brenda, he remembered, had tensed for the tip of his tongue as if girding herself for the hypodermic that would numb her gums before a root canal. Angela, by contrast, often, especially after a few drinks, could relax, revel in the attention, come explosively under his nose, even crush his skull between her thighs in spasmodic ecstasy to the point that he feared an imminent concussion; on other occasions, though, her curt tap on the noggin would alert Wade to the sad reality that his endeavors were this time unproductive, like a pitcher being pulled from the game when he didn't have his stuff. At least there was no one coming in out of the bullpen to take his place in full view of a jeering crowd.

"No theory. Plain simple fact. Black man, got him a hose like a fuckin' tree trunk, he think he the shit, don't got to get down there with no tongue. He figure he can just get hisself took care of anytime of the night or day, just show up, haul that big old thing out, and let the bitches stand in line, fight each other for access. Don't got to give back nothin' to get what he want. It ain't fair, it ain't right. Girl gonna give a blowjob, she got a right to get her pussy ate."

Wade took a breath, studied the open door and the blessed sanctuary beyond it once more, and then looked back at her. He risked a nod. "That's in *The Constitution*, isn't it?"

Carlotta grinned. "Nineteenth fuckin' Amendment. Shoulda spelled it out better, though. Motherfuckers, when they put in the right to vote, they left out the part about equal rights for your pussy. Course the brothers ain't read that shit anyway. They just be sayin' *get down there and take care of me*, then fall asleep on you soon as they fill you up, or jump on outta there and off to do the next chick. Or they think they only got to take care of a white chick, no tongue for a sister. You white boys got a better attitude, my experience. You know how to treat a girl right, give us what we need. Be honest now. Am I right? You don't have to say you *like* it."

"I didn't say I—"

"Nobody likes it," she continued. "But it's a trade-off, part of the deal."

"You sound like you've—"

"Done that? 'Course I have. Most girls have, even if they won't admit it. You want to get took care of right, you got to get a girlfriend to do it, everybody knows that. But you white boys is comin' along, I give you credit for tryin'."

Extra credit from Carlotta Baynes. Add a new bullet-point to Wade's slender resumé. He'd probably be needing to drag it out of mothballs soon anyway, now that this conversation had taken place. He glanced around the office, wondering if there was a chance she had recorded or filmed him for blackmail purposes; maybe that explained the reticence of her references.

"I'm just havin' fun with y'all, you know that, don't you?"

Wade knew nothing of the kind but nodded anyway and tried to smile. He pictured Sydney Carton grinning at the guillotine.

"Just givin' y'all a little taste of how us girls feel when you mens be hittin' on us all the time, makin' everything about pussy."

The woman had published; Wade marveled at the way she could go in and out of Ebonics.

"You tell Mr. Allenby to come see me hisself he got any more questions about African American Studies at CSU. But you want to be a little more personal, give me a call anytime. Hope I didn't hurt your feelings too much, what I said before. You actually kind of cute."

For a tight-ass, thimble-dick motherfucker, you mean? Wade headed for the door, freedom in reach, free at last, free to—

"Eat you some booty, too, I'll bet, dat true?"

Unbidden, he closed the door behind her parting chortle. A massive defensive lineman waiting outside it in a tank top and shorts grinned and prepared to knock as Wade brushed past him. Wade remembered him vaguely from a meeting with the football team and hoped the recognition was equally imprecise on the other end. The last thing he needed was a witness to whichever crime the political correctness police would surely charge him with for whatever the hell had just happened within.

"Sound like Carlotta in a *good* mood today."

"I'm Marcus Garvey," Wade said. "Son of Steve. You didn't see me here today, okay?"

"Didn't come to see you anyway. Marcus who? Harvey?"

"Maybe you'll find out in class."

CHAPTER 9

What does it matter, when you come to think of it, whether a child is yours by blood or not?

> —Jude Fawley, in Thomas Hardy's *Jude the Obscure*

If men could get pregnant, abortion would be a sacrament.

> —attributed by Gloria Steinem to a female cab driver who transported her and Florynce Kennedy in Boston

When Angela returned from her conference, Wade dutifully added adoption to the growing list of his research assignments. What he learned from his preliminary investigations provided few surprises. As anyone who paid even a modicum of attention to national and international news already knew, millions of children all over the world were waiting for help, and only a tiny percentage were getting it in timely fashion. Wade had been aware that there had long been a premium on healthy white babies; these, especially girls, it turned out, were still relatively easy to place, although they were getting harder to come by since Putin had banned the adoption of Russian children by parents in the United States. Children of color, those with medical issues, and those born abroad anywhere except in a handful of favored nations like China, Korea, and Ethiopia could expect to wait a very long time to get to the front of the line. Orphaned or abandoned black boys past infancy were far more likely to spend their formative years in serial foster care than to be permanently placed with a family. Adoption of children born in the U.S. was actually declining. About five percent of American women adopted children; many more were choosing childlessness. Republican conniptions notwithstanding, adoption by gay or lesbian parents had not significantly moved the needle in recent years; the trend for unwed mothers to keep their children instead of giving them up was the main driver of the current statistics. Without specifically seeking them, Wade came across his share of horror stories, but most of the statistics appeared to show that adopted children performed as well in school as children living with their biological parents and better than those living with only one biological parent. He was at his computer in his office at the end of his day, spending a few private minutes on CSU's dime, about to bookmark a site he had found with information about local agencies, when his phone rang.

"I'm in trouble, Dr. Wade."

Wade hadn't heard the scared, shaky voice on the other end of the line for more than a year, but he recognized his caller right away: Larashawndria Lewis, who had played a central if unpublicized role in the scandal resulting in the disgrace and departure of CSU's previous head football coach, Matt Lytle.

Larashawndria had come to CSU to play volleyball. Unlike Juke Jackson, she was not a great or multi-sport talent. She was tall, a good leaper, and a dedicated team player, but she did not have the supreme gifts of timing and anticipation that separated superstars from ordinary varsity athletes. She had worked hard to earn and hold onto a spot in the starting lineup by her junior year, but even Wade, who was no volleyball expert, could tell that she would never be an All American. Her ass, on the other hand, had been widely proclaimed All World, especially as showcased in the skimpy, skin-tight shorts that the CSU women's team disported in. At the home games there were always many admirers in the stands joining Wade in scrutinizing her distinctions.

"Always good to hear from you, Lara. Sorry about the trouble, though. How can I help?"

"Are you super busy like . . . right now?"

Wade had been moments away from shutting down his computer and heading home, with detailed instructions about the ingredients he was supposed to pick up for a salad to accompany the Mediterranean dinner Angela was essaying, but the urgency in Lara's voice stopped him in his tracks.

"I have time. Let me just call my wife, and—"

"You got *married*?" She made it sound like "You got *electrocuted*?"

"Stranger things have happened," he said, although offhand he couldn't think of many.

"Wow. Congratulations. I don't want to mess you up at home."

"No problem. I can be a few minutes late. Are you on campus, or—"

"I'm at the Pregnancy Resource Center."

"Oh."

"Want to take a wild guess why?"

Lara had a 3.5 cumulative GPA in a psychology major while competing in her varsity sport. Evidently another smart, disciplined woman had failed basic contraceptive science.

"My roommate dropped me off earlier, and she was supposed to come back and pick me up when I called, but her dumbass boyfriend borrowed her car without telling her and didn't bring it back yet. And she's fixin' to marry that fool."

"So you need a ride home?"

"I need a lot more than that."

"Let me call Angela, and I'll be right down there. You're on Chesterton, right?"

"No, that's Planned Parenthood. That's where I *should* have gone."

She gave Wade the directions, and he dialed home, wondering if his head was about to be handed to him. He made a quick pitch and prepared for the worst.

"Want me to come with?" Angela said, warming his heart with yet another unforeseen spontaneous gift.

"What about the big feast you've been—"

"I was just about to call you and tell you to forget about the radicchio and fontina. I think I've fucked up the spanakopita beyond human consumption. Let's go rescue the damsel and then you can buy us both dinner."

Wade pictured himself at table betwixt the two most beautiful women in the Central Valley. He worked on the caption: *Balding bookworm charms ebony and ivory goddesses, one preggers, one wannabe.* Close enough. "Deal. Maybe we can get a photo for Ripley's. I told you she's gorgeous, right?"

"You told me, fuckhead. Also half-a-foot taller than you. I'm pretty fucking gorgeous myself. Did I mention that I'm *very* fucking hungry?"

"On my way. Fat's okay after?"

"Over your dead body."

Wade arrived to pick up Angela a few minutes later and found the house full of smoke. He staggered in, fanning fumes out of his path to the kitchen.

"Shut up, Wade," she said before he could say anything. "I opened a window. Let's get out of here."

"Good idea to test the smoke detectors with some real—"

"Didn't you say we were in a hurry?"

Angela stepped into the bathroom, picked up an aerosol room deodorizer, and gave the kitchen a quick spritz.

Wade caught a brisk whiff of lavender mixing with the prevailing currents. "I hope that stuff isn't flammable. I heard that's how napalm was invented."

Angela fake-spritzed him. "Your turn at the grill tomorrow, Monsieur Bourdain. Let's meet this Amazon."

Wade could get lost going around the block, but with Lara's directions and Angela's kibitzing, he found the PRC, in a neighborhood no one would have visited except in desperate condition. He had envisioned a throng of troglodytes out in front, bearing placards proclaiming *Baby killers burn in hell, God will give you cancer,* or similarly subtle persuasions, perhaps jumping on the hood of his car as he drove up or terrorizing Lara when she came out, but he was relieved to see her waiting alone on the sidewalk. He swung his Civic alongside, bumping the curb, and then jumped out to open the door behind his for her.

"Thank God you came!"

She crammed herself into the back seat, and Wade closed the door behind her, then scooted his seat up as far as it would go, steering wheel pressed almost to his chest; he felt like the last sardine squeezed into the can. He grinned triumphantly at his wife, who waved him forward.

"My hero. Nice parking. Let's get the fuck out of here."

"Lara, the lady with the elevated vocabulary is my wife, Angela. Also Dean of Humanities."

"Wow! You're really beautiful. I never met a pretty dean before."

Here, here. Most academic administrators Wade had met looked as if they had dropped dead in the classroom after forty years, lain buried for several more, and then been dug up and disembalmed for further service at the discretion of a university president too small-balled to employ anyone alert enough to challenge occasionally his stupidest idea of the day. That was until Allenby came aboard at CSU anyway, started chopping out the dead wood, and hiring stars like Angela to light the way. "I like this girl already," she said.

Wade studied Lara in the rearview mirror. "What happened in there?"

"Did you know you can get pregnant if you take flu medication while you're on the birth control pill?"

"I don't think I can get pregnant that way," Wade said. "I've tried just about everything, but—"

"Shut up, Wade." Angela backhanded him across the seat, then turned to Lara and put a hand on one of hers. "Don't pay any attention to him. His idea of a joke is to name his car—"

"Is that information really necessary right now?"

"You men think this *is* a joke," Lara said. "You're not the ones who have to go through this shit."

It was indeed the definitive difference between men and women. Most of life's infinite array of alterations could apply equally to each gender: you could go hungry, go blind, go crazy, get tired, get fired, get hit by a bus, or get eaten by a bear, but at least if you were a male, you couldn't get pregnant. Yet. No doubt the transgendering teams were burning the midnight oil in their labs to come up with a male uterus to meet the demands of the future Caitlyns of the world, but that was one wonder Wade was fairly certain and fully unregretful that he would not live to see. In the meantime, *sufficient unto the day . . . .*

"I *did* know that about the conflicting medications," he told Lara. "The flu med prevents the birth control pill from doing its job. I had a student a few years ago that happened to, and—"

"What did she do?"

"She had the baby, and the guy married her a couple of years later. I think the baby was the best man at the wedding."

Wade watched in the rearview again as Lara nodded grimly. "Happy ever after."

"I heard they're divorced now, actually. Is that what happened to you?"

She shook her head. "I *wish* that what's happened to me. That's what a girl I met in there"—she pulled her hand free from Angela's and flung it back toward the clinic—"just told me."

"What *did* happen to you?" Angela asked.

"My *assbag* boyfriend took a needle and poked holes in the condom I made him put on. He made a bet with his fucking friends that he could give me a baby. Excuse my language."

"Jesus Christ!"

Wade had heard of girls using this tactic in order to get pregnant, but this was the first he had heard of a reversal of the roles.

"One of my girlfriends back home heard them laughin' about it at a party, then arguin' about when he was gonna get his boys to pay up. I guess they said wait till the baby pops out, make sure it's his, before they give up any cash."

Wade sighed and shook his head in disbelief. *The evil that men do.* Sometimes it was hard to accept that you belonged to the same subspecies. "Is this the same guy you told me about before, the one you were with when you came to CSU?"

Lara nodded. "Trip was supposed to come here with me to play football, but he couldn't get admitted, didn't have the grades. He finally enrolled and went out for the team at the JC back home. Tore up his knee in practice before the first game, before classes even started, and just gave up. Flunked out in one semester. Last time I went home for the weekend, I felt so sorry for him, all his dreams gone just like that. It was gonna be the last time we were together, too, I swear to God. I seen he wasn't gonna change, was never gonna grow up. Maybe he seen it, too—I mean, he seen that I was gonna move on."

Like Juke Jackson and many of her other contemporaries, Lara in speech routinely altered the simple past tense or elided auxiliary verbs. Wade wondered if she also did so in the essays she was earning A's and B's for in her psychology classes, but that was a topic for another time.

"So this was his brilliant fucking plan to hold onto me. We were together almost four years. I knew he had some issues, but I never thought he'd do anything as ghetto as that."

Wade looked into the mirror again. "Have you told your parents about this?"

"I *can't* tell them. They're like . . . the ones who invented church and made everyone else go. My dad's a damn deacon, and my mother hasn't missed a Sunday since Jesus was laying in the manger. I mean, I could've got this way gettin' raped by an escaped convict with AIDS and syphilis, they'd still tell me to have the baby. Hell, throw in Zika virus and anencephaly, they'd still say the same thing: *It's God's will.* That's how brainwashed they are: what kind of a fucked up God wants you to give birth to a baby with no brain? They'll for sure try to make me have it, probably try to make me marry that fool, too, even after what he did."

Wade tried to keep up. "So you didn't have the . . . procedure? What happened in the clinic?"

"They don't even *do* the procedure there," Angela snapped. "If you paid attention to anything beside the standings in the National League West, you'd know that. That place is run by the Catholics." She looked at Wade as if this was something he should have learned in pre-school.

Lara nodded. "That's right. It's just a place where they tell you about your options, try to talk you into keeping the baby. They make you feel like a real slut if you try to ask about an abortion. Said some shit about women could try to kill themself later if they get rid of their baby now."

"Did they offer you a referral to a real clinic?"

"I didn't even ask. I chickened out. I told them I came down there to do some research for my sociology class."

"Clever. I'll bet they never heard that in there before."

"Shut up, Wade," Angela said again. "What happened then?"

"I was talking to that girl I told you about, with the flu baby, and then these other women came over to us and started trying to give us all this Bible stuff. They were really pushy, and—"

"They really want you to have this baby," Angela said.

"Exactly."

"What do *you* want?" Wade asked.

"I went down there thinking it would be—not easy, of course—but not that big of a deal. Just tell somebody I got pregnant by accident and I need help. But you get down there and all the people inside are trying to talk you out of it, and—it makes you feel like some kind of a murderer or something."

"You're no murderer," Angela said quietly.

"They're just trying to intimidate you," Wade said, "get you to do what they want you to do, instead of what you want to do. Which brings us back to—"

"I don't *know* what I want to do. I guess right now I just want to go home and get some sleep. If I even *can* sleep. I hardly got a minute last night after I took the test."

"You want to come home with us and sleep in the guest room?" Angela made the offer before Wade even thought of it, the impulsive generosity one of the qualities Wade loved most about her. Brenda would have brained him with a frying pan if he'd had the temerity, during their union, to offer a night's lodging to a coed in distress. Wade also remembered, though, that Angela had been less keen to offer up the guest bed when he had suggested it for Jackson and Camellia, and he wasn't quite sure how to account for the difference now. Maybe she was more comfortable having just a woman under their roof.

"Thanks for the offer, but I'll be—"

"At least come have dinner with us," Angela persisted. "Then we can show you the room afterward and you can see what you think. You shouldn't be alone tonight."

Wade had to borrow a tie for the seating at Chez Marie, where Lara ate with more appetite than he had anticipated. Of course, the chow was a considerable upgrade from CSU cafeteria fare. Wade noted with approval that his wife took it easy on the wine. Afterward, Lara came home with them and agreed to spend the night. Wade fought off his latest *à trois* lunacy as he and Angela prepared for bed.

"That girl's drop-dead gorgeous, Wade."

"As advertised."

"Can you imagine what a beautiful baby she would have?"

"Before you go too far down that path, please remember that you haven't even seen the father. The guy with the *let's poke holes in the condom for a joke* genes."

"Maybe she has a picture."

"Are you serious?"

"We could raise this baby for her, Wade."

"Are you CRAZY?"

Wade stopped unbuttoning his shirt. He half-believed she was just having him on, but something in her tone told him to pay attention.

"We could solve two problems at once."

"Or create a hundred more. Don't you think the world is confusing enough for a kid without adding pigmentation issues into the mix? Shouldn't black babies be raised by black parents?"

"Don't be an idiot. Babies need food, shelter, clothing—and love—not coloring lessons."

"What makes you think Lara wants to give her baby—if she even wants to have it in the first place, which I don't think she does—to two white people she barely knows, one of whom is—"

"She thinks I'm beautiful."

"She said *pretty*. Get over yourself. And I'm old enough to be her—"

"You're not *that* old. Work with me here. I want a baby. Lara needs help. We can make this work. Maybe it's karma. The least we can do is ask her, give her the option."

Wade stared at his wife now as if meeting for the first time a creature from another galaxy. *Karma, for fuck's sake?*

Angela cuffed him on the shoulder. "Stop looking at me like you think I want to hack this baby out of her womb and steal it."

Macduff was from his mother's womb untimely torn. "Maybe we should try to go to sleep now."

"That's always your answer to every problem, isn't it?"

"*Always* and *every* in one sentence, Angie. You've hit the critical thinking jackpot."

"Fuck critical thinking, Wade. Fuck you, too."

"I guess this wouldn't be a good time to remind you about keeping our—"

"Sleeping bag in the—"

"—streak alive?"

"—garage?"

"I could always go down to the guest room."

"Dream on. That girl would break you in two. You wouldn't last ten seconds. Two minutes, tops."

"I seem to recall that someone lasted two *hours* the last time we—"

"I doubt if yodeling in the gully makes the cut in her league."

"Carlotta Baynes would beg to differ."

"Fine. Maybe you should try *her* guest room."

"Okay, okay, we'll ask Lara about—"

Wade stopped in shock. There, standing in the open doorway, was their guest, dressed for bed in Wade's much too small T-shirt, larger than anything Angie had to offer but still widely exposing a taut midriff and propulsing the swell of prodigious breasts. Wade averted his depraved gaze, looked at an equally discomfited Angela, then back at Lara, fiddled with the wedding ring on his finger, and said to himself, *All right, then, I'll go to hell.*

"Ask me about what?"

CHAPTER 10

Literature is mostly about having sex and not much about having children. Life is the other way round.

—Adam Appleby, in David Lodge's *The British Museum is Falling Down*

She wants the credit for being a mother without really liking children or wanting her life to be disrupted.

—of Georgina McCallister, in Justin Cartwright's *Up Against the Night*

"Stop gawking," Angela whispered fiercely to Wade, punctuating with a sharp slap to his slack, unguarded gut, before turning with a welcoming smile to their voluptuous interloper.

Lara held out a hand. Angela took it before Wade could decide if he should reach out himself and risk another shot to the breadbasket.

"I just wanted to make sure I told you guys how much I appreciate what you did for me today, and—"

Wait until you hear what a certain lovely someone wants to do for you tomorrow.

"—I wasn't sure I really acknowledged that. I know I was throwing a real pity party for myself when you two came to my rescue, and I hate that stuff. I mean, our whole dinner conversation was nothing but *me, me, me*. I don't ever want to be one of those ungrateful people who messes up and then expects everyone else to clean up after them and doesn't even say thank you."

"You're welcome," Wade said. "We didn't really do all that much." He looked at Angela and tried to decide if he was ready to hear her explain now how much more they were prepared to do. "We gave you a ride and bought you a dinner."

"And brought me as a guest into your beautiful home." She looked around admiringly at the wallpaper that Angela had selected for the boudoir with her customary *savoir faire*. Wade, in truth, wouldn't have noticed (or cared) if the surfaces surrounding him had been covered with purple polka dots or piglets playing parlor games, but he could tell that Lara was far more appreciative of his wife's refinement. "I feel sort of like Cinderella," she said. "Except I don't think she got knocked up by her retarded high school boyfriend."

The reference to her condition brought Wade the rest of the way back from Fantasyland. "Maybe we should adjourn to the living room, and—"

"How about the kitchen instead?" Angela said. "I'll fix us some hot spiced cider with rum."

"I don't drink alcohol anymore," Lara said, reminding Wade that she had abstained ever since nearly getting raped after a campus binge during her freshman year, "but I'd love some hot chocolate if you have it."

"Wade makes a killer cup of cocoa," Angela said, shooing him off to the task as she turned to sort through her robes. Good luck finding one to fit Lara. "He got the recipe from George Costanza."

"Who's that?"

"You have much to learn within these walls, my child." Wade placed a guiding hand on the small of Lara's back, promising himself this was the only tactile act he would indulge in, and then nudged her out through the doorway of dead dreams toward the kitchen. He fetched Bosco and soon had the beverages ready. Recalling Lara's punctiliousness about a distant Starbucks order they had shared when he was counseling her, he added a dollop of whipped cream and a sprinkle of nutmeg.

"You wouldn't happen to have a marshmallow I could melt on top of that would you?"

Cinderella indeed. "Fresh out, I'm sorry to report. But I can offer you a maraschino cherry to toss in there if you like."

"Go for it."

Angela joined them shortly, handing off to Lara a gift bathrobe Wade had never worn or glanced at twice but would see in sweet reverie for the rest of his days. Angela forswore her spiced cider and settled for sharing the cocoa, but Wade noticed that she tipped a splash of rum into her mug when she thought he was looking at Lara's tits, before they vanished into the folds of the robe. Maybe fortifying herself for the confab to come.

Angela took a swig and then said to Lara, "My husband has a proposal he wants you to consider."

Oh, good. My turn. Lara turned her wide-eyed gaze expectantly to Wade. He tried out, *You're pregnant and my wife wants your baby.* It was an improvement certainly on *My size two bride wants you to get fat as a hog and carry the weight for nine months so she can have a baby to hand off to my sister,* but it still didn't seem to strike quite the right tone to open the negotiations.

What exactly *were* they offering? Would Wade really make for Lara's child a better father than someone with forty more years of life expectancy? Just because Wade had a PhD and the condom-popper had dropped out of junior college, did that mean Wade was more qualified or motivated to guide a child—of color, no less—through the labyrinth of life in the twenty-first century?

How many other professionals who had navigated the path to a postgraduate degree had flunked the infinitely more challenging test of raising a well-adjusted child?

Wade would be seventy when the kid was ten, and eighty, if he lasted that long, when the kid was twenty and halfway through college, if he/she stayed on track, which hardly anybody seemed to do any more, what with gap years, semesters at sea, remediation (not likely in the case of a child reared, even remotely, by Angela), student loan debacles, and the virtually guaranteed multiple changes of major, the whole bewildering landscape of opportunities and challenges facing the current generation of college students. The average span of the CSU *four-year* degree was getting close to *seven* years. Wade could picture himself already, in his anciency, urging the adopted slug-a-dud to move out of the house before his/her father's departure for a nursing home. Of course, a man who had squandered a decade on his dissertation could hardly hope to set an undismissable example.

Then there was the question of his sister's involvement in the project to consider. Would Linda even want to leave the house she had inherited in clement coastal climes to move to the heat and dust of the Central Valley, just to have another child in her life? What was stopping her from staying put in paradise and adopting one of her own? She wasn't especially close to Angela, and even if the holocaust of family holidays with Brenda had broadened her perspectives on the saving graces of divorce, she had never forgiven their father for abandoning their family and might still harbor hostility toward Wade for accepting the choice. She was a very different person from Angela, a Christian to her core, and unlikely to see eye-to-eye with her on the values best inculcated in a child.

Maybe, Wade considered now as he watched their guest, awaiting his proposition, polish off her cocoa and extend her cup for a refill, that was the most promising escape hatch: even if Lara said yes, Linda could still say no. On the other hand, would that just make a stay-at-home job for Wade while Angela paid their way with her dean's salary or whatever other level of compensation she might ascend to if motivated by the presence of a prodigy to put through law or medical school or on the path to the Boston Philharmonic? Frankly, in that scenario, Wade was more worried about footing the bill for the psychologist who'd be needed later to sort out any child he had a significant role in raising. He glimpsed himself as Michael Keaton in *Mr. Mom*, demolishing his household, endangering his progeny; then as the superfluous, spastic clone in *Multiplicity*, a good idea gone off the charts wrong; finally as the cartoon superhero in *Birdman*, running to his entrance in his underpants, while his disenchanted daughter snogged with his despised and profligate rival. The three stages of fatherhood. Wade could hardly wait.

On the other hand, what if Linda said yes? Did Wade really want his sister to live with them? Were adult siblings really supposed to abide under the same roof? With a Christian sister on the premises, what would happen to the wild, spontaneous nights when Angela came sashaying from her computer to tempt him away from his own and into the sheets? Wade pictured instead the two women making goo-goo eyes at the baby, then taking pictures of his/her first step, first word, first precious independent poop, and posting all of the above on Facebook for the whole world to . . . throw up over. Meanwhile, lonesome Wade would be holed up on the hopper with a tattered *Playboy*, trying to recapture a fraction of Angela's magic with his own far less nimble fingers.

The plus side was that Linda was the only person he knew who lived and died with the Giants more than Wade did, so there would always be someone close at hand to dissect the day's game with or to explain the Infield Fly Rule to Angela if he got carried away with the fast forward button again.

As if reading his mind, Angela kicked him under the table. *It always comes back to sports with you, doesn't it, asshole?* She jerked her head in Lara's direction as the last of the chocolate disappeared through luscious lips.

Wade sighed, smiled at Lara, swallowed, and threw a dart at the board. "I know you said you can't talk to your parents about the—"

"Worst thing anyone ever did in the history of the world?"

"—baby, but maybe"—

"They won't listen to anything I have to say. I think they'd rather hear me tell them I'm goin' to prison for the rest of my life for selling drugs or something than hear that I'm not gonna have this baby. Like I said, it's like they've been brainwashed. Instead of looking around and seeing what happens to all of the other girls who had their babies with their pimp daddies, they just stick to the script that the damn church been handin' out forever. Girls wind up on Welfare or givin' their babies to their own mother to take care of, then they out trying to look for a job with no education behind them. All they can get is minimum wage, won't even pay for rent and food and formula for the baby. Come home tired and pissed off after gettin' yelled at all day by some fool of a boss who hates his own pitiful half-ass fast food manager job, she more likely to *bite* the baby gets dumped in her lap than cuddle and love it. I seen this many times."

Wade, too, had seen the parenting phenomenon Lara described, especially in the community colleges he'd flown the freeways among before finally getting on full-time at CSU. More than once desperate young single mothers had brought their infants into his classroom with them because they had no other child-care options. As much as he admired their determination to get an education, he couldn't help wondering: when did they ever sleep? How did they ever find an unharried minute to do their homework? What continued to mystify him was why these women, many of them otherwise apparently sensible, continued to put themselves and their children in this situation. With the thousands of products stacked on the shelves of every drugstore nearly guaranteeing to fend off reproduction before, during, or after the dirty deed, to conceive a child with an irresponsible partner seemed to Wade one of the stupidest things anyone could do. He had done his fair share of stupid things himself: locked his keys in the car with the engine running (twice), loaned money with the expectation that it would be repaid (more than twice), married a woman with a penis aversion she was *working on* (almost as ruinous as marrying a woman with a penis, as a hapless pal from grad school days had reportedly done), but at least he had not caved in to Brenda's demands and produced a helpless creature for her to abandon in the back seat on a hundred-degree afternoon in August when she met her idiot brother at a bar to wile away the hours until Wade came home to decontaminate the barracks and . . . bury the dead.

He looked at Angela, wondering if she was getting ready to relieve him yet. It looked more like she was getting ready to kick him again. Apparently the pitch was still up to him. Sometimes the starter had to reach down deep and try to go the distance.

He smiled at Lara again. "What if we"—he nodded at Angela, who gave him back a grim *get on with it, numbnuts* look—"told you we would like to help you with this baby?"

"For Christ's sake, Wade," Angela burst in, arrogating after all the closer role, "say it straight." She shot her hands out across the table and took both of Lara's in her own. "What he's trying to tell you is that we'd like to raise your baby."

"Oh, my God!"

Tears burst suddenly into Lara's eyes. Angela started to cry, too. Dry-eyed himself, Wade reached for napkins and handed them around. Lara pulled a hand free, took one, and dabbed at her cheeks; Angela swatted the offer away. *How can you be so cool? And why the hell aren't you bawling, too?*

"That's incredible," Lara said after a long moment. "Thank you. You don't know how much that means to me. I think this is the first time in my whole life that anyone ever tried to help me with something that really matters."

It sounded like an impossible hyperbole, and one that her parents, teachers, and coaches, let alone the doctors and nurses who had brought her into the world and treated her childhood ailments, would surely find shocking, but under the circumstances Wade thought he could forgive it.

Absolved or not, Lara rose abruptly. "If it's okay with you, I need to go to bed and try to get some sleep, so I can figure out how to deal with this tomorrow."

Lara came around behind Angela's chair, gave her an awkward hug, hugged Wade briefly as well, and then plodded back to her room. A lot to take in. Maybe they should have waited until morning.

Angela poured some more rum into her mug, not trying to hide it this time. Wade reached for her free hand.

"If she says no, there are lots of other babies."

Angela nodded and pushed the bottle toward him.

Wade poured himself a shot. "She'll make a good decision. She's got a good head on her shoulders."

"Not to mention a nice rack and a great ass."

That stopped his cup halfway to his mouth. "Oh? I hadn't really no—"

"Right. If you'd been salivating any faster, you'd have drowned in your own spittle, right at your own kitchen table."

"—ticed. Can't blame a guy for look—"

"I saw you touch her tush, too. I guess you thought you got away with that one."

Wade examined his guilty claw as if a crew from CSI would be popping into the episode imminently to check for residual evidence.

"I hope the thrill was worth it."

"I just hope it doesn't . . . impact our efforts to make history." He swapped out his caught-in-the-act confessional grimace for the thin beginnings of a lecherous grin.

Angela finished her drink, set the mug in the sink, and headed back into the bedroom. Wade rinsed up and followed her, wondering what the consequences of his innocuous contact, atop the inconclusive negotiations, might be.

His wife studied him from the bed. "You tried harder with her than I thought you would. I guess you deserve some credit for that."

"Oh." Wade brightened. "Then does that mean we—"

"Shut up and take your pants off, Wade."

This was by his rough count at least the third time today that she had ordered his silence, but the compounding of the predicate in this iteration certainly took the edge off. While she stepped into the bathroom, he complied with both parts of her command and climbed into bed, first shaking a figurative fist at the Yankee Clipper and then pounding on his chest as he inserted himself beneath the sheets.

"Not so fast, monkey boy," Angela said. She had stepped out of the bathroom, now nude. "I started my period."

"Oh." *Shit.*

"Wuss. Don't give up so easily. Do you have to check the rule book, or does a blowjob in the shower count?"

"A blowjob *anywhere* counts," Wade said, *as long as I'm the one who's getting it.* "Except maybe in the Oval—"

"Stuff it, Bubba. What about in the locker room?" Hands on hips, she leered at him, at once contemptuous and provocative.

Wade instinctively made a prune face, then tried to retract it, but didn't fool anyone, least of all Angela, who never failed to put his prejudices right back in his face. "Still *evolving*, huh?" she smirked now. "You're such a fucking 'phobe. Come on in here then, and let's get this over with."

He vaulted off the mattress in his best Olympic form but tangled a foot in the bedding, staggered, and then sprawled headfirst, spread-eagled at her feet.

Standing over him, Angela only partially suppressed a cackle. "Smooth move. If that's what you picked up from Pete Rose, I can see why they don't want him in the Hall of Fame." She reached a hand down to help him up. "Any vital organs damaged?"

How's your bird? Wade rolled over and saw a million stars.

"I think I may have fractured my spine."

"Rub some dirt on it."

As she pulled him up, a singular pubis came fetchingly into focus, the string from a tampon dangling as if to mock his concupiscence. He recalled a passage in an Updike novel, or maybe it was in one of his poems: when presented with this opportunity, the protocol for a proper chevalier was to go full speed ahead, gallantly tug the twat-stopper out with your teeth, as a prelude to . . . *BUT WHAT IF YOU SWALLOWED IT AND IT GOT STUCK IN YOUR THROAT, LODGED IN YOUR WINDPIPE, AND YOU COULDN'T GET IT OUT?* Wade pictured himself rushed to the ER, reaching it in tandem with the next batch of perforated gangbangers, being jumped in ahead of them, too late, as he turns purple and hears, as the last words spoken over him, *Poor horny bastard,* emended on his tombstone to *He died with a hard on,* to which some cemetery-creeping twit would no doubt add *And his mouth full.*

"What are you worrying about now?"

"Updike."

"Forget him. Up, dick."

"Already there. I'll see the trainer tomorrow. Anything for the team tonight." Back on his feet, he pointed proudly to the incipient bulge that her nudity had aroused and the face-plant had failed to dispel.

She shook her head and clucked, clearly less impressed than he by the dimensions on display. "Just so that you understand"— she released his hand, found another purchase, and turned to tow him toward the shower—"this one is strictly for the record."

Later, back in bed, streak intact, Wade was almost off to the Land of Nod when Angela murmured, "There's something I forgot to tell you about . . . one time I was with Ronnie."

"Do I really need to hear this *now*?"

"I'm sure you don't want to, but I need to tell you."

"Sounds like we need another drink first." He started to get up to fetch, but she reached out a restraining arm.

"Stay *here*. I really need to tell you this. It's the real reason I've been drinking so much lately."

"Oh. You mean it wasn't just about the baby you want to—"

Angela shook her head. "Ronnie and I—"

Oh, fuck. Got married after all—and never got divorced? I'm married to a bigamist. No, it's worse: Had *a baby?* Wade pictured a little Ronnie-monster wandering the streets with a switchblade in his tiny hands and Angela's perfect face. *No, thank God, they weren't together long enough last time for her to have given birth. But the asshole* could *have knocked her up. Maybe instead of having the baby they had—*

"—made a tape."

CHAPTER 11

I had rather be a toad
And live upon the vapor of a dungeon,
Than keep a corner in the thing I love
For others' uses.

—Othello, III.iii.

It's a simple operation.

—unnamed male to Jig, in Ernest Hemingway's
"Hills Like White Elephants"

Wade did not have to wonder what specific category of the representational arts his wife was talking about. "You *forgot* to tell me that you made a porno film?"

"A *tape*, not a—"

"Fine," Wade said. "By the way, Brenda called to ask if she and Tommy and their pet orangutan could come and move in with us. I said yes. I *forgot* to tell you."

"I knew you'd take this well. Okay, I didn't forget. I just didn't tell you."

"How the hell did—"

"Cammie Sanchez isn't the first girl who ever put herself in a compromising position. It was years ago, when I first got with Ronnie, before I ever even knew you. I was drunk, and I didn't really know what was going on until afterward. I tried to get it back from him, but I didn't. He told me he destroyed it, but of course he didn't. And now—"

"He wants you to buy it."

"Bingo."

"How much does he want?"

"A lot. We'll get to that. There's a little more you need to know first."

"Oh, good. It gets better."

"There was another—"

Oh, God, please let it be another girl, not a—

"—guy, and—"

"Oh fuck, Angela. How the hell did—"

"—he and Ronnie took turns with the camera, while I was with the other one."

Wade tried to banish the abominable image. "No double pene—"

"You know I don't go for that stuff."

"I'm not sure what I know or don't know about you anymore."

"So are you trying to tell me you never fantasized about doing it with two girls?" She lifted her head and nodded toward the spare bedroom, where, Wade guessed, Lara lay clueless of her presence in their conversation, wrestling with preoccupations of her own.

"I'm not telling you anything. I'm listening. Isn't that what a guy is supposed to do at times like this?"

"At all times it's not a bad idea. You can go make us those drinks now. Make mine a double."

Wade followed orders, came back, handed over hers, set his own down on the lamp stand, and watched her dive in.

"Take a slug, Wade. It might not help, but it can't hurt."

Wade took a sip. "It doesn't help," he reported.

"Come on, catch up."

He drank more deeply. "Still feeling the pain."

"So am I, Wade. Even more than you, believe it or not."

"Who was the other guy?"

"Does that really matter?"

"We're not talking Kobe or Derek in there with you and Ronnie, are we?"

"Do you think I'd share Derek Jeter with that asshole?'

"Just what I wanted to hear."

"Don't you think Ronnie would be blackmailing him instead of me if he was there?"

Wade thought Ronnie would blackmail anyone and everyone, including his own mother if he had one, but he conceded the point and nodded. "Which brings us back to who was the player to be named later?"

"Just some no-name friend of Ronnie's. In case you were wondering, I made him use a condom. And I *always* made Ronnie—"

"*There's* good news. Although it may cut down a bit on the commercial value of the—"

"Jerk."

"So how much does he want for it?"

"He wants a hundred thousand, but that's not even really the issue. How do I make sure that I get all the copies of the tape if I pay him?"

"You're not seriously thinking of paying him that kind of—"

"I'm sure we can knock his price down, but, as I said, the real issue is—"

Where to dispose of the remains after we castrate and dismember him.

"—how to make sure he doesn't—"

Bob to the top of the toilet bowl after we flush and say 'Amen.'
Wade had watched Coppola's *The Conversation* three or four
times. There was much to learn from the mistakes of other
well-intentioned murderers.

"—turn it into a regular monthly payment kind of thing. He
hasn't worked for years, and it's exactly the kind of scam he'd like
to cash in on forever."

"How do you know he doesn't have tapes of other girls with
the same plan?"

"I don't, and he probably does, scum that he is—but I doubt
if the other girls are deans."

Wade took another drink and then nodded. "Or have deep
enough pockets to make the extortion worth his while."

"So . . . what do you think we should do?"

"I could get on the phone and threaten to fly back there and
kick his ass."

"I can see him peeing his panties already. And after that?"

"How about we talk to Allenby?"

Angela frowned. "What would be the point of—"

"He, at least, could really kick Ronnie's ass, and his lawyers
could probably arrange for Ronnie to be incarcerated for a few
years—if you're willing to go that far."

"I'm getting there."

Wade took another drink. "I was there the first time he
slugged you."

"I threw a bottle at him first, remember?"

"A little prison time might have done you some good, too."
Girls who make sex tapes without me really belong there anyway.

"I don't think I want Allenby to hear about this, though."

"He's heard—and seen and done—lots worse. He was in
Vietnam, remember?" Wade didn't need to remind her about
the newspaper articles that had appeared when Allenby accepted

the CSU presidency. "A little naked flesh isn't going to send him into shock."

She nodded, appearing to consider this as she drained her glass, and then held it out for a refill. "So now you know: I'm a porn slut. Allenby's a war criminal. What's the worst thing you ever did? And please don't tell me about peeking at some online pussy or smoking a little dope with Brenda and her baby brother."

"A lot of dope, actually."

"Right. Like everybody else and his sisters and his cousins and his aunts. What else?"

"One time I claimed a deduction for a home office on my federal income tax."

"Oh, baby. Now you're getting me hot. You bad, bad boy."

"The IRS certainly thought so. They tried to lock me up for the rest of my life."

"I guess I'm not the only one who belongs behind bars then." She reached out, surprising him with a sudden stroke. "So when were you going to tell me about those threesome fantasies of *yours*? Erica Wiley is in there front and center, am I right?"

"I told you, *I only have eyes for—*"

"Bullshit. So am I busy with her, and you're sitting there watching, or what?" Another strategic stroke.

"What makes you think *you're* even there with—OUCH!"

"Don't get smart with me, buster. You're in an exceedingly vulnerable position."

"Touché."

"Okay. So what else were you going to tell me? There's got to be something worse than—"

"Actually, there's something else I wanted to *ask* you. Ronnie didn't . . . drop a log on you or anything in the tape, did he? Or the other guy?"

"Nobody pooped on anyone, Wade. It was just . . . sex." She stroked him again. "Do you want me to tell you—or show you?"

"Again? *Now*? You mean go back to the shower, or—"

"Right here. Just lie back and enjoy."

"I don't know if I—"

"Sure you can." She proved it with another squeeze. "But it looks like we're one short. Who's gonna be the other guy?"

Wade quit resisting and lay back. "Fuck you, Angie. Use your imagination."

"You mean like I do about the size of your—"

"Exactly like that. And thanks again for reminding me."

"No problem. It seems to be getting bigger now."

In the morning everyone, a doubly sated Wade included, was up early. Lara looked as if she had gotten even less rest than her hosts. Wade suggested they wait until after breakfast to resume their discussion, but Lara was ready to spill before the coffee had even been poured.

"I appreciate what you're offering me—I mean, offering my baby. I really do. I understand what it means to make an offer like that, and I can see what a great life you two could provide for a kid. I mean, your kid would have all kinds of opportunities that I never had and that I probably could never provide for my own kid, especially if I had one now. I know you'd make sure your kid gets a great education and lots of other great stuff—trips and vacations and summer camp and all that other stuff that people like you can afford to do. And that's not all, or even the most important part: I see what kind of people you are, and I know you'd give my baby love and encouragement every day, and good morals and respectable behavior that money can't even come close to buying."

Wade avoided looking at Angela when *respectable behavior* dropped from Lara's lips. He wondered how much money would be required to buy Ronnie's silence. How little anyone knew of the lives others led.

"I know all that," Lara said, "and believe me I don't discount it. But here's the thing: it's my life, too, not just this baby's."

Wade nodded and did look now at Angela, who nodded slowly, too.

After pausing to make sure that she had their full attention, Lara went on: "If I have this baby, I have to carry it for eight more months, lose a season of volleyball, lose the starting spot that I earned in practice every day for three fucking years, excuse my language, including my redshirt year when I couldn't even play in a real game. I'll probably lose my scholarship, too. Or even if I don't, I'd have to go back to square one to get back into shape and get my spot back. Do you have any idea how much weight I would put on if I carried this baby, how much that would change my body, how long it would take me to get back into the playing shape that I'm in now?"

"Other women athletes have given birth and regained their form," Angela, who didn't want to get fat either, said quietly. "It's not impossible."

"I know that, and that's great—good for them, because they chose to do it. They made a plan, had their kid, and set their time aside to get back into shape to resume their careers. But I didn't plan any of this. This baby only exists because my boyfriend played a stupid trick on me. He changed my whole life with his stupid fucking pinprick trick! It's not God's will that gave me this baby; it's my assbag boyfriend!"

Wade watched for a reaction from Angela, who'd had an assbag boyfriend of her own. She reached a hand across the table again toward Lara, but this time Lara declined the gesture and threw her own hands up in front of her face.

"I'm twenty years old! I should have my whole life in front of me. I seen what happens to girls who have babies at this age. I seen what happens to their lives. They get fat and nasty and angry at the world—and then they do the same thing all over again. They get trapped, and they never get out of the fucking trap. I should have a chance to get a good job and a place of my own and go on vacations and see the world and have fun and not be worrying about who's taking care of a baby that I didn't plan on having and that I tried hard *not* to have. I never let him touch me without a condom on, not one time. I never gave in to his *Let me get inside you for real just for a minute* or his *I'll pull out in time* bullshit. You have no idea how many times I had to fight that fool off—and not just him, either. Half of the athletes on this campus have taken a crack at my ass, and—"

Wade recalled seeing two or three CSU football players who had even tried to tap her at the memorial service for their murdered teammate, Marcus Foster.

"—not just the men, either. 'Course if I'd said yes to one of the bitches instead, guess I wouldn't be in this mess, would I?"

Wade laughed, in spite of the circumstances, and Angie cracked a little smile, too. Wade flashed first to Carlotta Baynes and then to Vera Farmiga in *Up in the Air* as George Clooney's well-versed lover: *Tried that. We're no picnic either.* In the wake of last night's revelations the topic seemed tepid now, but he'd often wondered if Angela had ever been to bed with another woman. He had never worked up the courage to ask. One thing the same-sex team had going for it was that at least nobody had to worry about getting pregnant.

Lara picked up her napkin and wiped her eyes again, then blew out a deep breath. "One thing I want you two to know for sure is that this is *not* about race. I mean, my parents might still talk some smack about how black babies need to be raised by black parents, but—"

Wade gulped, remembering that more or less the same words had come out of his own mouth.

"—I never bought into that. It doesn't matter what color the parents are if they are good people—and if they *aren't* good people, it won't do the baby no good just because they're black. Doc here already proved to me what kind of man he is when he stood up for me against that crazyass football coach—even though he's a white man, too." Lara looked at Angela. "And I already know how special *you* are, and of course I can see how much Doc loves you. Any fool could see that he's crazy about you, and any baby would be real lucky to have two parents who love each other like that. So it's not about color, and it's not about me not understanding what you two could do for my baby. It's about me, about my choice, for *my* life. And if that sounds mean or selfish, okay, I'm gonna say I can live with that. I have to do what I think is right, right?"

"Right," Wade said. He looked at Angela, still teary, who bit her lip and nodded. "We support your decision."

Two days later, after one more futile attempt to persuade Lara to speak with her parents, Wade accompanied her to the Planned Parenthood clinic. Again, he feared a mob of militants; instead he and his passenger were met by half a dozen smiling women, one dandling a pink-cheeked cherub, who gently offered Bibles or pamphlets, which no one attempted to strike them with or cram down their throats when they brusquely declined. Wade looked around suspiciously. Was this it, or was there a sniper concealed in the nearby trees or a suicide bomber en route to blow them both to kingdom come as soon as they passed within the forbidden walls?

"Let's get to it," Lara said, putting up a hand to fend off one last persistent offer of salvation. Sometimes, Wade had to concede, there were benefits to having a less fervid imagination and a less active awareness of the world's inventory of atrocities.

He tried to read while the procedure was performed, but today even the sports page failed to divert him from contemplation of the consequences of his actions. He'd been unabashedly pro-choice for as long as he had understood anything about the vagaries of human reproduction, but to be caught up in the actual process of a termination, even as a mere driver of the delivery/getaway car, hit him harder now than he had anticipated. God only knew what Lara was going through now and would feel later. Even if it was the right thing to do for a thousand reasons, it might still be hell on Earth for her afterward. He wondered if she would ever be able to tell her parents. Would keeping a secret like that, if it was even a possibility given the foibles of the would-be father, haunt her for the rest of her days, or was that just anti-feminist propaganda? Wade wasn't sure, but he was thankful again to have been born without a womb.

For the immediate aftermath, Angela had offered the guest room once more, but Lara had elected not to impose further on their hospitality, so when it was over Wade took her back to the campus. At the entrance to her dormitory, he accepted a lifeless hug and left her, hoping he had done the right thing but feeling like . . . what? Accessory? He could always rationalize the matter by conjecturing that someone else would have stepped up to take her if he had refused, but on some level he knew that his support had meant more for Lara than mere transportation. A year, or ten years, from now, would she thank him or curse him for it? What if she never had another chance to be a mother? As unlikely as that seemed, it wasn't impossible. There were no ends to the ways you could beat yourself up for trying to help another human being.

It was murder not telling Allenby. Wade was used to confiding in his great friend about every major issue in his life, but he had promised Lara to tell no one, so Angela and the unreliably affianced roommate were the only ones outside the clinic in the know. How the boyfriend/father would be dealt with Wade wasn't sure, but in view of the intellect indicated by his behavior and GPA, an alien abduction tale seemed at least worth a try. Or maybe his gambling partners would solve the problem permanently for all involved when he couldn't pay off on his bet.

Angela had decided not to enlist Allenby's aid in her dealings with Ronnie at least for the time being, so Wade had two secrets to keep when he met with the president to review other matters. Wade supplied an edited version of his meeting with Carlotta Baynes and explained that he had signed Juke Jackson up for Introduction to Business on the premise that it wouldn't hurt him to get a little training in management of the assets his physical prowess would shortly be yielding. Allenby listened without apparent consternation or even surprise to the Baynes update and briskly nodded approval of the news about Jackson. He obviously had other matters on his mind.

"We've heard from Camellia Sanchez's parents. They're planning to file a civil suit against the university for failing to oversee our athletic programs properly, specifically the behavior of our male athletes."

Wade whistled. "Wow. Art Briles is in hot water for that at Baylor, and—"

"His Holiness Ken Starr may go down with him," Allenby added. "Couldn't happen to a nicer guy. Of course Starr will keep his full professorship at the law school and his big fat salary, but it's definitely a sign that we need to take this stuff seriously."

"Is she—or are her parents—going after Dawes, specifically, this time or—"

"We don't know all the details of the accusations yet, but they're threatening to name Juke Jackson as one of those who abused her. It makes sense from a financial standpoint: Dawes is out of here, so they probably figure they can get more money out of us if they put the pressure on the presumptive starting QB of the football team. They'll also probably file against Dawes separately, try to get some of that Dodgers money."

"What are we going to do?"

Allenby shrugged. "We'll almost surely settle out of court and make a payment. The U's lawyers will tell me it'll be cheaper in the long run."

"I don't know if Juke will be on board with that. The girl stole his fucking furniture. *She's* the one who ought to be held liable for—"

"She didn't punch herself in the face, though."

Wade nodded to concede the point, wondering how Jackson would take the news of his lost love's latest betrayal.

Allenby sighed. "We've got to find a way to get these boys—these young men—we bring to our campus to treat women—to treat *everyone*—with simple common courtesy and respect. What good are all the abstract lessons in the classroom, all the degrees we hand out, if our students can't even be counted on to do that?"

He sighed again and then picked up a folder from his desk.

"There's more on the accreditation front, too. What you were telling me about Carlotta Baynes may complicate this visit considerably. We may have to shut down her program."

"A black president shutting down the Black Studies Department? Do you want to line up now for tar-and-feathering?"

"Just be aware that if I close out Baynes, she may come back at you, too. I probably should've taken that bullet myself."

Wade was beginning to regret editing his report. He wondered if anyone had ever called Allenby a porch nigger. And then in the next breath offered to jump into the sack with him.

"In the meantime, if this suit by the Sanchez clan goes viral, we'll be at the center of the firestorm over abuses by college athletes. You'd better let Jackson know that he may be getting some heat again soon. How's he doing in that summer class you signed him up for? He's not going to flunk out on us and make all this other stuff irrelevant, is he?"

Wade flipped his hand back and forth in the *could go either way* signal. "He's struggling with the basic math involved, but he's working on it every day, going to every class, doing his homework, going for tutoring. He's giving it his best shot."

Jackson was doing all that while working out twice a day, four or five hours total, to get ready for football. Wade found him at his minimally refurbished apartment after his second workout of the day, poring over the chapter in his textbook to be featured in an upcoming quiz. Before Wade could deliver the breaking news about Camellia, Jackson surprised him with an update of his own, straight from the source.

"She pregnant, Doc."

"Yours?"

"So she sayin', anyway."

"How far along is she?"

"Say she just found out. Missed her period. Look like four, five weeks."

"That would put it right around the time of the shit with Dawes and his crew."

"What I'm thinkin'."

Of course, it was also true that Jackson had been with her the night before. Obviously, he had made the same calculation.

"You may have to go back in for another DNA test."

"Don't they keep that stuff for a while?"

"I guess we'll find out."

"Girl is fuckin' crazy. First she 'cuse me of rapin' her, try to ruin my life, now she want me to marry her, have this baby, might not even be mine. *Probably* not mine—we was real careful. *I* was anyway. Like I told you, I never did nothin' with her without protection."

That sounded like a prudent policy for a number of reasons. "When did you hear from her?"

"Today. She texted me, man. I was in class when I got it. Almost lost it in there." Jackson waved a hand at the pages beneath him. "Hard enough to concentrate on this shit without her comin' at me again."

"I wonder if she and her parents are on the same page about how to handle this."

"She say she hates 'em. Spends her whole life runnin' away from 'em, then runs back to 'em when the shit goes down. Don't know what she'd do if she had no mommy and daddy to clean up her messes."

"It doesn't seem fair that you should be the one to clean up this one."

"If it's mine, I'll pay to get it took care of. Or to support the baby, if she want to have it. Or I'll raise it myself, get some help if I have to. No way, though, I can marry that girl after what went down before."

Let alone what's going down now. Wade decided to save the news about the lawsuit for the next counseling session. In the meantime he wondered whether Cammie had sent the same message to Johnny Dawes and his date-raping frat brothers, to see if any of them would claim responsibility for her child, and whether *Reply All* was an option.

Jackson had another update for him: "JD beat her up again when he found out she pregnant. She almost lost the baby right then."

Perverse as the notion might seem to some, Wade couldn't help thinking that a miscarriage might not have been the worst outcome in the case. On the other hand, he reflected, as he left Jackson to wrestle with his arithmetic, if Cammie went ahead with the birth, maybe her family would sell HBO the rights to film the whole damn thing, right through to the delivery room, her baby famous before its eyes were ever even open to behold the *brave new world* it was entering.

CHAPTER 12

His life will never be the one that he dreamed about and worked so hard to achieve. That is a steep price to pay for 20 minutes of action out of his 20 plus years of life.

—Dan A. Turner, letter to Judge Aaron Persky, urging a reduced sentence for his son Brock, Stanford swimmer and Olympic hopeful, after conviction for sexually assaulting an unconscious woman on campus. Sentenced to six months in jail, Brock Turner served three.

I am not what I am.

—Iago, *Othello*, I.i

It was Cenon Aquino whose continuing investigation ultimately got to the bottom of the Camellia Sanchez case. With the city cops overwhelmed by the daily challenges of preserving a semblance of law and order in a culture ruled by guns and drugs, and their own investigation blunted by Sanchez's contradictory accusations, Aquino had quietly persisted with his interrogation of parties known to be associated with Johnny Dawes. The shortstop himself was off to Utah to play on the Dodgers' rookie league team, a stopover in Mormonia perhaps just the ticket to curb his off-field improprieties. Aquino had asked around and tracked down the three fraternity brothers seen with Dawes on the night of the assault. With all three intent upon evading responsibility for the crime and continuing their education at CSU, Aquino had interviewed them separately and eventually established a convincing version of what had transpired. After meeting with the police chief and the district attorney to file his report, he returned to the president's office to brief Allenby and Wade before the news would hit the headlines.

"One of the kids cracked and gave up the others," Aquino said. "He admitted that all of them had intercourse with Sanchez after Dawes doped her with Rohypnol."

"Christ," Allenby said, "what did you do to get that out of him, waterboard him?"

Aquino shrugged. "I just talked to him. He started out wanting to stay in school and graduate on time. Now he's hoping to stay out of prison."

"These three kids are all white, aren't they?" Allenby asked.

"Affirmative." Aquino handed Allenby a folder that included photos of the culprits.

Allenby studied the photos and then passed the folder to Wade. "We'll terminate their enrollment immediately, let them take their chances in court. If they were black, they'd probably be looking at fifteen years, like that kid from Vanderbilt."

"Dawes is the only black kid in the fraternity," Aquino said. "There are a couple of Asians they probably let in to give the frat's GPA a boost, but the rest are all white."

Allenby turned to Wade. "That frat's been in trouble before, hasn't it?"

Wade nodded. "They've pretty much been on permanent probation. They had a chugging contest a couple of years ago, and a pledge fell off the balcony and broke his neck. I think he won the contest, though."

Wade looked at Aquino, wounded so grievously in the service of his country, to see if the veteran would register his contempt for the level of idiocy that led some to squander so casually the blessing of intact health that he would never again know.

Aquino ignored Wade's glance and stayed on task. "All three of the other kids say Dawes is the one who did the doping and that he participated in the sex."

Allenby sighed. "Blame the black guy, huh?"

Even when he's three-quarters white.

"There's more confirming evidence," Aquino continued. "The kid who cracked first used his cell phone to film the whole thing, except his own participation in the sex, or maybe he figured out a way to delete that part if one of the other guys filmed it. He thought he'd deleted all of it, but he emailed it first to one of the other frat members, and that guy saved it on his computer. When I found the computer guy, that's how I got the leverage to break the others down. The cops will subpoena the kid's hard drive, and it will be pretty tough stuff for any judge or jury to ignore, even if Sanchez recants just about everything she said."

"This is going to be wonderful publicity for our university and our baseball program," Allenby said to Wade, after thanking Aquino for his report and sending him back to work. "There's one good thing: at least Juke Jackson should be completely in the clear."

"Not exactly." Wade hadn't had a chance until now to tell Allenby about the little surprise in Camellia's text message.

"Oh, great. Just what a kid trying to play quarterback and center field at the same time needs to add to his cart."

"I wonder what the Dodgers will do about Dawes."

"Fuck the Dodgers," Allenby said, the refrain becoming music to Wade's ears. Some songs you never tired of hearing. "Let's focus on what we're going to do about *our* programs. How are we doing with our graduation rates?"

"Slate has improved it for football," Wade reported. "We've pulled ahead of Cal now."

The Stanford man grunted. "That's setting the bar pretty fucking low. What are the Golden Bears at now, 40%?"

"Something like that. Classes there are tough."

"They don't worship football in Berkeley, so the profs don't cave and give away the grades. I'll bet the same kids would be doing just fine in Tuscaloosa. I wonder what the GSR is *there*."

"I'll find out," Wade said. "I don't know if Alabama graduates them or just sends them straight to the penitentiary when their football eligibility ends. Did you see that photo the 'Bama running back sent out on Instagram with his new Dodge Charger? I guess a full ride goes a long way in the Deep South."

"About the same at all the big football schools, I imagine," Allenby said. "Hard to keep kids from doing stupid stuff."

"Anyway, we're near 50% and trending up in football and basketball. Slate and Cody are doing a solid job with their study hall programs, and we've hired and trained more tutors."

"Glad to hear it. What do you know about Eduardo Alvarez?"

Wade blinked at the abrupt transition and took a moment to scroll through his mental files before replying. "Infielder, utility type, came up with the Angels, I think, bounced around the bigs for a long time, played on a couple of World Series teams at the end of his career. Great glove, decent hitter, a guy who could steal a base or get a bunt down."

"That's the way I remember him, too."

Wade went on with the scouting report: "Dominican, isn't he? Played with the Padres for a year or two when Bochy was managing them, before Boch came to SF and became a genius."

"I hope you're not going to hold that against him. What would you say if I told you Alvarez was available to coach our baseball team?"

"If I didn't know better, I'd probably ask if you'd been overindulging in that medical marijuana you don't have a prescription for. I thought we already had a baseball coach."

"*Had* is correct, as in past tense. Sharky Sheehan has agreed to step down. After this Sanchez fiasco and the noises the faculty senate is making again about shutting down the program, he's ready to call it a career. He doesn't want to face that kind of heat."

"Let me guess: a generous settlement has fallen from the heavens and landed in his cap."

"He gave me some grief at first when I broached the idea. I asked him about the fight between Dawes and the second baseman, and the gun in Dawes' locker. First, he denied both, so I told him there were multiple credible witnesses to each incident—which there are, thanks to your research. Then he said—wait for it—*That's the kind of stuff you have to deal with when you add black players to a team.*"

Wade covered his face with his hands. "He said that to *you*?"

Allenby turned his palms up. "So I pulled a few strings and got him a nice cushy P.E. gig. You know I've been trying to expand the Physical Education course offerings for the general student population anyway, so he'll get a few sections of coed Ping-Pong and a couple of weight training classes, which even he can't find a way to fuck up."

"The man once lost 26 games in a row," Wade reminded him, "including one to Menlo College and one to Cal Tech. He's never even beaten the Banana Slugs. Are you sure we can trust him to station a spotter for the cling-and-jerks?"

"We'll surround him with teaching assistants. He can sit in the bleachers and chew on his chaw, tell stories about how he discovered Juke Jackson and single-handedly coached CSU to the brink of the College World Series. Alvarez is coming here to kick the tires on taking his place. I talked to him over the phone about getting more black kids on the path to MLB with our two-sport plan, and he's interested in the project. He's been working with the Dominican national team, and he found a couple of great prospects who'll be in the majors soon. Some of the stuff he's been working on with them might just transfer to our own kids. He'll be here this afternoon. I want you to meet him. We may be the smallest hiring committee in CSU history, but if he's up for it, I just might exercise my executive authority to fill an emergency vacancy and make him an offer today."

"This is sort of a weird question to raise in present company," Wade said, "but I wonder why he still wants to work after all the dough he raked in before." Willie Mays had topped out at about $200,000 per year; even utility infielders made more now in a single year than Mays had made in his career.

Allenby shrugged. "He's got six kids to feed."

"Think he might want to put one up for adoption?"

"The dean's still on that kick, huh?"

"*There ain't no let up, the live-long night and—*"

"I can't picture you changing didies at this stage of life."

"Join the club. I thought maybe Eduardo could spare one who's already potty-trained."

Wade hadn't learned yet whether Allenby shared Erica's concerns over Angela's drinking. He decided to find out now.

Allenby shrugged again. "I'd drink heavily, too, if I were married to you."

Wade went to lunch and came back to find Allenby engrossed in conversation with the candidate. Eduardo Alvarez stood up to greet him. He was not much taller than Wade and didn't have much more hair, either. He did have a magnetic smile, and he won further points with just the right handshake. Some ex-jocks you met wanted to prove they were still by far the better man by crushing you with a grip you would be feeling for weeks.

"I was just asking Eduardo about playing for Bochy—and telling him how much you love the man's managing style."

The Giants' mastermind was getting a lot of love from fans and media, eventual Hall of Fame enshrinement a foregone conclusion. Wade felt the causal analysis there might be a trifle shaky. How much of the Giants' success in recent years was attributable to their manager? Angela had taken to calling him Einstein whenever the appearance onscreen of the skipper's macrocephalic image, to highlight his deliberations, occasioned Wade's grumbles.

Alvarez was still smiling. "Hard to complain about three championships."

Wade nodded. "Even harder to believe they won them with the lineup they put out there, after never winning one in the sixties with five Hall of Famers."

Allenby chimed in: "A lot of great teams in the NL back then. Plus no playoffs until the end of the decade. Win the whole league or go home. The Giants didn't have the pitching depth to match the Dodgers and the Cardinals."

"Or the table-setter at the top," Wade added. He had grown up watching Maury Wills and Lou Brock steal pennants from SF's slugger-laden lineup.

Now Alvarez bobbed his head. "You guys know about Matty Alou?"

Wade and Allenby nodded in return. The second of three brothers from the Dominican Republic to be signed and then traded away by the Giants, he had won a batting title with the Pittsburgh Pirates.

"Everyone in the D.R. know this story. Matty come up with Giants, he little guy, my size, 'bout five-foot-eight, maybe less, he try to hit home run every time, try hit the ball out of Candlestick, wind blowin' in like a hurricane. No way, man. Nothing. He get traded to Pirates, coach there, Harry Walker, teach him to hit the ball on the ground, chop it down, use his speed. Different player. All-Star now. Could've played that way when he was leadoff man for Mays and McCovey."

It was a familiar tale. Matty's older brother Felipe, also traded away by the Giants, had finished second to him in batting average and twice led the league in hits. Since their day, multiple generations of Giants' hitters had come and gone, swinging for the fences or bust. The current team was on a pace to set a new record for hitting into double plays. Wade pointed this out to Alvarez and asked if the manager didn't bear some responsibility.

"Bochy good man. I play for him in San Diego. Smart, calm, no crazy shit—he never gonna flip the spread or embarrass his guys with the media. I learn a lot from him."

"Is there a chance that I hear a *but* coming?"

Alvarez smiled again and then grew serious: "He very cautious. Is not the way I like to play. I like to be more aggressive. Got to have some *machismo* to play baseball, to coach it. Got to take a chance, try something different sometimes. Bochy love long ball, wait for it, wait, wait, wait—even when nobody in his lineup can give him what he waiting for. Before San Francisco, in San Diego, Petco Park, 411 feet to the wall, more wind blowin' in, he still wait for long ball. Not gonna happen. You guys remember Klesko?"

Wade and Allenby nodded in unison again.

"Pretty good hitter, got some pop, but man, he messed up by that ballpark. Sometimes he *kill* the ball, damn wind knock it down, they catch it easy, not even warning track. No way to play in that park if you want to win. Got to play small, take some pitches, steal some bases, move the—"

"Does Bochy even have a *Take* sign?" Wade had been wanting to ask this for years and couldn't pass now on the chance to get the answer from someone who might actually know.

"Sometimes for the pitchers," Alvarez said, with a laugh. "Not always even for them, though. I see him let them swing 2-0, 3-1. Think he gonna get a home run in Petco from the pitcher?"

"Maybe Bumgarner," Wade had to concede. "But—"

"What other role models did you have as managers or coaches?" Allenby cut in to ask.

"You pay attention, you learn something from everybody. Everybody in the game got somethin' to teach you. I talk with Omar Vizquel every chance I get. Very smart guy, he know how to play the game. He work hard make himself into .300 hitter. When he first get to Cleveland, he tell me he can barely hold onto the bat when the big fastball come. But he learn, he adjust, he figure it out. Same as Ozzie Smith. Those two, not just great fielders, best ever maybe, but they make themselves into offensive weapons, too. Use their speed, use their brain, help their team win, both side of the ball."

"Not just famous guys like that, though. Lot of other people teach you if you listen. Smartest guy I know in baseball is college coach. His name Reed. I play with him in minors. He never get to majors—last guy cut in spring training one year by Giants. That some serious heartbreak right there. Some guys get mad, get sad, give up, but he figure out another way to make a career in the game. He go to Air Force Academy, coach there, very successful, then come home to California. He take community college team nobody ever heard of, beat all the teams from L.A. and San Diego and San Jose—because he smart, hold his best pitchers back, save them for state tournament. Other teams got more talent, maybe much more talent, but all their pitchers got dead arm from too many innings, can't finish the job. Reed keep his boys fresh, got one boy never even pitch during the regular season, save him just for the tournament, and his team go in there and steal a state championship. Lot of community colleges in California, lot of teams—that's when you know a man can coach. No *rico* owner to buy wins for you, just your guys against their guys."

This was the program Juke Jackson would have played in had he stayed in Stockton. Wade wondered if the fundamentals he would have picked up there would have helped him more than the coaching he'd had so far from Sharky's staff at CSU.

"I still talk to Reed, watch his team play whenever I can. Learn something every time. Last year I watch some MLB playoffs with him. We see guy go up to try sacrifice bunt. Shit on the screen tells us he no try sacrifice all year. Reed say, *So how he gonna do it now against this stud pitcher throwin' 95 in on his hands when he never even tried to do it one time all year before?* No way. He miss one, then pop one up foul, runner still at first base."

Might as well swing for the fences there, eh, Boch? Wade remembered being amused by national network wonks who would broadcast a Giants game every other month or so; if they happened to bump into a bunt by a position player or see a baserunner take off on a 3-2 pitch with less than two outs, they would rave about Bochy's mastery of small ball, ignoring the reality that this might have been the only time he had called for a sacrifice or started a runner in the last two weeks. In 2014 the Giants, according to one credible account, had attempted in the 162-game regular season a total of eleven hit-and-run plays. Even with catchers league-wide throwing out less than thirty percent of attempted base-stealers, Bochy, like so many of his peers, would anchor his runners and wait for home runs. Wade wondered how many coaches who understood the nuances of the game labored in obscurity and would never get a chance to shine in the spotlight of MLB, where the same old codgers seemed to be recycled season after season. For every Joe Maddon who tried to do something different once in a while, there were a dozen cookie-cutter guys playing the same old lame game. The curse of Earl Weaver looked like it was going to live forever: *If you play for one run, one run is all you get*, the Orioles' manager had famously decreed, settling the prevailing style of managing for generations to come. Waiting for the three-run homer might make sense when you had Frank Robinson and Boog Powell in the middle of your batting order to deliver it, but how many teams had a tandem like that? Sometimes one run was all you needed, and *every time* one run was a hell of a lot better than none.

"Strike out if you lucky there, double play if you ain't," Alvarez continued. "You got to put the bunt down in February, March, April you want to see it in October. You got to send some runners, too. You ain't gonna take no bases in the playoffs if you don't run all year. Reed say, one-run game against that stud pitcher you gonna see, you better be able to get a bunt down, steal a base, give yourself a chance to score on a fly ball or a groundout."

Alvarez stopped, grinning widely. "Maybe you no hire me, you hire him instead?"

Allenby laughed. "Sounds like he's got a good thing going where he is."

Wade was pretty sure Alvarez had the job when he went out the door. Once Allenby sat down again after escorting him to the exit, Wade said, "I sort of thought you were hoping to go three-for-three, hire another African American for the head baseball job, to join Slate and Cody."

"I won't deny that I gave it a try," Allenby said. "But you have to hire the best man—or woman—you can find. If he accepts our offer, Eduardo will be the second Latino head coach in any sport on this campus, after we added Estrada in softball. We've still got a lot of catching up to do there, too." Allenby produced a grin to rival the one Alvarez had laid on him. "He's darker than I am, anyway."

"I'll tell him to put that on his resumé."

When he got back to his office, Wade found a voice mail message asking him to return a call to Tennessee State, in connection, he assumed, with his race-related sports research. This was the school where John McLendon in the 1950s, before John Wooden's dynasty had begun, became the first basketball coach to win three consecutive college national championships, with an NAIA team featuring Dick Barnett and John Barnhill. One of the pioneers of the fast break, McLendon had later been, briefly, the first black coach of a professional basketball team before Steinbrenner had canned him. Wade had always wondered what Wilt Chamberlain's teams might have achieved in the NBA if he'd been coached by McLendon instead of the likes of Butch Van Breda Kolff.

"I just retrieved this message from my department secretary," Curtis Roberts said when he came on the line. "Sorry for the delay. I was at a conference and then on vacation. You called about a reference check?"

"Oh." Carlotta Baynes, of course. Wade had forgotten for the moment that Nashville was one of the stops on her *curriculum vitae*.

"So Carlotta finally made it to the Promised Land."

"Sort of," Wade said. "CSU isn't exactly UCLA."

"Well, TSU isn't exactly the Ivy League either. It's pretty amazing that someone who couldn't cut it here could find another college job anywhere, actually."

"Carlotta was fired?"

"Well, she didn't make the tenure cut, which is more or less the same thing—and pretty much unheard of around here. I was the chair of her committee. I almost got run out of town myself for the decision, but we really had no choice."

"What happened?"

"Some background first: Carlotta was a very, very popular teacher on our campus. This may have had some connection to the fact that she was the most generous grader in our department and probably in the university as a whole."

"That sounds familiar."

"Our administration loves that stuff, though. The problem was her scholarship."

"I thought she had published a book and some—"

"Right. She basically published her dissertation. But we found out that she stole a good chunk of it, copied it basically word for word, from another thesis by someone at Ole Miss."

Who the hell reads dissertations? It was hard enough to get the members of your appointed committee to move their eyes over your pages, or pretend to, let alone find anyone with time to scrutinize crap from another campus.

"We've got a guy in our department who keeps tabs on folks he went to grad school with, and he spotted the plagiarism in an article that Carlotta published after she chopped up the book and sent out the chapters individually to journals to try to get more credits. Then, once we began looking more closely into what she had published, we found out that the parts that *weren't* plagiarized were full of all kinds of errors—names, dates, basic stuff like that. How anyone decided it was publishable is a miracle."

Wade sighed and scratched his head. "I know everyone's leery of lawsuits these days, but it sounds like you had the goods to back up the decision not to tenure her. You're the first person who was willing to talk to me about any of this. One of your colleagues I talked to acted as if *his* next call was going to be to the Witness Protection Program."

"That was probably Enoch Robinson."

Wade didn't remember. "Sounds right."

"He's the guy who was hired to take Carlotta's place. He'd been an adjunct here forever, had originally come in second when Carlotta was hired, almost jumped off a bridge when he didn't get the job back then. Once he finally got it, he was probably worried she'd accuse him of retaliation if she found out that you'd spoken with him about her. I imagine you know what a few years of part-time teaching status can do to someone's psyche and the potential for paranoia."

No shit. "Okay, that accounts for Robinson. But why was everyone else so close-mouthed when I called about her?"

"Carlotta was *very* friendly with the higher ups, our dean and a VP in particular, if you get my drift."

"She's a friendly girl," Wade agreed.

Roberts' chuckle suggested intimate familiarity. "If you spent any time in her company, I imagine she offered to—"

"All of the above," Wade said. "Would I be correct in assuming that she also targeted *you* for—"

"I'm gay, Dr. Wade. Carlotta decided, quite insistently, that I must be bisexual, but somehow her charms failed to . . . engender the experiment."

Wade laughed. "Maybe that explains the publications. Maybe—"

"It wouldn't be a shock to learn that the offer was put forth. Whether it affected the decision to publish her rubbish, who knows?"

Or cares. Wade gave his caller a quick overview of the turmoil Carlotta had caused at CSU, including her counterattack against Allenby.

"Black university presidents are few and far. If you want to help your friend, there's something else I can tell you about

Carlotta. It's quite personal, and I had planned to keep it to myself, but under the circumstances—"

"If you're going to tell me she used to be a man, I don't think that matters much around here anymore. We're pretty cool with sexual orientation issues in California."

"This is not about her sex, Dr. Wade. It's about her race."

Wade remembered his first impression. "Are you saying—"

"She's no more African American than Hillary Clinton is."

"You mean—"

"Carlotta Baynes is white."

CHAPTER 13

I'm a big football fan, but I have to tell you, if I had a son, I'd have to think long and hard before I let him play football.

—Barack Obama

Baseball is like driving: it's the one who gets home safely that counts.

—Tommy Lasorda

Juke Jackson's first chance to redeem himself after the botched ending of CSU's baseball season came in the last week of August, before fall classes had even convened on campus, when the football team went on the road to take a payday beating from Nebraska. After spurning *the primrose path* to Carlotta Baynes' class, Jackson had survived in the business course Wade had found for him, even knocking out a B to be proud of, maintaining both his scholarship and his eligibility. In a development less likely to be celebrated, given the circumstances, DNA testing had revealed that Jackson was indeed the father of Camellia Sanchez's forthcoming child, a stark reminder that the failure rate of condoms (even those unsabotaged) remained in the range of seven percent. Thus had another unintended conception been added to the three million or so in the nation's annual total, accounting for nearly half of U.S. pregnancies, in spite of all the science available to prevent them. As Allenby had predicted, the Sanchez family's lawsuit against CSU had been headed off, and an out-of-court settlement was in the works. The criminal case against Dawes and his fraternity brothers was ongoing but not expected to reach court until spring. In the meantime Wade had filled Allenby in on what he'd learned from Curtis Roberts.

It turned out to be a controversy over Carlotta Baynes' candidacy for office in the faculty union at TSU that had drawn attention there to her ethnicity. Her opponent had done some research and outed her when he discovered parents in New Jersey of Polish and Italian extraction. After a series of miscarriages following Carlotta's birth, they had adopted two black children, one boy and one girl. The boy had not embraced his new home and had turned into one of the adoption failures that terrified Wade, winding up in jail several times before a stint in prison for possession of narcotics. The adopted sister, on the other hand, had proven a great success. A natural beauty, showered with affection from infancy, she had thrived in school, earned a scholarship, launched a lucrative career, and made a lasting marriage. A displaced Carlotta had grown up in her new siblings' shadow, her parents alternating consternation over her brother with adulation of her sister. The eventual result had been the stratagem of recasting herself as a black woman, culminating in a graduate degree and then teaching positions in African American Studies and even a low-level leadership position in the NCAAP. Three marriages to black men had ended in divorce, with accusations of adultery on both sides in each case. She had kept the first husband's surname, presumably because it rang truer to her sense of self and/or her ambitions than the Lipschitz she'd been born with.

Wade had reported the news to Allenby the next day. "The first time I saw her I thought she was light, but I never thought about her trying to . . . pass."

"She always looked white to me," Allenby agreed. "I don't judge people on their color, but if you're applying to teach African American Studies, being black yourself is probably a pretty good place to start."

"And of course, at the HBCs like Tennessee State," Wade said, "it's probably still a lot easier to get hired in any job if you're at the politically correct end of the palette."

"I'm glad we found out about this. For now, let's just stick with the facts about the grade distribution and the plagiarism when we communicate with the accrediting team and our grievance committee. That ought to be enough to hang her and protect us. I don't want to make an issue of her race or of her misrepresenting it unless we have to. Maybe now that we can choose whichever bathroom we want to go into, we can choose whatever race we want to be, too."

Perhaps preoccupied by the prospect of impending father-hood, Jackson had failed to earn the starting quarterback position to start the season. After one year to get his grades up and another as a redshirt to grasp the full-throttle Spread offense that Coach Slate had installed, it had been widely expected that Jackson would emerge as the starter in spite of missing spring practice for baseball. Slate had delivered news to the contrary personally to Allenby in a meeting, before the road trip, that Wade had been invited to attend.

Slate was a slight, fit, no-nonsense type who in his first head coaching job had undertaken the daunting task of improving the football team's performance on the field and in the classroom after his predecessor had been caught up in the scandal involving Larashawndria Lewis. Since making an initial splash by nearly engineering a victory over USC in a bowl game, Slate was making slow but steady progress, though not enough to satisfy some of the more vocal alumni, who accused Allenby of hiring him with insufficient experience because he was another African American and wondered why the hell CSU hadn't been to the Rose Bowl yet on his watch. Slate had no delusions about New Year's Day in Pasadena but was clear on the concept that, like other coaches, he would be measured ultimately by wins and losses. He was working round-the-clock to improve the program, and when Wade saw him now in Allenby's office, it was impossible to miss how much the stress had aged him in just a few years; it was almost like comparing the grizzled Obama nearing the end of his second term with the rock star who had hit the scene at the beginning of his first.

"Jackson's got the instincts and the physical tools, obviously," Slate reported. "He's head and shoulders above the other quarterbacks on the team—and in our league—in those regards. And he's done well learning the plays. After his struggles academically, we were a little worried about that, but he's worked hard and done really well picking up our system. The problem is"—Slate paused, sighed, and looked Allenby in the eye—"hero ball."

Allenby nodded, as if this was no surprise.

"He's so gifted athletically that he just has a hard time learning when to give up on a play. He wants to turn every down into six points. We're not trying to turn him into Tom Brady or Peyton Manning: we want him to use his feet, of course, but we're trying to get him to pull back, to play like Aaron Rodgers or Russell Wilson, throw the ball away or get out of bounds when there's a chance to avoid a sack or a big hit. So far, I'm afraid, he's playing more like Michael Vick."

Wade remembered when Vick had nearly won a national championship as an electric freshman at Virginia Tech. His early heroics had long since been overshadowed by his animal abuse conviction and an up-and-down, ultimately unsatisfying NFL career, marred in recent years by one injury after another.

Slate continued: "Vick is the most physically talented quarterback, possibly the most physically talented football player at any position, that I have ever seen. But he can't stay on the field."

Allenby nodded again. "The last time I saw him play, he was roaring downfield to throw blocks for his running back—in an exhibition game."

"Heart of a lion," Slate agreed. "But he's never learned to live for the next play. That's what we're trying to teach Jackson—and I'm sure he'll get there, soon. But he's not ready to start against Nebraska."

Since relocating to the now bloated and misnomered Big Ten, Nebraska was no longer among the premier programs in the country, with other finishing schools exceeding in recent years its efforts to recruit and stockpile scholars who could bench-press their body weight twenty times or run the forty-yard dash in 4.5 seconds. Nevertheless, the Cornhuskers were loaded as usual. Their huge, deep squad was full of athletes from across the nation who would never have considered sending a game tape from high school to Slate's staff. CSU would net nearly a million dollars from the savaging of flesh and spirit that was about to unfold. It was the kind of scheduling travesty that had begun to diminish Wade's enthusiasm for college football, once his favorite sport to watch.

Allenby had declined the Nebraska administration's offer of a luxury box, and on game day Wade was sitting with him in a tiny contingent from CSU, mostly coaches' wives and parents of players, amid a sea of red. Awaiting the 7:00 p.m. kickoff in 90 degrees and 80% humidity, Wade knew that everyone of the locals crazy enough to sit in this steam bath instead of under the

AC in their living rooms was fully expecting the home team to prevail by fifty or sixty points. They would be upset if the visitors' offense crossed midfield; if CSU somehow scored even a single touchdown, panic might set in. The absurd chase to catch up in the rankings with Ohio State and Alabama before their seasons had even begun would commence as soon as the ball was kicked off tonight. Wade comforted himself perversely with the thought that if the Cornhuskers actually played one of those elite teams they dreamed of overtaking, they'd probably face a mismatch nearly equal to the one CSU was about to endure. The Buckeyes had won the first true *settled on the field* national championship with their third-string quarterback replacing two injured All Americans. What hope was there against teams stacked like that? And what did it say about human nature that anyone wanted to watch?

Allenby pointed down at the field, where the size differential was obvious among players lining the opposite sidelines. No doubt the CSU players were taking note as well. "This is probably how the Christians felt when they were sent in to meet the lions."

Wade nodded and mopped his brow. "I hear they drew big crowds for that, too. I hope they had better weather, anyway. Who could *live* in this?"

Allenby looked around, shared the wonder, and shook his head. "The kind of man who can put on red pants, apparently. Even *you* would have more sense than that."

Wade laughed and then flashed to Jason Compson's timeless lament: *what kind of a damn man would wear a red tie?* If the nation didn't start paying attention, pretty soon we might have a Commander-in-Chief who wore nothing but.

They had flown out on Saturday morning, Wade's first-ever first class flight. After his last plane ride, trapped between a talkaholic and a four hundred pounder with perspiration issues, he had promised himself he would never fly again; this he now revised to a commitment never to go back to coach. To have actual legroom seemed nearly a miracle. No one had shoved a seat back into his face or spilled a drink on him or tripped over him and fallen into his lap trying to get to the toilet. It was true that the upgrade didn't extend to the quality of the entertainment—Allenby had promptly turned on his Kindle while Wade tried and failed to sleep through Hollywood's latest comic book-misbegotten imbecility—but all in all it was a glorious interlude. Then they had landed in Lincoln, and Wade had been treated to a foretaste of hell.

Sweat was soaking his clothes by the time they had made it to the sanctuary of the rental car. Once they had checked into the Hyatt Place, Wade was half-wishing they would stay put to watch the game from their rooms—or possibly from the hotel bar once the score got lopsided and libation would come in handy to anesthesize the pain. He knew, though, that there was no way Allenby had come this far to settle for television; nothing Nebraska could throw at him would faze a man who had survived Corpus Christi and Kae Sanh.

The game began with the usual flurry of mistakes and penalties common to season openers and especially common to the abomination of football before Labor Day. The Cornhuskers moved the ball with evident ease against the CSU defense but squandered their first few scoring opportunities with a third down holding call, a fumbled hand-off, and an end zone interception. CSU's offense failed to capitalize on the early opportunities it was presented, as the starting quarterback who had beaten out Jackson misfired on his pass attempts or failed to elude the rush of the Cornhuskers' massive defensive line. When the QB got up unsteadily after the third time he was sacked, Jackson raced onto the field to replace him.

"Well, we didn't have to wait long for the prodigy after all," Allenby said.

"Third and long," Wade pointed out. "Not the most auspicious of circumstances for his debut."

Jackson's first pass was on target but was dropped by a wide-out open at the first down mark. Wade drew Allenby's attention to the receiver examining his hands afterward as if an RPG had just passed through them.

"Looks like Juke needs to take something off the fastball."

"He threw that one like he's still trying to strike guys out," Allenby agreed.

A chip shot field goal finally put Nebraska on the scoreboard just before the end of the first quarter. Ever faithful Midwestern fans applauded dutifully but without enthusiasm: 3-0 wasn't exactly their idea of the launching pad for a push to the national championship. Then, on the ensuing possession, CSU's second-string quarterback gave them something to tell their grandchildren about.

On third down, after two more of his passes went awry, Jackson dropped back to try again, but was almost immediately swarmed over by the Cornhuskers' rushers. Three of them reached him almost simultaneously, one from his blind side; Wade feared they would literally break him in half. Somehow, as if by transubstantiation, Jackson disappeared from their grasp, reemerged briefly in the clear, then juked a late-arriving linebacker into a complete whiff, and seemed about to take off downfield. Instead he scrambled parallel to the line of scrimmage and gestured for a distant receiver to keep going toward the end zone. After somehow dodging more Huskers, Jackson pulled up, a foot or so to the legal side of the line, and fired the ball just over the reach of the deepest defensive back to the receiver, who didn't have to wait long for its arrival. Touchdown. CSU had taken the lead over mighty Nebraska. So much for the Cornhuskers' hopes for a number one ranking.

Wade had never seen Houdini slip his underwater chains, but he had watched a lot of football, dating to the days of Johnny Unitas. "I've read that Willie Mays threw a ball eighty yards in a high school football game," he said, "but that might have been the greatest pass I've even seen."

Allenby had seen even more football and could count Otto Graham, Bob Waterfield, and Norm Van Brocklin among the legends he had observed. He wasn't easily impressed. "Forget the pass," he said. "The getaway is what made the play."

Along with the stunned Cornhuskers' fans, they watched the replay on the giant screen in the stadium. They counted seven would-be tacklers Jackson had evaded to get the throw off. Wade was reminded of the epic upset that Appalachian State had pulled off before 106,000 or so disbelievers in The Big House at Ann Arbor when Armanti Edwards had run circles around the cumbrous Wolverines. CSU, too, had nearly won its bowl game against USC when the late Marcus Foster had done the same against the Trojans. A shifty quarterback with sprinter's speed—like Juke Jackson—was the one element that could give you a chance in hostile surroundings against a vastly superior team.

Unfortunately, there were still nearly three quarters to play. In the second quarter Nebraska settled down, punched in two touchdowns, and took control of the game. Jackson connected with a few receivers and scrambled for a few first downs, but CSU was unable to sustain a drive. With a minute to go in the first half, Nebraska blocked a punt and recovered it in the end zone to push the score to 24-7, a midway margin almost acceptable to the carnivorous fans and possibly even the pollsters. After the kickoff was returned to only the fifteen yard-line, Jackson attempted to work another miracle, evading multiple rushers again to launch another laser far downfield. This time, however, he would not witness the result: just after he released the ball, he was hit from behind at the knees and felled as if struck by a deer hunter's cartridge. The pass fell incomplete downfield, but Wade and Allenby had eyes only for the crumpled figure writhing at the five-yard line.

"Fuck!" Allenby said. "I hope to God that wasn't a Theismann break." Lawrence Taylor's infamous hit had ended the Washington Super Bowl quarterback's career with a compound fracture.

"Broken leg might be better than a blown knee," Wade pointed out grimly. He could still picture Gale Sayers, the most elusive open field runner he had ever seen, sprawled on the field at Kezar Stadium after Kermit Alexander's flying tackle consigned him to playing on one leg for the rest of his career. Surgical techniques had improved a thousand-fold since Sayers' days, but the spectacle of a great athlete cut down in his prime was still heart-wrenching. Wade flashed to Bo Jackson's being dragged to the turf from behind, fracturing his hip, instantly ending his NFL career and curtailing what might have been one of the greatest baseball careers ever.

Wade left the stadium right away and took a cab to the university Medical Center's hospital, where he had learned that Jackson would be taken by ambulance. Allenby stayed to endure with the rest of the CSU party the humiliations of a second half with their third-string walk-on quarterback at the helm.

Wade inquired unproductively about Jackson's status, then, exhausted from unfamiliar travel and clime, slumped into a waiting room chair and promptly fell asleep. He startled himself by waking later with an erection. He realized he had been dreaming about Angela and wondered if she was missing him half as much as he was missing her. What craven creatures we were. *What kind of an asshole gets a hard-on in the hospital?* With Jackson's leg and future possibly in ruins in an adjoining room. *How could I be thinking of anything but that?* Then Wade remembered, after each of his parents died, that feeling of impossible, inconsolable, end-of-the-world desolation, when you felt you would never smile or laugh or want to eat anything again, and the thought of ever making love again was a million miles from your consciousness. Then a week went by, or maybe it had been a month, and your body's urges slowly returned in spite of your heart and your brain, and eventually you did make love again and even enjoyed it, maybe even relished it all the more because of the reminder of mortality you had just endured.

Wade's erection subsided, and he fell asleep again. He woke to find Allenby and Slate at his side, comparing catastrophes. It seemed truly irrelevant in the context of Jackson's injury, but the Cornhuskers had run the scoring gap to sixty points before mock-mercifully inserting their scrubs with two minutes to go.

"It's the last time we schedule those motherfuckers, I promise you that," Allenby said. "They were throwing the ball all over the field in the fourth quarter when they were up eight touchdowns."

Slate shrugged. "Par for the course. Puffing the stats for their All American wannabes."

"Good luck to them with that. I hope Wisconsin gives them a taste of their own next month."

Wade unslumped and jumped in. "Too bad they don't play Oklahoma this year."

"Sleeping Beauty at last arises."

Allenby and Slate had already visited Jackson in the recovery room. Wade leaned forward to hear the report, guessing that they had spared him the initial shock and fearing the worst.

"He's still in and out of the anesthesia," Slate told him. "It's a broken femur. They set it, think it'll heal fine."

Wade nodded and sighed in relief. "His knee's okay then?"

"There's some swelling, but the surgeon thinks his knee is sound," Slate said, before turning back to Allenby. "I'm really embarrassed about the way that game turned out. I thought we were better prepared for . . . what hit us."

Allenby shook his head. "It's my fault. I should have canceled that game when I saw it on the schedule. It's not worth the cash to take a beating like that. Two quarterbacks knocked out, and how many other guys beat half to death in the first game of the season?"

Not to mention men in red pants and the worst weather this side of Abbottabad.

"The kids want to compete against the best," Slate said. "We won't get the athletes we want to play for us if we don't schedule high profile teams."

Wade didn't want to hear any more about human sacrifice. "What's the prognosis for Jackson's healing time?" he asked. "Is he going to be okay in time for baseball?"

"Too soon to say for sure," Slate said, "but normally with this kind of break, he'll be up and running in a few months. If the knee's okay, he should be good to play baseball in the spring. Maybe not the start of the season, but sometime before it's over."

Allenby and Slate, with many other duties to attend to, left. Wade went into the recovery room to find a groggy, glum Jackson and tried to figure out what he could say to cheer him up.

"I'm thinking of signing you up for an extra class."

"What for?"

"I figured you'll have more time to study while you're rehabbing. You need a speech class to knock out a graduation requirement."

"Man can't even take a nap around here without gettin' more work put on him. Don't you think I got enough to do, get this leg back in shape for baseball?"

"Just give it a try, okay? You can drop the class if it doesn't work out." It was a pitch Wade found himself making regularly these days.

"You always pushin' extra work on guys who get hurt?"

"Not always," Wade said. "Some guys can handle a push, and some guys can't. I figured your uncle would see it my way if he were still with us."

"You right about that. He be hangin' right over this bed, askin' me when I'm gonna get back to work."

Wade started to put a hand on Jackson's shoulder but settled instead for tapping the bed. "You'll be out of here and back on the field for baseball before you know it."

Jackson studied his blasted limb, looked away from it and perhaps from more, then nodded. "Baseball. I'll be ready."

Back in his hotel room a few minutes later, Wade was still thinking about how quickly and drastically life could change. One minute Jackson had been on top of the world, completing a miraculous play against some of the stellar athletes in the country—and the next he was flat on his back in a hospital bed, wondering if the speed that had set him apart from everyone else would still be there when he took the field again, or if an operation would be required to restore it. Wade almost felt the surgeon's blade himself, a reminder not to waste any more of the healthy days he had left.

He was looking forward to getting home and getting things figured out with Angela. Since the negotiations with Lara and the revelations about Ronnie, she had been concentrating on her new book, preparing for the new semester, figuring out a way to deal with her blackmailer, and making some midsummer history, while prodding Wade to continue his research on adoption options. Maybe it was time to tell her that he was ready to take the project more seriously. He saw the light on the hotel phone blinking and picked up to retrieve her message but found instead one from Erica Wiley and another from Allenby, telling him to call Erica. What the hell was so urgent with her? Hemingway wasn't going anywhere.

"It's about Angela," Erica said, ending the mystery, as soon as Wade reached her. "She was in a car accident."

Oh, my God. Please don't tell me—

"She's . . . all right, Wade. She wasn't hurt seriously. Her back and her neck are sore, but—"

Wade felt his heart start again. He allowed himself to breathe. "Please don't tell me she totaled her Bimmer."

"This is not about her car, Wade." Something in Erica's voice now made him shiver and kicked the relief he had just felt into a distant corner.

"Of course not. What—"

"You *really* need to get a cell phone."

Another county heard from. "I will, I promise. What happened to—"

"Her father had another heart attack, and—"

"Oh, no."

"—she was rushing to the airport to go to him. On the way out of town, in her hurry, she tried to squeeze past another car, and she hit a parked car. Apparently she was speeding, and—"

"Oh, Christ!"

"—her blood alcohol level was—"

Wade closed his eyes, racked his brain to recall the legal limit.

"—0.25."

"Are you telling me—"

"She was driving drunk, Wade."

PART II: 2016

If I knew back then what I know now, I would have never played football.

—Bo Jackson, quoted by Bob Nightengale in *USA Today*

My son, if you aspire to be a servant of the Lord, prepare yourself for testing. Set a straight course, keep to it, and do not be dismayed in the face of adversity.

—*Ecclesiasticus 2:1-2*, inscription near the entrance to the Negro Leagues Baseball Museum, Kansas City, Missouri

Today we are seeing more people killed because of opioid overdose than traffic accidents.

—Barack Obama

I love her, and God damn me for it.

—Frank Sinatra, of Ava Gardner

CHAPTER 14

But oh! as to embrace me she inclined
I waked, she fled, and day brought back my night.

—John Milton, "On His Deceased Wife"

We wouldn't care how much people thought of us if we
knew how seldom they did.

—John Lanchester, *Mr. Phillips*

Wade woke with a start, knocked the clock to the floor, fumbled for it, tumbled from the bed, stumbled on the blaring alarm, and then savagely snapped it off, demon technology ruling his life yet again. Maybe two hours of true sleep, he guessed. He tossed the tangled covers back onto the bed, shivered, peed, staggered to the mirror, and terrified himself. The bags under his eyes seemed to have had babies again. He didn't dare stick his tongue out for fear of seeing a shade best saved for the other side of the grave. Maybe he had died in the night and this was actually his corpse staring back at him. *Good thing Angela isn't here to see this. Good thing Angela is . . .*

Gone. He said to it himself again, the same thing he had said first thing every morning since the end of August. January now.

Empty, endless, joyless Christmas break over with at last. Up and at 'em, time to go to school, fake his way through another day, another week, another month—Christ, was it going to be another fucking semester?—without Angela.

Her father had briefly survived his second heart attack but had succumbed a day later. After her release from jail for the drunk driving arrest, Angela had flown to Baltimore to assist in the funeral arrangements and to comfort her mother, who was devastated in spite of the multiple divorces removing her from her first husband. With Allenby's approval, Angela had arranged to take an indefinite leave of absence from CSU, and then had stunned Wade by electing to arrange her court-ordered treatment in Maryland. This had swiftly led to a decision to seek psychiatric care for the depression presumed to be causing her alcoholism. After a few desolate phone calls, she had cut off virtually all communication with Wade. Now that he finally had a cell phone, it never rang, except when somebody he didn't know wanted to sell him solar paneling or a cemetery plot. He found himself studying the phone, almost as assiduously as his students had studied theirs while faking attention to his lectures, as he waited helplessly for the ringtone or the revelatory text that would restore his life, bring her back. His requests to visit her had been ignored or rebuffed, and he had been left to contemplate whether he should be seeking psychiatric care himself or saying yes to one of those enticingly affordable plans to cremate his remains.

One of the things Wade had most missed in his life, and that he craved profoundly now in Angela's absence, was a sense of belonging to something bigger than himself. This yearning for purpose was not hard to pinpoint. Both of his parents had sprung from backgrounds where fellowship was a fundamental way of life. His mother had been born into a community of dirt farmers whose members pitched in routinely to help each other cope with the ceaseless array of variables that defined their way of life, and she had carried that ethos with her into suburbia. His father had served in the U.S. Navy during World War II and then in a seemingly infinite list of service organizations: the YMCA, the PTA, Kiwanis, even a club in which he had instructed youngsters in rifle safety. Wade shuddered now to recollect the level of responsibility his parents had taken on, both within and without their family. He had never been tempted to try to equal the quantity of their good deeds, but at the same time he knew he was missing out on something important.

The creation of a sense of community should have been possible within the walls of a university, it would seem, but Wade had never found it at CSU. Of course, most of his years there to date had been spent as an adjunct faculty member, and it was hard for part-timers to feel part of anything except the urgency of getting to class on time, getting it over with, and getting off to the next class on the next campus in time to keep that job as well. A few exceptional souls like Erica Wiley reached out to welcome newbies of any caste, but there had never been any collective effort at CSU to integrate the adjuncts who taught more than half of the classes on the campus. Whether there was any more sense of harmony among the full-timers, given the in-fighting over tenure, promotion, sabbaticals, release time, and assorted other perks—penny ante by Wall Street's standards but sources of boundless contention in the small world of academia—Wade had yet to gauge conclusively, but early returns had not been promising. His split-duty appointment had occasioned some grumbles about favoritism that had reached his ears, and the general disdain among the professoriate for the Athletic Department types who outearned them so spectacularly was probably not helping his cause. Even though his own salary was pegged to the academic scale, it seemed likely that Wade was tarred among his peers with the same brush as the shitcanned football coaches who were still costing the university millions of dollars annually in severance pay. Allenby had noted the flagging *esprit de corps* in the CSU ranks and had kicked around with Wade some ideas about how to improve it, but, as on many other campuses, decades of dysfunctional relations between the administration and the faculty and staff would pose a formidable obstacle to any swift, meaningful change.

In Angela's absence, Allenby had prevailed upon Erica to step up temporarily into the dean position. One of her first acts in her new post had been more or less to insist that Wade keep his Hemingway class on the spring schedule, no doubt believing that it would provide at least a minor distraction from his marital woes and give him a chance to work with students again in the way that he had been trained to. The feeling of contributing to a community within a classroom came along sporadically with any teaching assignment, but, at least in Wade's experience, it wasn't something you could count on. His most heartfelt feelings about his default profession came at the end of each term. After working steadily, burning up mental energy and life's precious allotment of days and hours to build a connection with his students and to help them achieve their goals, however grand or modest those might be, what Wade often felt at the end of the semester was that he had mostly been wasting his time. Only a handful of students kept in touch, usually when they needed something, most often letters of recommendation. Most of the students you taught, you never saw again after the final exam. Then you powered up and started all over again with a new group in the next term, knowing you would never see *them* again when they finished your class. Since he had made the move into guidance, with many of the athletes he was trying to advise, as with the students in his classes, he couldn't avoid the feeling that he cared more about and invested more in their education than they did themselves. Many of them evidently regarded him as just another obstacle, his counsel (like his classes) just another box to be checked off in the path to a degree, which in and of itself might be worthless in the economy they would be entering anyway, once their mostly pie-in-the-sky plans for professional playing careers fell through.

Wade had always wondered if he would find more fulfillment in teaching an elective class than in staring down the conscripts in composition sections. Until Angela had crashed and then vanished, he had been looking forward to the seminar that Erica had prevailed upon him to offer. Now he was numb to the possible pleasures of that project, as to everything else. He was listlessly looking over his notes for the first meeting when he heard a tentative knock on his office door.

"Am I interrupting you?"

He looked up to see a vaguely familiar face but found, as so often these days, that he couldn't put a name to it. College teachers typically had hundreds of students each semester; students had five or six teachers at a time to keep straight (not that they always managed to do even this), so they had you at a pronounced disadvantage. Still, it was embarrassing when they remembered your name and you couldn't call up theirs.

"Norma Rodriquez. I had you for bonehead English a few years ago."

"Of course," Wade said. *You're not here to complain about your grade, are you?* He tried to remember if she had passed his class or if he had given her a D and forced her to repeat it.

"I just filed my petition to graduate at the end of this semester."

"Oh. That's great news. Congratulations."

"I came by to let you know and to say—"

Fuck you. You flunked me but I made it anyway.

"—thank you for giving me the push I needed."

"Oh. That's nice to hear."

"I almost dropped your class about ten times. That C you gave me was the hardest grade I ever earned."

"I'm glad you—"

"You beat the crap out of my essays, but I learned something. I got a B in English 1A, and I even got some A's in my essays for other classes. You'll be glad to know I never tried to use a semicolon again after I left your class."

"Best news I've had in a long time," Wade said. "I really appreciate your taking the time to—"

"I'm trying to show a little more gratitude these days. I just got back from a month in Mexico."

"Oh?"

"I went with our church group to spend the holidays in the village where my mom grew up and help out with a house we were building. It was pretty intense."

"Primitive?" Wade guessed.

"You could say that. They have to worry about really basic stuff. Like, is there enough hot water for me to take a shower today? Stuff like that. I used to complain to my mom all the time when I had to walk home from school here, on days when she was too busy to pick me up. It was like a mile, less than that, from our house. There the kids walk four miles every day to get to the school in the nearest town. I went with them the last day of school before Christmas, just to see what it was like. I wanted to borrow my dad's truck and take a bunch of them, but my mom said I should walk. I always used to tease her about dropping out in the fourth grade. She said I should find out why. She said I could use the exercise anyway. Hard to argue with that."

Norma was not petite. She slapped a hefty thigh and laughed. Wade smiled.

"It took more than an hour to get there. It was *so* cold. You don't feel it so much when you're walking, but there was no heat at the school either. Nobody complained, though. It's just normal to them. It seems funny to me now. Here at CSU people freak out if the temperature in the classroom is a little too high or a little too low. They should try freezing their ass off in a class in La Tuna Manza sometime."

Wade nodded hypocritically. He had fired off the occasional useless complaint himself when an inferno or an arctic blast blew through CSU. A previous administration had shaved a few more bucks from the facilities budget for their own salaries and perks by purchasing the cheapest HVAC system they could find, reputedly from a Crimean black market vendor, and it was maintained (to use the word in its loosest possible construction) by a subcontractor headquartered in Ohio. When the classroom temperature varied from levels tolerable by Californians, you had to call someone in Columbus and pray for a response before heat prostration or frostbite set it. As often as not the result was an overcorrection that turned torpor into a deep freeze or vice-versa. By the end of class students practically trampled each other in the rush to escape into the fresh air, often leaving a detritus of jackets, sweatshirts, and hoodies behind.

"Some of the kids there don't even really have any winter clothes. They just go to school in a shirt and jeans. And their shoes are so crappy you can't even believe it. We took a bunch of old coats and sweaters and sneakers and stuff with us to give to them, and you can't believe how happy they were to get them—I mean, just stuff we would have thrown away or given to the Salvation Army here. It was like a miracle to them. And the house we helped to build, it was really more like what people here would consider a shed, or a place to keep a dog. But the family was so grateful—it was like we built them a palace or something."

Wade nodded again. "What was it like at the school, besides cold?"

"It was okay, actually. The teacher treated me like I was some kind of celebrity. She asked me to give the kids a lesson in English. I taught them some of the stuff you showed us—making subjects and verbs agree, that kind of stuff. My Spanish is pretty basic—they laughed at me a few times—but I was able to explain it pretty good, I think."

Pretty 'well,' Wade autocorrected, but he swallowed it and tried to put the solecism into perspective. Had he ever done in his sixty years anything half as selfless as what Norma had just described?

"We take so much for granted here, you know?" she continued. "Here we worry about whether the car we drive is cool enough or if our big screen TV is big enough. We worry about whether we're getting enough sex and if the person we're getting it with is hot enough."

Or if the hot person we're NOT getting it with is . . . getting it with someone else. And possibly preserving it for posterity.

Wade forced his thoughts elsewhere and pointed at the newspaper open on his desk. "In parts of Africa, girls still have to worry if a witch doctor will carve out their clitoris before they even find out what it's for. In Pakistan, girls are worrying about whether their own mother will burn them alive if they look twice at the wrong boy."

"There was a girl from the village who moved to Mexico City. She tried to testify in a case against the drug dealers who killed her brother. They cut her head off and dumped it on her parents' doorstep."

"Christ! Were you there when—"

Norma shook her head. "That was two years ago. They still talk about it, though." She closed her eyes and shook her head, as if in exorcism. "I don't mean to talk about all that stuff, though. How have you been doing, Dr. Wade?"

"Fine," he said. *My wife got drunk and smashed her car last year, and my life has been a clogged toilet ever since.* He held up his Hemingway notes. "I'm mostly a counselor these days, but I'm going to be teaching a new class this semester."

"I'm glad you're still going to be teaching. A teacher like you really makes a difference for students like me. You know that essay we wrote for the final in your English class? You made us read it out loud in front of—"

Wade held up a hand to demur. "I don't think I *made*—"

"—the whole class?"

"—you read it aloud. I *invited* you to share it with your classmates, unless you—"

"Yeah, right. And we'd have been like the biggest wuss in the world if we didn't read ours when everybody else did. You know what a wuss is, right?"

Wade knew what a wuss was. He had grown up hearing the word, had probably uttered it a few times, and had certainly applied it to himself in more than a few internal monologs. It was (or, *shit*, had been) among Angela's favorite terms of endearment for him. He was mildly surprised that Norma used it. Perhaps, in deference to his years and ears, she was euphemizing for a more contemporary choice.

"When you banned the *b* word in our class, that's what I came up with instead."

Chalk up another triumph in vocabulary building for English X.

"Anyway, that essay you assigned was about a major decision in our lives. I wrote about trying to figure out how to tell my parents I like girls. It was the first time I ever said it in public."

Wade remembered her clearly now, recalling across the years her shallow breathing and halting reading. "The class was pretty supportive, if I remember right. No stoning anyway."

She nodded. "I was sure they were gonna clown me. I was practically shaking up there. But they all acted like it was no big deal, nothing to hide. Some guy in the front row even gave me a fist bump when I finished and sat down. There were a couple of big-time born-agains in that class, but if anyone thought I was going straight to hell, they kept their mouth shut."

Wade tried hard to keep the evangelicals from saving souls in his classroom, but an occasional sermon had been known to slip through. He was glad none had tainted the response to Norma's narrative. "I think everyone respected your honesty that—"

"That day in your class, as hard as it was to share that, it gave me the courage to talk to my parents the next time I went home. After all the years of hiding who I really was from them, I finally told them the truth."

Wade smiled, hoping this was the right response and he wasn't about to hear that her family had banished her from their household on the spot or signed her up for conversion therapy. Sometimes your writing assignments could have unintended consequences. "And?"

"They already knew."

"Aha." *What a surprise.*

"They just assumed that *I* knew that *they* knew."

"I see." *Imagine that, parents who paid enough attention to figure out their own child's sexual orientation.*

"I kind of figured my mom probably had some clue, but my dad—I mean, I thought he might have a stroke or something, or try to find out if it wasn't too late to put me in a convent. All he said was, *Whatever makes you happy, mija.* Then he asked me if I wanted to go out and play catch in the driveway, just like we always used to. I spent all those years worrying about nothing. How sick is that?"

Wade shrugged. "I've wasted a lot of time worrying about stuff I didn't need to, too. Can you believe I used to worry that I'm not as tall as Elvis?"

"Yeah, but you're straight—right?"

Wade nodded, accustomed, as a male English teacher, to confirming this aberration.

"It's not the same thing."

Wade shrugged again. "When it comes to relationships, anyone who ever couldn't get a date can relate. *One touch of nature makes the whole world kin.*"

Norma frowned. "Isn't that about *dying*, not dating?"

"Sometimes they're pretty much the same thing. I see you know your Shakespeare, though."

"I had Professor Wiley for English 1B. That lady knows her shit."

"Agreed. Did you know they made her a dean this year?"

"I heard that. It's good she got promoted, I guess, but a lot of students are going to miss out on a great class. She was probably the best teacher I ever had. No offense: you were a cool teacher, too."

"None taken. There's always somebody better to look up to. I'd probably lose if I went one-on-one with Michael Jordan, too."

Norma laughed. "He's hella old now, though. You guys should probably just play H-O-R-S-E, unless you got a ambulance standing by."

"Good idea," Wade said. "Our president probably knows him. I'll see if I can set it up. Maybe we can do it at halftime of the student-faculty basketball game, sell some extra tickets."

"Do they still play that on donkeys?"

"Right. Can you imagine what an autographed photo of Michael Jordan on a diapered donkey would be worth?"

"I'd buy a ticket to see that myself." Norma laughed again, looked away for a moment, and then looked back at Wade. "There's another reason I came to see you today."

"Oh?" Another letter of recommendation request appeared imminent. "I'd be happy to write a—"

"I don't need a letter from you, Dr. Wade, at least not yet. Maybe when I apply to grad school or something. I'm here because I heard you got in some kind of trouble with one of the other teachers. Some b.s. about Dr. Baynes suing you for discrimination."

"Something like that. She filed a complaint against me."

In December, a few days before Christmas, Carlotta Baynes had turned in, along with her customary set of incendiary grades, a letter to CSU's grievance committee accusing Wade and Allenby of racial discrimination, sexual discrimination, impugning her academic integrity, and infringing upon her academic freedom. Angela on his mind night and day, Wade had barely noticed this bit of holiday cheer and couldn't bring himself to care. That might change when he was hauled before a tribunal packed with PC police in a month or so and forced to waste a few hours proving that he was not now and had never been a member of H8Machine, the Sons of the Confederacy, or the Ku Klux Klan. Whether he could do so without disclosing all he knew about his accuser could prove tricky.

"What happened?"

"All I did was tell her that I don't care what color she is or her students are, but she can't give A's to all of them. She's invoking academic freedom to say she can give her students whatever grades she pleases."

"That sucks, but . . . don't teachers usually get to decide on their own grades?"

"Of course they do. And in most cases they grade at least semi-responsibly, although grade inflation has been an issue around here—and everywhere else, really—for a long time. How much do you think your A's will be worth, the ones you worked your ass off for, if other students are getting them just for signing up?"

"I didn't get too many A's in my courses, to be honest with you. I said I got a few on papers. I'll graduate with a little over a 3.0. cumulative GPA. I was happy to get B's. But I had to work for almost every one of them. The classes I had, there were only one or two teachers who gave everyone a free ride. But—"

"Very glad to hear that."

"—Dr. Baynes was one of them. I took her class last semester, and it was a total joke."

"How'd you wind up taking a course from her?" Wade remembered Norma well enough by now to know that she wouldn't want her time wasted.

"I wanted to take Mexican-American History or History of Latin America, but all the sections were full. So I got on the waiting list for her Black History class. I went on the first day and she took everybody from the wait list, must've been fifty of us. I guess she gets more money or something if she takes more students?"

"Bonus units," Wade confirmed. "It's a popular feature of our contract."

"We did like nothing in that class. We had one paper and one test, and she didn't even mark the papers, just handed them back with a grade on the last page. I got a B on mine. I went up to ask her why, and she just snatched it out of my hands, didn't even look at it, just added a + to the B, then said, *There? Does that make you feel better?*"

Wade shook his head. "I'm guessing it didn't."

"I worked hard on that paper. I know I'm not the greatest writer in the world, and maybe it *was* a B instead of an A, but I thought I had a right to know why. God, Dr. Wade, after all the stuff you wrote on my papers to help me get rid of the stupid shit I started out with, I thought she'd at least offer to take the essay home and read it again."

"I'm afraid a lot of teachers don't provide much in the way of feedback around—"

"I hope you're not defending her now."

"No, Norma," Wade said gently. "I'm trying to expose her. That's what got me in trouble in the first place, remember?"

"Sorry. I'm still pretty bummed about that class. What really pissed me off was that I asked around and all the black kids in the class got A's on their paper. All the Mexicans got B's, or at least all the ones I asked. Some of the jerkfaces in there should have flunked out of kindergarten. They'd come in late, halfway through class sometimes, and talk with each other the whole time the class was supposed to be going on. I saw some of those papers they got back, too. I swear, a jock in that class could wipe his ass and turn in the toilet paper, she'd put an A on it."

Wade couldn't stifle a snort. "I'm sorry you had to go through that."

"No, *I'm* sorry, I didn't mean to go into so much detail. I really just wanted to say, if this case against you is serious and you need someone to stand up for you against that bitch—sorry, but that's the right word this time—you can count on me."

Wade felt sudden moisture in his eyes. This student, whom he had not heard from since she was a freshman and had not so much as thought of twice since she sat in his class, had reached straight across the years and reduced him to tears. Unwilling to trust his voice, he nodded his thanks.

"I know it sounds really cheesy now, but you were there for me then. You pushed me, encouraged me, helped me get through my first year here, which was really tough, especially when I got cut from the softball team in the tryouts. All the spots were already taken by girls that were recruited. A walk-on like me didn't even have a chance. Do you remember what you told me?"

Wade drew a blank. "I probably told you not to give up, to try again next—"

Norma nodded. "Yeah, you did, but everybody told me that. You also told me to find an intramural team to join in the meantime, to have some fun with my sport and keep playing. At first I was too pissed off to take your suggestion, but the next spring I got on a coed team. I grew up playing with my brothers, playing with guys all the time, so it was really natural for me. The team I was on wound up winning the intramural championships twice in a row. The second year, which was last spring, the new coach for the women's softball team, Connie Estrada, came up to me after I hit a couple of home runs in the championship game. She asked me if I wanted to try out for the varsity again. I'm going to be on the team this year, even got a shot at starting catcher. My dad's so proud he can hardly wait for the games to start."

"That's great, Norma."

"The softball team is just a bonus for me, though. This spring, I was telling you, I'm going to graduate. I'm already the first person in my family to finish high school, let alone college. I've got cousins my age who dropped out in the ninth grade. Some of 'em have five kids now. That's all they do is make babies, feed them, clean up after them, and then make some more."

Wade thought about Lara's giving him the same summary about her set of friends. There were hillbillies in Arkansas, Latter-Day Saints in Utah, and Aryans in Idaho following the same reproductive path, but for ethnic minorities the challenges accompanying birth into such circumstances seemed especially daunting. How were we ever going to break the cycles of poverty and neglect when ignorant proliferation continued at such a pace? Norma, at least, would not be contributing to that problem.

"Of course, I wasn't going to get knocked up, for obvious reasons, but I still could have given up that first year and dropped out. I wouldn't be here today, this close to graduation and with a chance to play on the team, without your help. I owe you a ton."

Wade felt the tears again and fought them back. "You don't owe me a damn thing, Norma. I was just doing my job. And just by turning up here today and telling me about what you've accomplished, you've given back more to me than you can imagine. Your dad's not the only one who's proud of you."

She suddenly sprang forward and wrapped her arms around him. Wade wasn't sure about the protocol for hugging lesbians in your office, and the absolute last thing he needed was another complaint from another aggrieved woman of color/no color, but under the circumstances it seemed right to return the embrace and in any case impossible to avoid it. The biceps of a prospective starting catcher were not to be denied. Too bad there was no photographer on hand to preserve the moment. This one could go right into the scrapbook next to the shot of Wade coming up about to the waist of Marvin Walker, the seven-foot six-inch center from Harlem who had taken his class a few years before, albeit with a less uplifting outcome.

"I want to take a picture of us together, Dr. Wade." Norma released him with one arm and with the other fished in her backpack to produce her cell phone. Wade had forgotten: in the age of the selfie, there was *always* a photographer on hand.

An abrupt knock on the open door announced Juke Jackson, who couldn't avoid a double-take as he stepped in.

Wade performed the introductions as Norma handed her phone to Jackson and addressed him: "Can you take a decent picture?"

An indecent one would be more fun. And just what was needed to add a dash of Latin/Sapphic spice to Wade's delinquent campus diversity rating. He raced right to the caption this time: *Tortillera backstop gropes wedo prof in office.*

"Shoot it," he told Jackson, smiling for the mugshot.

After Norma left, with a photo in her phone, a promise to send Wade a copy, and a promise in return from Wade to attend her team's first home game, Jackson explained the purpose of his visit. He had decided to add Wade's Hemingway class.

Wade couldn't conceal his surprise. Jackson read his expression immediately.

"You don't want me in your class?"

The bluntness of the follow-up question took Wade aback even more sharply than had the original announcement of intent. "It's not that I don't *want* you in the class; it's just a question of whether it's a good choice for you."

Jackson had been working hard on his writing since he had first arrived at CSU. Wade recalled verbatim the report from Dixon James, the first tutor with whom Wade had matched him, about Jackson's initial essay for a remedial class: *He wrote the whole thing as one giant sentence.* "I've seen worse," Wade had said then, and he tried to recall now if he really had. There had been progress, to be sure, but whether Jackson was ready for an upper division English elective was debatable, at best.

"You'll miss a lot of classes for baseball," Wade reminded him now.

"That's true for any class I sign up for," Jackson pointed out. "At least if I take your class, you'll know I'm not making up excuses for why I can't be there."

Ah, yes, students and excuses: as he geared up for his return to the classroom, Wade had been thinking of including in his syllabus a contest for the most compelling alibi of the semester.

Past contenders, delivered via email, jumped to mind now, the real calamities in his students' lives richer than any fictive efforts to which they might have turned their hands:

> Dear Dr Wad i will not be able to attend class today, i am having a terrible week, my car was stolen and wrecked by my ex bf, and last night my mom got her truck taken away for running from the police i have to find a ride to work or i will be fired please understand and i was wondering if i am still able to turn in my paper for credit.

> Dear porfessor wayne please excuse my absence today my fiancé has to go to court again for drug and abandonment charges and will not be able to care for our child, please understand that my life is one big circus that I'm trying to piece together I hope we are not doing anything important in class today please let me know and I hope I can still get an A, I need it to get into the nursing program.

Wade saw himself on his deathbed in the hospital, his meds tended by this aspirant to the healing corps. Maybe better to step in front of a speeding train, sever a few limbs, get it over with quicker. He pushed a copy of *In Our Time* across his desk toward Jackson. "Did you read any of Hemingway's books in high school?"

Jackson frowned. "He didn't write *The Scarlet Letter*, did he?"

"Too bad he didn't. That's Nathaniel Hawthorne."

"Glad to hear *that*. You ever try to read that book?"

"I imagine I got about as far with it as you did."

"I guess it's supposed to be some kind of masterpiece or somethin', but excuse me, that's some boring ass shit there."

Wade laughed, then on impulse scanned his shelf and pulled off a copy of Tom Perrotta's *The Leftovers*. He opened it to the page with the bookmark where he had left it, handed the volume to Jackson, and pointed to the passage that had been worth by itself the price of the book. The protagonist, assigned to read *The Scarlet Letter* in high school, had become so frustrated with it that he had attacked it with a steak knife, explaining to his onlooking sister that "he was trying to kill the book before it killed him."

It took him a mildly alarming while to get there, but Jackson laughed when he reached the end of the paragraph. "That's about the same with me, only I didn't take no knife to it. Book belong to the school. Plenty of other people got to not read that copy." Jackson closed and then hoisted Perrotta's novel. "Okay with you if I borrow this one?"

Wade smiled in surprise and then nodded. Students rarely asked to borrow any reading that wasn't required.

"I'm tryin' to read more. Lot of people, includin' you, told me that's the most important thing to work on." Jackson grinned, then added, "'Cept for my slider and change-up, of course. You think I'll like this?"

"I'm pretty sure you'll find it more pleasing than *The Scarlet Letter*." Wade wondered if he had just managed to reset the bar for damnation with faint praise.

Jackson put down Perrotta and picked up *In Our Time*. "What other Hemingway books we gonna read in your class?"

Okay, so that was settled. "We'll start with the stories in there. Then we'll read all the novels he wrote and some more of his best stories. You might find some of it pretty interesting, actually. He wrote about baseball sometimes. Big fan of Joe DiMaggio's."

Jackson frowned again, trying to place the name. "I heard of him before. Yankees, right? Hold some kind of a record, don't he?"

He used to. Wade thought about Angela again, for the first time in the last, oh, fifteen seconds or so, then nodded, in spite of knowing better, and signed the form to add Jackson into his seminar. "See you in class."

CHAPTER 15

I just hated school so much, hated everything about it. I'm starting to think that was what was fucked up, a lot more than me? Keeping us locked up all day, treating us like children, making us learn a lot of shit about nothing. I think it made me sort of crazy.

—Billy Lynn, in Ben Fountain's *Billy Lynn's Long Half-time Walk*

What teaching has done for me is make me not want to read anything, written by anybody, for the rest of my life.

—Mike Magnuson, author of *The Right Man for the Job*, qtd. by David Gessner in "Those Who Write, Teach"

In February, in spite of Angela's continuing absence and his uncertainty over her plans, if any, to return to hearth and home, Wade began to feel a little bit better, as he always did when the year's first bitter month was behind him. Along with longer and at least slightly warmer days, with occasional hints of actual sunshine, came the promise of baseball. MLB pitchers and catchers would be reporting to spring training soon, and the whole annual ritual of preparations for the pennant race that had governed

Wade's calendar almost from infancy would commence anew. *Wait until next year* (or, on Chicago's North Side, *Anyone can have a bad century*) would yield once again to *hope springs eternal* (Alexander Pope's contribution to the grand old game) as Wade and millions of others across the nation and the world invested their hearts and minds in their uniformed heroes. Even Angela, after all, had been seduced by the game. Wade wondered if she would still be interested in the Giants when he saw her again. *If* he saw her again, he reminded himself.

The college baseball season had already begun in earnest. Constricted by a spring semester that ended in May or early June, the schedule for most teams began in mid-winter. Most of the major universities played their early games in rain or freezing wind, not exactly the conditions typically enjoyed by the big leaguers training in Florida or Arizona. Wade didn't even like to sit in the stands to watch a game played in foul weather, and he certainly didn't envy the athletes on the field attempting to cope with the elements. As with some of the professional sports, a season half as long would have made much more sense, but the joined forces of tradition and economics would likely prevent for the foreseeable future any improvements beyond those Allenby had already enacted.

If you were going to play college baseball, you had to play when the other schools were playing. Schedules were typically set years in advance, and there were many contractual and financial implications involved in making changes in the agreements with other colleges. As interim A.D. before becoming president, Allenby had waded in personally to save CSU some money and to cut down on the amount of time student-athletes would spend away from the campus. He had coughed up some cash—offset in part by the elimination of travel costs—to cancel a few road games, dipping into his own pocket for some of the restitution, in order to produce a more manageable schedule. The first four games had been knocked out, getting CSU out of the insanity of baseball in January (a sin against nature on a par with football in August). After failing to cancel a trip to the East Coast when the contracted opponents declined to accommodate his request, he had negotiated with universities in the Pacific 12 to discontinue two series that would have taken the CSU squad to Oregon and Washington for a likely water-logged week as prohibitive underdogs.

"The kids won't like it," Wade had pointed out, when Allenby first ran the plan by him.

"Fuck 'em. Tell 'em to stay home and study, work on getting a degree, something that might actually lead to a job, instead of worrying about a scout who's going to notice them striking out three times or popping up if they get lucky against a Pac-12 pitcher. We'll put Oregon State back on the schedule when we're ready to compete with them—and when they're willing to come here for a home-and-home."

Last year's surprising surge had elevated local and national interest in the baseball program, but Juke Jackson's injury had diminished expectations for the current season considerably. Wade decided to hold off until Jackson's return to the field before going to a game. When he emailed Norma to let her know of his intent to attend her softball game, she emailed him back to say that she, too, had suffered a setback in the form of a jammed thumb. Wade told her he would come to a game when she was healthy. April looked about right. In the meantime his role in the accreditation charade and his Hemingway class had been keeping him busy.

Wade had filed another shitload of reports for the visiting poohbahs, who had come and gone in February's first week without his seeing hide nor hair, just as Erica had predicted. He didn't know and didn't care if what he had written had been or would be carefully considered or scanned in a glance; it was much the same as he had felt when he delivered the final draft of his dissertation at Berkeley. He was just glad to get the goddam thing out of his hands. Allenby, of course, had played a far more prominent role in the process. He had taken the accrediting team out to extravagant dinners, plied them with liquor, let them sit around the table and tell him how brilliant they were, and, after a few hours and a hefty bottle count, how impressed they were with his campus. It was tried-and-true methodology, and whatever self-loathing Allenby had to endure in resorting to it was offset by the enhanced prospect of a favorable report and no more than token interference from ignorant outsiders with the reforms he had set in motion.

With the bulk of his own bureaucratic obligations concluded, Wade found that, in spite of the gaping hole in his private life, he was having fun in the classroom. Having suffered, like everyone else, from far too many teachers who told him far more than he needed to know about their feckless pets and exes, insane neighbors, and incarcerable boomerang children, he made a point of keeping his own remarks short and trying to draw ideas out of the students before they fell asleep pretending to listen to his. Jackson had provided some nice surprises for Wade in the class discussions. Initially quiet and deferring to others, he had begun to respond with some welcome insights to Wade's persistent attempts to engage him in the discussions. Jake Barnes, Jackson had argued, could have taken a lesson from CSU's Cenon Aquino: there was no use dwelling on an incapacitating injury. All you could do was work hard to make the best of what you had left. Wade realized that Jackson, pushing his limits every day to rehabilitate his leg and maintain his upper-body strength, was probably giving himself a pep talk at the same time. It was hard to be sure if he would utter the same upbeat assessment if afflicted in the particular way Jake had been, but at least Wade was glad that Jackson had shared Aquino's story with those in the class who had not known of the genuine hero in their midst.

Jackson's essays, on the other hand, like much of the writing submitted in the class, were more liable to make Wade want to pluck out his own eyeballs. When he passed back the first paper, festooned with marginalia more pertinent to linguistic atrocities than to matters of substance, he invited Jackson to come to his office to review the abuse. Jackson had somehow made it through his high school English courses, as well as a remedial section and English 1A at CSU. The tutors Wade had found for him had no doubt helped considerably with the latter. Out of professional curiosity Wade asked Jackson now what the writing assignments in his high school classes had been like.

"We didn't really write too many papers, didn't get 'em back if we did."

"What did you do in there?"

"Same as everybody else: messed with my phone, checked out the chicks. We had a bunch of little quizzes. Spent a lot of time gettin' ready for the state test. Watched a lot of movies. High school just a waste of time, really, 'cept for sports, of course."

"Did the teachers give you any feedback on your writing skills at all?"

"Was one teacher, my sophomore year, thought she was hot. She let me know I could stop by her place anytime, you know, for some extra help."

"Generous," Wade said. "Did you take her up on it?"

"Shit, no. I ain't never been that hard up. She *old*, like thirty or somethin.'"

"Practically one foot in the grave." Wade was reminded again that he must seem a truly ancient mariner to the generation he was attempting to engage.

"She hook up the next year with a guy on our basketball team, our center. Got pregnant from him, got her ass fired. He got kicked off the team, too, messed us up in the playoffs."

Wade remembered that Jackson had scored something like thirty points in a losing effort in a quarterfinal game for the state championship, en route to multiple college offers for scholarships in basketball as well as the sports he was competing in at CSU. With that kind of success on the courts and playing fields, how much could you blame him for paying less than full attention to the *little quizzes* in the classroom? There was so much crap you had to sit and listen to in high school. The only classes Wade himself had enjoyed back then had been in P.E. All the time he spent in other classes, staring at the walls or ogling girls he would never have the guts to ask out, he was just dying to get out onto a field or into the gym for another chance to run around and have fun, however unheroic the results that attended his efforts. He wondered what his own GPA would have been if he had made so much as a single varsity squad, let alone been his school's superstar in each of the major sports. He probably would have been so full of himself that he wouldn't have noticed anyone on campus besides the chicks fighting in line for next licks.

He spent half an hour going over Jackson's essay with him. Jackson appeared to listen carefully, took some notes, and wanted to know how he could improve.

"We've talked about this before. The more you read . . . ." Wade gave him again the standard spiel.

"You know, before I took this class, I never really read a whole book before in my life. 'Less you count the Bible."

"If you've read all of that, you're one up on me."

"Just *The New Testament*. Too many crazy old dudes in the other one."

Wade found Volume II equally batshit but kept the opinion to himself.

"I like this stuff Hemingway wrote. Feel like I understand it pretty good, too. This class helpin' me a lot."

This was Wade's favorite part of teaching. Of course, it was a good deal less gratifying when students hated the books you picked or couldn't be bothered to read far enough to figure out if they loved *or* hated them, but, even for an irredeemable heathen like him, there was something almost numinous about sharing literature that you loved with a student who began to enjoy it, too.

Jackson picked up the essay Wade had annotated, stood up to leave, and then said quietly, apropos of nothing, "I'm a father, Doc."

"Congratulations," Wade said automatically. "Boy or—"

"I got a little girl."

"Healthy, I hope?"

"Baby fine. Her mama crazy, but baby fine. Want to see a picture?"

Wade wondered if ever in the course of human events anyone had declined this invitation. "Sure."

Jackson pulled out his cell phone and showed him a photo. "Think she look more like me or more like Cammie?"

Wade was just glad she didn't look more like Johnny Dawes. "Looks like she got the best features from each of you. What's her name?"

"I wanted *Michelle*, you know, like the President's wife, but Cammie picked *Arabella*. Sound like a terrorist to you?"

"Maybe to Fox News." *Make sure to keep her birth certificate handy.* "I wouldn't worry about it. I think it's a nice name. What happens next?"

"Cammie's parents gonna help her. Live about a hour from here. Plus she got a sister live here, few miles from school, was takin' some classes here back in the day, when *she* got a baby. Now she got three. Don't make no difference to her help out with one more, I guess."

"I see." *New family formation, California Plan.*

"I be able to see my baby a lot, anyway."

"That's important."

"I'm scared, though, Doc. I'm only twenty, got no steady job. I didn't plan on this."

"You'll have a steady job soon," Wade said, "with a nice fat paycheck. You're going to do just fine. I'm sure you'll be a good father." *Your kid will still have a crazy mama, but—*

"You never wanted to have no kids?"

Never. Was that why Angela hadn't come home? "My wife and I are—*were*—talking about adoption, but—"

"I'm adopted, more or less. My father never signed the papers, make it official, but my uncle is the one who raised me after my mama got killed in the Army. Closest thing to a dad I had. He the one told me I got to stand up, be a man, if somethin' like this happen." He waved the cell phone, then clicked off the image of his daughter and pocketed the phone. "Taught me how to do all that good shit with my hands, too." Jackson hefted his copy of *Winner Take Nothing.* "Too bad I didn't pay more attention in high school, though. Make it kind of hard for you to catch me up now, don't it?"

"You're doing well. Just keep working on it, get a little better every day." *I sound like a fucking fungo coach.*

"I plan to. Thanks again for your help."

Jackson left. Wade headed home, hoping they had made some progress. After a beer to clear his head, he sat down at the kitchen table with the new batch of papers he had collected. He found on top one from Monica, a buxom lass who had added the class on the last possible day after bailing on Contemporary Poetry. Wade didn't blame her for the defection. Other than Dr. Seuss, he didn't have much use for the poets who had come down the pike since Pound and Eliot had, as Frost lamented, relegated their genre to the academics.

Monica had missed a class or two after the late add and been tardy to a few more. Wade encouraged students to connect their own lives with the literature they were supposed to be reading. Sometimes the results were more edifying than others.

> I don't see why Lady Brett and Jake can't work out there problems if they just have an honest, open discussion, after all communication is always the key to relationships. When the Jake in my life and I have a fight, we always make up and we never go to bed mad, that's the Golden Rule of Relationships, in fact as a women I feel that sex is a great way to communicate, honestly, I can't think of a better one, too bad Jake and Brett didn't give it a try!

Clearly, beer wasn't going to get the job done today. Allenby had turned Wade on to Scotch. He poured himself some now and counterattacked with relevant page numbers, spelling, and punctuation, wondering how Big Pharma was coming along with that prototype for a pill to knock out run-on sentences. If the drug lords could figure out how to burn off ten pounds in twenty minutes, grow hair on a golf ball, or give an eighty-year-old an all-day boner the size of Babe Ruth's business tool, why the hell couldn't they concoct something that would stimulate students a class or two from a college degree to put a fucking period at the end of a fucking sentence? Wade took a slug and tackled the next paper in the stack. One of the Christians in the class had decided to weigh in again on "A Clean, Well-Lighted Place." Wade had not treated her first draft kindly. So much for getting better every day. *If at first you do not succeed, shut the fuck up and go away.*

> The theme of this story is very subtle, it is an analogy about the birth of Our Lord Jesus Christ. As i said in my previous essay (in which i disagree with your grade with, by the way) eventho his name is never specifically mentioned in the story, the point that is obviously trying to be made is that the café represents the manger where the baby Jesus—

Climbed up on the crucifix so he wouldn't have to read this shit. At least it was comforting to know that the Holy One, his inviolate mother, and his cuckhold dad were cozy in there; Wade hoped they also had central heat and air. He managed not to make a note to that effect in the margin of the essay. He was pretty sure that this student already had him slotted for eternal damnation anyway, but he didn't need another petty grievance to go along with roasting in hell forever. Lacking hemlock in his liquor cabinet, he was reaching for more malt and the next revelation when the landline rang.

"Wade, it's Brenda."

"I know. I can see your number."

"You finally got fucking Caller-ID?"

"It came with the wife."

"That's right, you married the titless wonder, didn't you?"

"Mellow as ever, I see. What's on your mind? Did you get my check? I'm afraid that's all I can—"

"I got your fucking check, Wade."

"Oh, what is it then that—"

"It's Tommy. He O.D.'d again."

"Christ, what did he—"

"He took carfentanil."

"What the fuck is—"

"It's the drug they use to tranquilize elephants."

Of course. How could our Tommy resist that?

"It's a hundred times stronger than fentanyl, the drug that's been killing all the heroin addicts. He thought he was buying *that*."

Wade knew about fentanyl light. It had been prescribed for his father, near the very end, when nothing else could ease his pain after cancer of the prostate had metastasized into five other kinds.

"Please tell me you didn't give him the money I—"

"Do you think I'm *that* fucking stupid?"

Wade had often heard it said that there was no such thing as a stupid question. Even in the unlikely case that this were true, some questions clearly were best left unanswered. Despite the suds and spirits sloshing within, he had enough discretion to leave this one alone.

"I just wondered where he got the—"

"He . . . stole the money out of my purse."

Which you, of course, just happened to leave lying around the house I'm paying for that you SHARE WITH A FUCKING HEROIN ADDICT. Perhaps in an envelope with a nice little note in your third grade curlique cursive, FOR YOUR NEXT FIX, LITTLE BROTHER. It sounded like a story she was making up. How pathetic was that? She had to cover her ass for funding the treat that sent her own sibling to the hospital again. By now Tommy ought to have his own wing in there.

"I see. Where is he now? Back in ER, or—"

"He's dead, Wade."

Wow. Wade's jaw half-dropped. So the odds had finally caught up with Brenda's little brother. Wade tried to figure out what he was feeling. Not shock, really. Not grief, no use pretending that. Maybe just mild surprise that Tommy had turned out to be mortal after all, that after a lifetime of experimentation with every narcotic known to man, in quantities inconceivable and in combinations lethal to every other form of the species, the sheer blind stupid luck that had spared him before had finally run out.

Wade settled on a white lie. "I'm sorry to—"

"Wade"—something suddenly vulnerable in her tone warned him, more trouble on the way—"I can't do this without you. I need you to come to Stockton and help me bury him."

ARE YOU FUCKING KIDDING? Just cremate the cocksucker. Douse him with cheap booze, shove a bong into his mouth, light a match, and get it over with, just like he nearly did to himself a thousand times before.

"Of course," Wade heard himself say. *Fuck me again.* "When's the service?"

CHAPTER 16

Never [. . .] go on trips with anyone you do not love.

—Ernest Hemingway, *A Moveable Feast*

For some reason, I AM COMPELLED TO ASK, "do u know how to change a tire??"

—Bria

Wade was putting a note on his office door to explain his impending absence when Jackson appeared in the hallway. He had stayed home to focus on his classes and hit the weight room while his baseball teammates cuddled in snowy Colorado and waited for the make-up games to pile up.

"Trainer say I can run full-speed next week, maybe play in a game by the end of the month."

"That's great news," Wade said. "I'm heading out of town. Got to go to Stockton to help my ex-wife bury her brother."

"Sorry for your loss."

Wade nodded acknowledgment of the conventional condolence, obviously sincere in this instance. He had uttered the phrase on more than one occasion himself, but remembered now just how stiff it had sounded when others had said it at his parents' funerals. Applied to Tommy, on the other hand—

"Was you real close to him?"

I dote upon his very absence. "Not really." Wade didn't waste breath on qualifying the dimensions of his grief. "His sister's all alone there, so—"

"Think I could hitch a ride with you?"

"To Stockton?"

Jackson nodded. "Where I grew up. Someone there I need to see. I'll split the gas with you, how's that?"

"Not necessary," Wade said, realizing he would be glad to have the company but puzzled about why Jackson wanted to go with him.

Jackson read the confusion. "I let Cammie borrow my car, and she—"

"Wait a minute. You let *Cammie Sanchez* borrow your car after she—"

"—backed into a garbage truck. I can fix it myself, but the car got impounded. She didn't have no license with her."

Wade paused to let the info sink in. He thought of his deceased brother-in-law's legendary roadway exploits, which Tommy had somehow always managed to survive. "Could've been worse, I guess. Could've been a fire engine she—"

"Main thing is, nobody hurt too bad."

Wade admired the equanimity on display, even if he could never have matched it. He couldn't resist a follow up question. "How come she's driving *your* car after—"

"Dawes sold her car after she drove out to Utah to be with him. Probably had to pay off some gambling debts he had."

"What about his bonus money?"

"Shit, he probably blew through that in Vegas on his way out there. Cammie's father pretty pissed. He the one paid for that car, not her, and—"

"Certainly not Dawes."

"—he wouldn't even go get her after Dawes beat her up again. She had to take the bus to come home. JD got hurt, couldn't get out the way on a double play, messed up his knee. Pretty bad, I heard. His baseball might be done."

"At least he has his trial to look forward to," Wade said. Dawes and his entourage had a June court date. "Maybe he can finish his degree in prison."

Dawes had completed ninety-some units with a GPA of 2.02. Only the five classes from Carlotta Baynes he had presumably held his nose through, if he had bothered to grace the lecture hall at all, had kept him barely eligible.

"You talkin' 'bout that General Studies major he signed up for? That shit don't pay no bills."

Wade had recently seen a statistic cited by a sports agent who claimed that, in spite of the millions they earned, 68% of NFL players and 72% in the NBA were bankrupt three years after they retired. Baseball players historically had the reputation of being a little more savvy with their earnings, but how many of them wound up where Dawes was heading? How many student-athletes would learn enough in the classes they completed to manage a solvent life after leaving the groves of academe? Wade wondered how Jackson would fare once his big paydays began.

He wondered, too, who it was that Jackson needed to visit in Stockton, but didn't press for details now. They arranged a rendezvous, and Wade went to speak briefly with Allenby.

"Stockton, huh? Is your life insurance paid up?"

The seat of San Joaquin County had made national headlines by joining Akron and Detroit among the most violent cities in the nation, and anyone could be a target. A high-end crime spree there was three punks phoning in an order, ambushing Domino's delivery boy, beating him half to death, and stealing his merchandise.

"I hear the local gangs don't usually shoot up funerals," Wade said. "Weddings, birthday parties, picnics in the park, toddlers in the street, those they cater to pretty regularly, but—"

"I'm not so worried about gangbangers taking you out. They pretty much keep to their own kind. I'm more worried about your ex. Does the phrase *Hell hath no fury* ring a bell? Are you sure you're prepared to see her on her turf?"

"At least I can leave when it's over."

"It's never *over* with an ex."

Wade shrugged. "Juke Jackson's coming with me, by the way."

Allenby blew out a sigh. "Just make sure you don't get him killed, too. *You* we could probably replace with a phone call or two; him the baseball team is going to need in the playoffs."

"Duly noted. It's nice to be appreciated."

"Don't let it go to your head. Are you taking that deathtrap Japanese shitbox of yours, or is Juke going to—"

"That's a tale for another day," Wade said, heading for the door. "Did you know Cammie Sanchez is back in town?"

"Oh, crap." Allenby sank into his chair, shaking his head. "Don't come back to this office until you have some better news to report, understood?"

Wade picked Jackson up and they hit the road, running into construction delays almost immediately. California's bill for deferred maintenance had fallen well past due, and anywhere you went on the Central Valley's bombed-out war-zone freeways these days, a backup was almost inevitable.

"You been to Stockton much?" Jackson asked, as they emerged from one slow-down only to run directly into another.

"Not for a while," Wade said. Among California's cities, Stockton was the second most populous, trailing only equally abused step-sister Oakland, without its own state university main campus—and without the consolation of a world class UC in spitting distance. Several surveys had declared it the least literate city in the nation and several others the most miserable place to live in the lower forty-eight. Wade hadn't spent much time there in recent years except to attend a few conferences at the majestic, immaculate campus of the University of the Pacific, which by comparison made CSU's look like a spittoon. "I've got some fond memories, though."

Like the site of CSU and other Central Valley cities, though it could be fog-ridden in January and hot and dusty in the dog days of summer, Stockton was often glorious. Spring and fall were spectacular. Indian summer in a good year could last nigh unto Thanksgiving. All but the hottest of true summer days turned into balmy, walkable evenings. Winters were mild for the most part, especially by contrast with those in Madison, Minneapolis, and other cities somehow ranked far higher in *livability* surveys. Wade remembered Ulysses Grant's description of the climate America's early settlers had endured (*nine months of winter and three months of cold weather*) and recalled also the joys of Memorial Stadium in August. He wondered if current lifestyle surveys included respondents who had to dig their vehicles out of a snowbank in minus-20 degrees at dawn for months on end just to dice with death on frozen freeways to get to work, or those who had to outmaneuver mosquitos the size of baseballs in humidity that never diminished when the summer sun finally surrendered. He had spent enough time in other places to know that living in interior California beat the hell out of living almost anywhere else. Whatever its reputation among pollsters shivering or sweltering afar, Stockton still held a place in his heart.

"My dad used to bring my sister and me, sometimes along with our friends, to go water skiing in the Delta," he said. "We had a blast."

"Water-skiing, huh? Probably a good idea to know how to swim before you try that shit, right?"

"You never learned?"

Jackson shook his head. "Had a cousin, my uncle's youngest boy, year older than me, went fishin' out there one time, fell in, got his ass drowned. Scared me off. I never tried to learn after that."

A century and a half past the end of the war that freed their ancestors, many urban blacks still did not master this simple skill. Jackson was an elite athlete capable of performing at the highest level in the most competitive sports in his culture, yet apparently he couldn't crawl across a backyard pool, and maybe wouldn't even dare to dip his toe in a river to cool off on a summer day. Wade might not have survived the first cut for baseball, but in order to graduate from high school he had been required to swim fifty laps in a competition pool and to tread water for an hour. It wasn't just English and math that black kids were falling behind in right from the start. Wade wondered how many of them went to schools that didn't even have pools.

Distracted by his ruminations, he failed to swerve in time to avoid a suddenly looming crater. Jackson was thrown against him in their seats. A minute later Aborto began to wobble.

"Think you got a flat tire. Better pull over."

Wade flipped off the fuckwit tailgating him and drove onto the narrow shoulder, which looked like a perfect spot to get sideswiped or carjacked. Thank God Jackson was riding shotgun.

Since the blessed advent of radial technology, Wade had not been obliged to deal with the particular humiliating inconvenience at hand. He made sure that his car, otherwise abjectly neglected, always had tires that were relatively fresh in order to forfend his utter ineptitude in coping with their dysfunction. He realized now that he had left at his bedside the cell phone that never rang. *Fat lot of good it was going to do there.* He asked Jackson if he could borrow his in order to call the insurance company's road service number.

"You don't want to fix it yourself?"

"Not in my skill set."

Jackson looked dumbfounded. "You can't change a tire?"

Wade shook his head in chagrin. It was one of a thousand simple manly tasks he had never mastered. "I tried once. I didn't secure the—whatdayacallit?—*jack*, and I dropped the end of the car on my leg. Almost broke my ankle."

Jackson's turn to shake his head. "Nobody never taught you how? Your father didn't show you?"

"He was too easy on me. I gave up on stuff that didn't come naturally to me." For the same reason, Wade hadn't even learned how to ride a bicycle at the age when other kids did. He had fallen off at the first attempt and given up, then lived with the sickening shame for years. "He should've pushed me harder, but he was too . . . gentle."

Jackson nodded now. "Sometimes a father got to kick your ass, teach you shit you don't really want to learn."

Wade had no use whatsoever for men who raised a hand against their women or children, but he had to agree that a little discipline from his father might have gone a long way toward equipping him to deal with the world more competently.

"Want me to show you how now?"

"Sure." Wade would have far preferred that his passenger simply hop out, tend to the chore, and report its completion, but he sensed that it would be bad form to decline the lesson. He popped the trunk, got out of the car, and tried to stay out of the way as Jackson set to work.

"You got one of them little midget tires, come out of a gumball machine." Jackson held up the spare disdainfully. "You only supposed to ride on this shit for a few miles, get you to the auto shop."

"That's what came with the car when I bought it."

"You bought this car? Thought you said you took it off the Japanese at Iwo Jima." Jackson set the tire down and picked up the jack. "Come on over here, and I'll show you how to do this. It's simple, but you got to do it yourself if you want to learn."

"Okay."

Wade followed instructions and fumbled his way through the process, Jackson stepping in to steady his efforts at several points. The car looked lop-sided once the toy tire was in place, but Jackson said it was safe to drive for a short distance. Once they were back underway, a road sign noting the scant mileage to their destination, Jackson turned the subject again to his home town: "One thing about Stockton, we got some hot women there."

"Well, the only woman I really know there wouldn't exactly fit into that category, but that's always good to hear."

In counterpoint to the misery index reports, another survey picked up by the Associated Press had recently claimed for Stockton the highest percentage of beautiful women of any city in the country. Although it was not the kind of *news* Wade generally paid attention to or placed any faith in, he mentioned the study to Jackson, who hadn't read the newspaper but had seen for himself.

"The races all mixed up there. Got a lot of hot girls half-Asian, half-Mexican, or half-black, half-Mexican, shit like that. Lot of hot Filipino girls, too."

"Wouldn't be one of those you're going to see by any chance?" Jackson had remained cryptic on this subject. Wade hadn't wanted to pry but risked the question now.

"High school, there was one really fine girl I knew, part Filipino, part Vietnamese."

"Was she someone special to you?"

Jackson nodded. "Some guys used to get on me, sayin' why you want to be with such a skinny girl? Shit like that. One friend of mine always sayin', *Once you made love to a big-tit woman, you can't go back to itty-bitty.* He full of shit, you ask me. Don't matter the size up top: it's the girl inside gonna tell whether you can spend some time together."

Wade had a hunch that his own experience in this department was quite a bit less extensive than his junior traveling partner's, but was inclined to concur. Although he would be among the first to admit that large breasts were hard to ignore and were indeed conducive to arousal, once the act itself was underway, their importance seemed to subside. He had adjusted without a great sense of sacrifice to Angela's modest proportions.

Jackson continued: "Way I look at it is, once you've made love to a woman who likes it, it's hard to go back to one who don't. You know how some girls just lay there with their eyes closed, waitin' for it to be over?"

My first marriage in a nutshell. Wade wondered how old Jackson had been when girls first started tossing their panties at him. According to multiple media accounts, many youths reported their first intercourse at thirteen or fourteen now.

"Girl I was tellin' you about, Emma, she my first one, really, sophomore year. When'd you get started, Doc?"

"Not until college," Wade admitted.

"You didn't mess around none before then?"

"All the girls who were interested in me in high school wanted me to walk them home from French Club or go to Mass with their family, stuff like that. They definitely weren't interested in helping me . . . get started. It's hard enough getting shot down asking for a date without having to hear *We'll be praying for you* afterward." The venerable European tradition of fathers' taking their sons at puberty to a brothel had never seemed like such a bad idea to Wade, especially by contrast with the *Marry early or you'll burn* approach that the Puritans and other fun types had brought with them to the New World when they came to escape the repressions of the Old. "The cheerleaders and party girls I was wanking over wouldn't even look at me—or looked at me as if I was an insect, if they happened to catch a glimpse." It still made Wade wince to recall how the meanest (and, of course, hottest) of them would sneer at him or make the gagging sign if, heaven forbid, any inadvertent eye contact took place.

"I had a few cheerleaders," Jackson said. "You didn't miss nothin' special there. Spend more time lookin' in the mirror before and after than gettin' down with you."

"In college—actually I was almost finished with college—a girl finally . . . took pity on me, I guess you would say, and helped me get it over with."

"She hot?"

"I don't remember too much about her face, to be honest with you."

"How you get her to . . . you know?"

"I helped her with a paper for her history class. The truth is I more or less wrote it for her. She basically just put her name on it."

"Sound like cheatin' to me, Doc. You get caught?"

Wade shook his head in shame again. "I think the teacher was trying to get into her pants, too. That paper was a true piece of crap, but he gave her an A- on it." *And she gave* me *a—*

"Make it kind of hard to call out your students for doin' the same shit, don't it?"

Wade was not, in practice, soft on plagiarism. He tried to steer a middle course between the colleagues who wanted to settle for a slap on the wrist at the first offense and those who favored amputation at the elbow. His policy was to issue an F for the copied assignment; if the culprit protested or pled innocence in the face of blatant evidence, Wade wrote a letter recommending dismissal from the university. This he had done half a dozen times even as an adjunct instructor; usually the bleeding hearts on the discipline review committee overturned the recommendation and issued a stern warning (always good for a cackle after) instead. On the other hand, if he encountered confession and contrition, Wade was usually willing to let the student stay in the class, take the F on the assignment, and try to do his or her own work on the next one. Maybe it was lingering guilt over his own complicity in salvaging a fellow student's GPA that had led him to this moderate approach. She wasn't the only one he had helped too much, he remembered now—just the only one to *pay him back* in the currency of that occasion. Quite a few others over the years had asked for his aid and wound up pressing him to edit (translation: rewrite) the garbage they had written for their classes, or, on the travesties known as *group projects*, to write far more than his fair share.

Fortunately, Jackson didn't probe Wade's conscience on that score any further but turned back instead to his own regrets. "That girl, Emma, I thought she really liked me. We was friends, then we got together for a while. But then she met this Chinese dude was goin' to Pacific, gonna be a pharmacist. Her whole family like fell in love with him. They didn't never want to see my black ass around her again after he come along. He be makin' a lot of money someday."

"You'll be making a lot of money someday, too. Someday *soon.*"

Jackson nodded. "But a pharmacist, that's steady, that's every month. You get that license, you set for life, thirty, forty years. A ballplayer, you never know. You blow out your knee, your arm if you a pitcher, you done in a minute. Look what happened to my football season."

"You could be a pharmacist," Wade said. "You'd just have to take—"

"All them science courses? Shit, that stuff 'bout fry my brain. I was lucky to make it through Biology in high school. Girl I was tellin' you about, she my lab partner, help me out quite a bit in there. Chemistry, I bet that shit would kick my ass."

"It's a tough course," Wade, who had never been inspired to take it himself, said. "But I'm sure you could get through it. You've got the aptitude for science. I can see that from the way you—"

"You goin' graduate me from changin' a damn tire to gettin' through Chemistry? I don't think so, Doc."

They neared the Starbucks where Jackson had indicated he wanted to be dropped off. Wade tried again: "All I'm saying is, you're not limited to sports. You can do a lot of things."

Wade didn't see anyone waiting. Jackson started to step out of the car, then stopped and turned back toward Wade.

"I 'preciate you sayin' that. I never heard shit like that from my father."

Wade nodded, feeling for maybe the millionth time the swell of gratitude that came from having had himself a dad who knew what an encouraging word could do. You could forgive a lot, even the mortification of being the last kid on the block to ride a bike, when the trove of better memories kicked in.

"Thanks for your help today. Good luck with your . . . visit. I'll find a phone and give you a call when I'm ready to head back."

"Cool. Don't forget to get that tire replaced. Good luck with your ex."

"Why in the world would I need that?"

CHAPTER 17

Many brief follies—that is what you call love. And your marriage puts an end to many brief follies, with a single long stupidity.

—Friedrich Nietzsche, *Thus Spoke Zarathustra*

I hate a dumpy woman.

—Lord Byron, *Don Juan*, Canto I

Dating back to last year's delay, when their plans had been thwarted by her father's first heart attack, Wade and Angela had been planning a trip to the Hotel del Coronado for this year's spring break. It would have been his first real experience of the revels that students and colleagues had been celebrating with (he presumed) hyperbolic abandon for as long as he had been in academia. Most of his own recesses in recent springs had been devoted to catching up on grading the papers that had piled up in the first half of the semester, or fighting through the alternate stacks of paid bills and bank statements to concoct his annual creative writing projects for the IRS and the Franchise Tax Board. In the years before Brenda had divorced him, they had tried a few mini-vacations, usually to motels of dubious repute, in accordance with their budgetary constraints, inevitably with Brenda's late baby brother tagging along or turning up *by accident* at their destination. Tommy and Brenda would then instantly get the party started, before anyone even had time to unpack, and instead of basking on the beach or by the pool, Wade would spend the vacation/hell-week mopping up their vomit, checking occasionally for a pulse, and wishing he had stayed home to watch a rerun of *Fun in Acapulco*. With Angela gone again now, he realized, his trip to bury Tommy would be the closest thing to a spring break he would get this year.

The abode that Brenda now called her own would never be featured in *House Beautiful*, but viewed externally at least, it was less of a pit than Wade had envisioned. Built in the early 1950's for perhaps $2,500 and sold originally for $5,000, it had been resold for $350,000 at the peak of the real estate bubble in 2007 and turned into a grow house. Pending the incarceration of its previous owners, Brenda had bought it in foreclosure for $80,000, Wade's cash and Allenby's counsel making the deal possible. She had made a few modest improvements, including a fresh coat of paint and new carpeting. Double-pane windows had been next on the list before she lost her job teaching third grade when a round of layoffs in the Stockton Unified School District wiped out a spate of dubiously qualified recent hires in favor of retaining, in her version, a core of geriatric dipsos and pedophiles retired on the job for the past twenty years. As with the other dwellings on her street, the original panes were cracked here and there and did little to provide insulation from summer or winter extremes, but it was a house, it was her name on the deed, and it was a step beyond anything she had ever lived in before, including crappy apartments with Wade—and certainly a vast upgrade from the circumstances of her rearing by (Wade's version) inbred rednecks who rented from trailer trash.

Brenda met him at the door, no longer quite filling the frame. She appeared to have lost about fifty pounds. Pharmacology, cosmetics, or an aesthetician's torch had all but eliminated the rebarbative little mustache that for a while had given her an uncanny resemblance to Hitler's sister. Wade stood on the stoop, not knowing exactly what was called for. A kiss on the still chubby cheek, a high five, condolences for the dear departed (sibling, not pounds), or—

"Aren't you going to give me a hug?"

Problem solved, Wade complied.

"Did you notice that there's less of me to hug?" she said, as she stepped out of his limp embrace, essaying a semblance of a twirl to showcase the redistribution of her assets.

At her heaviest she had packed nearly three hundred pounds onto her five-foot two-inch frame. The result of her transformation was that she looked less like a Sumo wrestler now and more like a nose-guard. Wade recalled a scene from Kingsley Amis's *Jake's Thing* in which an impotent middle-aged husband was examined by his personal physician seeking the cause of his disaffection. The first question the doctor had asked: *How much does your wife weigh?* This, of course, was not merely a problem in English novels. Wade had read that after age twenty-five, the average American woman put on a pound per year; Brenda, obviously, had exceeded that norm four or five times over. It was conceivable to Wade that a man could sustain romantic interest in a woman who was far overweight, but there *were* undeniably limits. His students, especially the females, had often written essays extolling *unconditional love* and castigating any fictional characters or actual newsmakers who fell short of this lofty standard. Wade turned the tables: he wondered what their thoughts on this subject would be fifteen or twenty years down the road when their soulmates brought their bulging beer bellies into the boudoir or lost their jobs and spent their days in the basement or the garage playing video games and surfing for porn featuring nymphs who looked nothing like their *unconditional lovers.*

Life was unfair, in this regard as in every other, of course. For every ten or twenty rotund Brendas, there was a freak like Angela, who could eat like a horse, anything she wanted, all day long (while of course monitoring the nutritional value of every morsel *he* consumed), but never show the effects, her weight fluctuating wildly between 105 and 106 pounds. Wade had no science to draw on, but he conjectured that her metabolic rate must be somehow connected to the hyperactivity of her brainwaves. The intensity's wondrous carry-over onto the mattress bounced back to remind him now—*Angela's gone*—as he stood face-to-face with his first wife and dredged up their so-called sex life.

Like many other fools, Wade had begun life with a healthy libido and had envisioned marriage as a pathway to regular satisfaction of it. During their courtship and honeymoon, Brenda had tolerated his intrusions without too much complaint, but within a shockingly few weeks (or had it been even a matter of days?) her preferences had turned emphatically elsewhere. Lacking the fine motor skills required to broil a chicken breast, steam some vegetables, or open a can of soup, she had quickly renounced learning how to cook. Fast food and television became her preoccupations, until dope and cocaine had come along to supplement them. Wade soon tired of the effort to arouse her; it was profoundly disempowering, to turn the buzzword of the day on its backside, to be abed with a woman who took so little interest in the pleasures of the flesh. And as the flesh beside him multiplied grotesquely, Wade's own interest diminished, *gradually, then suddenly,* until he lost all desire to touch her or to seek her touching him.

"You're thinking about all those great days we had in the sack, aren't you?"

"How could I not?" Wade said. "But shouldn't we concentrate on Tommy now?"

Brenda had been close to her brother in spite of—or perhaps because of—the addictions and deviations that had defined and ultimately destroyed his life, but she seemed strangely unemotional now. Wade had anticipated wailing; it didn't look as if she had even been weeping.

"I don't really want to talk about him now."

"I thought that's why I was here."

"There will be plenty of time for that later. Let's catch up first, okay?"

Plenty of time. That sounded ominous. How long was he in for? "What time have you scheduled the service for?"

"Can't we just take a few minutes to enjoy being together again before we take care of the other stuff? Are you even going to say it's good to see me?"

"You look good, Bren." *The truth might set you free, but a lie could keep you from getting socked in the stomach.*

"I heard your new wife left you."

So much for dodging the gut punch. "She's . . . taking a sabbatical."

"I thought she just got started again at CSU."

Wade hadn't realized his ex-wife would be tracking developments with the currently estranged version so closely.

"It was sort of a special arrangement."

"I'll bet," Brenda said, managing to convey with a major juddering of her badly plucked and boldly dyed eyebrows the clear implication that Angela had slept her way to whatever agreement had been reached. "How have you been coping?"

"I've been"—*smoking dope, drinking Scotch, and jerking off every day when I wasn't too wasted to find my own dick*—"doing a lot of walking."

"See! We should have done more of that when we were together."

How many times, Wade couldn't remember but also couldn't forget, after giving up on getting busy in bed, had he tried to coax her out for a walk instead, only to be shushed or swatted away in favor of eating, sleeping, shopping, or watching a soap opera depicting delectable women half her size having performed upon their persons by impossibly perfect stallions preliminaries to the very feats of carnal delight he had proposed to perform upon her own far more substantial form?

"If we had walked more, maybe I wouldn't have got so"—she paused, perhaps waiting for him to toss in a healing euphemism: *obese? humongous? ginormous?*—"out of shape."

"We could have done a lot of things differently," Wade conceded.

"We should've spent more time in bed," Brenda said. "We spent more time fighting than we did fucking."

"I'm sure that's true for most couples."

"Fuck most couples, Wade. I'm talking about *us*."

There is no us, remember? "I understand. Maybe we shouldn't talk so much about what's past."

"Okay, here's what new: I learned how to give a blowjob."

"Oh. That's . . . great." *About twenty years too late, give or take, but—*

"Tommy taught me."

Wade had imagined that nothing Brenda could tell him involving her brother could shock him at this juncture, but here she had at least come close. Then he remembered how Tommy had selected the occasion of their wedding reception to unburden himself about his boyhood fantasies, prominently featuring a peep through the bathroom keyhole in their family's hovel to ogle his pre-pubescent sister in the tub. Wade had come to think of it as Tommy's version of Greek tragedy: *The Myth of Sis's Tits*.

"I'm glad he accomplished something before he died."

"I don't mean I actually *did* it to him. He just . . . *talked* to me about how to do it. Which is more than *you* ever did. You never even tried to—"

"Right." *Never* as in a few thousand times he had begged her to give it a shot.

"And please don't tell me again that it's not rocket science."

"Don't worry, I won't." Wade tried to remember if, amid their many fruitless conversations on the subject, he had actually resorted to the cliché he flayed his students for.

"He told me that I have to use my hands more to do it right." Brenda made in the air a squeezing motion that Wade supposed was intended to be erotic. It looked more like a choke hold on a hapless intruder, or a desperate attempt to drain an extra ounce from an empty bottle of mustard. She followed the gesture with a meaningful glance in the direction of Wade's crotch and poked the tip of her tongue through her lips, seductively she perhaps imagined. "Want to give it another try?"

Wade thought of a plump lizard on a hot rock in the sun, about to flick in a particularly slow-witted fly. His own role in the analogy could hardly have been clearer.

"Thanks for the offer. Maybe another time." *Maybe another life. Maybe a billion years from now, on Mars or Pluto, if you and I are the only surviving life forms and there's nothing to watch on TV.* What an irony: after all the times he had cajoled her, here she was freely offering, and he wasn't even slightly aroused. Indeed, he was repelled.

She reached out to touch the uninspired object of her gaze, but Wade stepped back, and she pulled her hand away as if she had burned it on the stove. "You weren't exactly Casanova in that department yourself, you know."

"I'm sure I wasn't." Wade wished he could snap his fingers and summon up on the spot a video to show her of Angela writhing in ecstasy under his ministrations—but of course it was Ronnie who had that kind of evidence. *Fuck.* Meanwhile, somewhere, presumably nearby, Tommy, tutor in the erotic arts, was waiting to be laid to rest.

"Shouldn't we talk about—"

"Getting back together?"

"I've remarried, Brenda. You have to accept that—"

"The bitch took off on you, just like she did last time. Right now she's probably fucking that football player she dumped you for before."

"Thanks for reminding me. Maybe we could focus on the funeral now. When—"

Brenda's cell phone beeped. She picked it up, checked a text message, and then sent one, Wade wondered to whom. He couldn't imagine that her parents could've mastered the technology involved. He wondered if they had made the trip from Taft to send off the prodigal son. Who else could it be? Brenda had mentioned vaguely a couple of acquaintances she had made at the school where she'd been teaching before the funds ran out. He couldn't imagine anyone who had ever met Tommy giving a shit that he was dead, but maybe one of her new crew was coming over to accompany them to the service, wherever *that* was. By comparison with the current interrogation, Wade was beginning to look forward to it. A eulogy for Tommy: now *there* would be the challenge to test all forensics contest entrants for generations to come!

Brenda set the cell phone down without saying who was in touch. She shared other news: "I have to go potty."

"Feel free." *It's your house, but thanks for the bulletin.*

Based on past experience, this could take a while. Wade settled in for a wait/siege and looked around, remembering what it had been like to share a habitat with Brenda (*the very rats instinctively have quit it*). Her tidiness did not appear to have improved with ownership, although of course having her unhousebroken brother underfoot would have posed a significant impediment to progress. Wade was no neat freak himself, to be sure, as the disorder awaiting Angela, *if she ever came back*, to their house could attest—in March, after six months of her absence, he had arranged maid service to keep the dust in the living room from burying him alive—but at least he could still usually find a place to sit down. He looked for a newspaper or a magazine, finding only a *Cosmopolitan* with a lead story of "Top Ten New Sex Tips." He didn't open it to see if Tommy was credited.

A moment later there was a knock on the front door. Wade steeled himself to greet the grieving parents, just in case, recalling past disasters. They had fully reciprocated his disdain, believing him unworthy of their precious doily, and in contrast to his silent suffering, had always found a way to let him know. Brenda's father had kept most of his own hair and was prone to open with a bald shot, usually followed by accusations of niggardliness when Wade declined to purchase any of the home-brewed hooch or second-hand underwear he peddled out of the hatchback of a prehistoric Pinto. Her mother would typically poke Wade, far too hard, in the gut and make a crack about his lack of a six-pack *and hey, by the way, could you get me one?* From the moment of learning of his profession in their first meeting, she had never let pass an opportunity to boast of her contempt for grammar and for those tasked with enforcing it. In the darkest depths of his bondage to Brenda and entrapment in her clan, Wade had taken counsel from Lord Byron: *I should, many a good day, have blown my brains out, but for the recollection that it would have given pleasure to my mother-in-law.* He started to move toward the window now to pull back the curtains to take a peek, preparing himself for the prospect of assault on multiple fronts.

Brenda stopped him in his tracks with a bellow from the throne: "Can you get that, Wade?"

How the hell had she heard the knock through the bathroom door? Was she still in the habit of leaving it ajar while she was conducting her business in there? *Best not to ask, never to know.* Wade went to the front door, braced himself for a blast from the wretched past, and pulled it open.

Angels and ministers of grace defend us!

The Antichrist had risen.

CHAPTER 18

If you'd have married her you would have had to marry the whole family.

—Bill to Nick, in Ernest Hemingway's
"The Three-Day Blow"

There needs no ghost, my lord, come from the grave
To tell us this!

—Horatio, *Hamlet*, I.v.

"You're supposed to be dead, Tommy."

Since the last time Wade had seen him, Brenda's brother had lost his front teeth, no doubt to the methamphetamine epidemic similarly afflicting so many other denizens of the Central Valley. His breath, never less than pungent to begin with, had not been improved by periodontal disease, and combined with his B.O., *the rankest compound of villainous smells that ever offended nostril,* was almost enough to knock you over. His hair, once a wild, fecund growth that Wade could only envy, was suddenly going fast, and, as was his way, he had managed to find a style that made the creepy worst of it. He was wearing glasses now, which he had needed but neglected for years, partial cause of many roadside entanglements with competing cars, bicycles, pedestrians, and pets, not to mention trees, telephone poles, parking meters, and on one especially memorable occasion in Golden Gate Park, a mounted policeman. He had somehow survived all of them—and evidently wasn't yet finished cheating death.

"Is that any way to greet your long lost baby brother-in-law?"

Wade viewed the ruins and wondered what to say next. *Maimed any thoroughbreds lately?*

Tommy helped him out: "Was this a great stunt or what?"

Wade digested the truth of the ruse and kicked himself for falling for it—*Show me the body*, he should have insisted, a photo ID before getting on the road. "Brenda said you O.D.'d again, and—"

"That's the *stunt*, man. I'm clean! I couldn't possibly O.D. I don't do drugs anymore. I don't even smoke pot—or cigarettes. Shit, man, I don't even drink coffee or caffeinated sodas. I'm like totally chemical-free. I'm a new man!"

A man can change. Wade heard in his head Dean Martin's *boracho* Dude, to John Wayne's Chance in *Rio Bravo*, still his all-time favorite movie. Change, though, was far more credible on the silver screen with Dino and the Duke than in your ex-wife's living room with her cretinous sibling grinning toothlessly in your face. "You're supposed to be dead," Wade said again. "Aren't you due for embalming or something?"

"It was my idea to say carfentanil. I knew you'd fall for it."

"Good one, Tom. When I heard it can put a pachyderm down, I figured it was the perfect choice for the guy who'd tried everything else."

"I'd never touch that shit. Do you think I'm *that* stupid?"

Once again Wade bit his tongue. Like LeBron, he was finding it harder and harder to hold to the high road.

"I knew it was the only way to get you to come here, to get you back," Tommy continued. "My sister still loves you, man. Even though this house you bought her is a little cramped, to be honest with you—have you seen the room I sleep in? It's like a fucking cupboard, man. Sometimes I have to go and climb in bed with Bren just to get some—"

Wade closed his eyes, wished he could close his ears.

"—rest. She still cares about you, wants to get back together with you. I don't know if the three of us can live here together, might be kind of tight quarters, but you gotta ditch that stick you hooked up with, and—"

"I'm married, Tom." *And my wife is in fucking Baltimore. And you're supposed to be fucking—*

"In the eyes of the Lord, you're still married to my sister, Wade."

"What did you do, go back to Mass?"

Tommy had told far too often the tale of being molested in childhood by a priest, while a naked nun looked on and made notes in her devotional, *his* version of a three-way. He periodically dipped back into spiritualism of assorted kinds in the effort to expunge a fraction of his many tortured memories, sins, and delusions.

"None of that Catholic crap, Wade—I've been to Joel O.'s church in Texas!"

"Hallelujah."

"You have to come with me and hear him speak sometime. The man is worth fifty million bucks! He has a house worth ten million! Beats the crap out of this little roach-trap, believe me. And it's all paid for with donors' freely given dollars. I've been inspired, man. I'm going to start my own fucking church. Sorry, I don't really say that word any more. I gave up swearing, too."

You were supposed to give up breathing.

"Hell, I mean, *shit*, I mean, *shoot*, I might even make myself a Cardinal or something."

"I think the Catholics have that one covered. Are you going to start your own religion, too?"

"Nothing is impossible, my friend, as long as you believe. The power of faith can work miracles."

As if on cue, Brenda emerged from the can. Wade tuned out Tommy, straining in hopes of hearing a flush behind her in case, as seemed likely, he needed to visit the premises urgently himself for an upchuck. She waddled over to join them, grinning like a banshee who had got her signals crossed. She high-fived Tommy, then put a hand, which Wade hoped she had remembered to wash, on his shoulder. His flesh didn't exactly crawl under her touch, but even this slight portion of the weight of her felt like far more than he could ever bear again.

"Tell the truth," Brenda said. "You missed us, huh?"

While you were taking a dump with the door open, you mean?

"How can you tell?"

"It's love, man," Tommy said. "That never goes away."

Wade wondered how he could make Tommy go away. The fucker had come back from the grave. Was he going to haunt Wade's life forever?

"We want you to come back to your family, Wade. I'll cut you in on the church I'm gonna start, and you can help out with the sermons. Quit that nitpicky crap you put out about *passive tense* and *dangling indents* and *subliminating conjunctoids,* and—"

"You forgot *randy moodifiers.*"

"You should forget 'em, too, and say some shit that actually matters half a rat's ass, make a difference in some people's lives. *Plus* bring home some real bacon instead of the peanuts they pay you at that backwater bus stop."

Tommy had never held a job for more than six months. He had never earned more than ten bucks an hour except from selling drugs, and his profits as a dealer had been substantially eroded by his propensity for looting his own stash. Now he was dispensing financial advice.

"Let me see if I have this right: you want me to quit my job, move to Stockton—"

"Divorce your bitch wife number two," number one threw in.

"—start a church, and—"

"Get rich as Jesus!"

"I think you mean Croesus, Tom."

"Whatever. The point is, there's millions to be made. All we need is a little start-up cash, and—"

I wonder who's the lucky fuck that's coming from.

"—we'll be on our way. Joel did it! There's no reason we three can't do it, too. Do you have any idea how many fucking sinners there are in fucking Stockton? Sorry for the language, but—"

Tommy's abandonment of obscenity was apparently a work in progress.

"—it's like a fucking gold mine here. Whores, pimps, gang-bangers, thieves, murderers, crooked politicians, trigger-happy cops, teachers who knock up their students, preachers who can't keep their hands off the children in their congregation: we got 'em all. Hell, we got a mayor accused of playing strip poker with the kids at his youth camp and taking pictures of their pee-pees and hoo-hahs. They all need saving, Wade. And who's to say they're not better off spending their money on salvation than on—"

"What fucking money, Tom?" Sentimental attachment notwithstanding, Wade had a clear-eyed view of the Delta city's limits. "Isn't this the town that went bankrupt because it couldn't pay its bills? The town where pensions promised to public employees turned into pennies on the dollar? Aren't most people in this town still trying to figure out how to pay their overdue mortgage with the minimum wage job they lost?"

"*Exactly* why they need *your* comfort and advice in *our* mega-church, Wade! We'll give 'em the power of positive thinking, and they'll give us—"

A swift trip to the penitentiary.

"—mucho deniro."

Wade didn't bother correcting him. Tommy had watched *Taxi Driver* four hundred times and had crossed the border in search of affordable stimulants almost as many. His spelling and linguistic issues transcended all boundaries. Brenda claimed her brother was bimodal and could kick ass in math. Wade had never put this claim to the test, but he had his doubts based on Tommy's inability to track the tally of self-injections likely to *shuffle* him *off this mortal coil.* Somehow the *coup de grace* always eluded him, as it had yet again now, the false hopes raised by Brenda's little jest notwithstanding. Back in school-age days Tommy had been kicked out of six or seven high schools and arrested at several others, and he had never set foot on a college campus except to pick up drugs or indiscriminate sex partners. (To Wade's way of thinking, anyone so deficient in critical thinking skills as to blow off English 1D in order to jump into bed with Tommy deserved whichever among his extensive collection of STDs he was currently communicating. If you really got lucky, maybe Tommy would even offer to share a needle.) He was just the sort of project some of Wade's counseling colleagues at CSU would go apeshit over; they would probably offer him a scholarship, maybe even start a new major. Tommy could be the first to pursue a degree in Perversity Studies. He could serve as a primary case history in the very textbooks he would be pretending to read. Throw in a couple of core courses on public masturbation and child pornography, add a prerequisite covering dope, coke, and hash, top it off with an advanced seminar on speed and smack, and hell, Tommy would breeze right through the program. He would come back as a guest lecturer and be made a full professor in no time. Students would line up around the block to sign up for his classes and purchase his product. Many of CSU's students were unofficially double majoring in this stuff already anyway, so why not tap the body count and make the chancellor happy?

"You know what Joel tells people when they complain?" Tommy was still talking about his latest inspiration. "Be glad you weren't born in some fuckhole in Africa, or with two heads and no dick. Although he doesn't say *dick*, of course, and—"

He probably doesn't say 'fuckhole' either, although if you live in Houston it had to be a hard word to avoid.

"—I really shouldn't say that word either. I'm still working on improving my vocabulary. You can probably help me out with that, right, teach?"

This, of course, as for anyone who spent time behind a lectern, was Wade's very favorite of all the signifiers applied to him in and out of classrooms over the years. *Right. Here's a pop quiz. We'll start with an easy one: define 'congenital moron.'*

"Anyway, forget the words—"

Fine. Just point with your thumbs.

"—you know what he *sells*? The air, man. The fucking air that we breathe. That's *it*. That's—"

"The air that we breathe just killed 1.6 million people in China last year," Wade informed him.

"—all! But we're not *in* fucking China, are we, Wade-o? We're in—"

Fucking Stockton. That cowshit you're inhaling here ain't exactly alpine clear.

"—the fucking U.S. of A., the greatest fucking country in the history of the world, where every man—and woman"—he nodded at his sister lest she be offended by the initial exclusion—"is born free to go forth and—"

Stultify.

"—make his—or her—fortune. And do you know what his product costs him?"

"Are we still talking about Brother Joel?"

"Hell yes we are. Do you know what it costs him to sell this stuff?"

Let's see: his self-respect, any shred of dignity he might have been born with, and—

"Zero. Nada. Buttkiss."

Bupkis, Wade knew he meant. Tommy had once similarly misnamed a brain-damaged Doberman retrieved from one of his garbage can forays, thinking he was honoring the Chicago Bears' legendarily malevolent middle linebacker. Fortunately, the animal's mortification, as with most of Tommy's pets, had been short-lived, because his master, high on crank one evening, had found and fed to the four-month old pup an entire box of See's candy that Brenda had been planning to polish off for her midnight snack. The consequence had been similar in speed and scope to the effect achieved years earlier when Tommy had either inadvertently (as he claimed) or vindictively (as seemed rather more likely) dumped rat poison into the dish of the enormous, incontinent cat Brenda had deprived of a far more dignified quietus when she accepted it from a misguided community college rescue program staffed and funded by delusional neurotics sublimating their incapacity for meaningful human interaction by foisting upon the already far too crowded planet an endless plague of feral felines. Wade, truth to tell, had not been unduly distressed by either dispensation, and he had actually been relieved to be free of the terror of Buttkiss's hauling ass abruptly from any direction to savage his buns or groin, or Fatman's clambering on top and peeing/leaking on him when he was asleep, then clawing him viciously when he tried to reposition the beast to Brenda's side of the bed or (best case scenario) onto Tommy's face, if brother-in-law happened to be lying about amid one of his innumerable *pop-ins* of indeterminate length and incalculable devastation to Wade's otherwise merely miserable domestic lot.

"You should listen to Tommy," Brenda said to him now. "He's not as stupid as he looks."

Wade shrugged, declining to call a loser in that neck-and-neck contest.

"That hurts, Sis," Tommy said, grinning hideously, gums aflame, to show that it didn't really. Wade grimaced at the view and noticed that Brenda did, too.

"And *you* should see a dentist," she told Tommy.

Stop in to see the barber, too, on the way to the lobotomist.

Wade wondered how all those coeds of his who wrote with such conviction about *unconditional love* would fare with Tommy as the object of their permanent affection. William Faulkner had written, as Obama had noted and quoted, *The past isn't even past.* When were you officially allowed to say *It's over*, to put into the past someone you had loved, or thought you loved, or someone you inherited because he came attached to someone you once thought you loved? How about when they were too stupid to take care of their own teeth? Given the transparent desirability of being able to nourish oneself until the whole ridiculous charade was over, this one seemed like a no-brainer. Hair you really couldn't do much about. That was in the hands of God or whatever sadistic subdemon had been deputed to decide such matters. Even a billionaire like Trump couldn't buy anything to put on top that made him look better with than without. Teeth, at least, you had some input with, especially if you refrained from coating them at every opportunity with corrosive sodas, caramels, tobacco, or crystal meth—or in Tommy's case, all of the above, sometimes simultaneously. Maybe the undergraduates who swore to love so everlastingly would allow one condition, after all, if pushed hard enough: *I promise to love you forever, as long as you don't turn into fucking Tommy.*

"I can't believe I wasted my time to come here."

Tommy tried for a sophic smile. "Everything happens for a reason, Wade."

Of all the stupid things that all the stupid people in his life regularly said to Wade, this was possibly the very stupidest. *Of course* there was a reason for everything; that didn't mean the reason made any fucking sense. The pathetic attempt to put a positive spin on unspeakable, random catastrophe inevitably made him cringe. What reason could explain his mother, kindest person he had ever known, who had spent every waking moment looking for ways to help others, losing a decade to dementia? Or his father, war hero, public servant, friend to anyone he ever met, surrogate dad to hundreds sired by the disengaged, ravaged at the end by six different kinds of cancer? Somewhere on the globe, even as the honeyed platitude came out of Tommy's foul mouth, a child was coming out of a womb with no fingers or no eyes or no brain.

"What *fucking* reason?"

"We don't say that word in this house any more, Wade."

"You just said it yourself about ten times, Tommy."

"Well, we *try* not to say that word in this house. Joel says, *Profanity is the effort of the feeble mind to . . .*—oh, fuck, I forget the rest."

"*Express itself forcibly,*" Wade finished for him. "Actually Spencer W. Kimball said it, but I'm sure your new hero feels free to steal from him and every poindexter who preceded him. Do you think Richard Pryor had a feeble mind?"

Tommy stroked his pimpled chin, striking the air of an Oxford don about to weigh in on Kant or Kierkegaard. "Well, the dude *did* set himself on fire."

Wade didn't mention that he had envisioned a similar, if more conclusive, fate for someone near and dear. "Sorry I missed your funeral, Tom." *I liked you better when you were dead.* He turned to Brenda. "I'm out of here. I'm not coming back."

"You don't really mean that," Tommy said to Wade, nodding toward his sister. "You'll get horny again someday and—"

"Shut up, Tommy," Brenda said, for once saving Wade the trouble of silencing her brother. It wasn't quite as satisfying as the cremation Wade had come for, but the stopped yap was enough to raise his spirits for the moment as he studied the now truly wounded expression on Tommy's face. He looked like a kid who had been caught with his dick in the cookie jar. Wade was about to tell him as much when, flabulous arms akimbo, Brenda stepped between them. Over the years she had invariably backed her brother in the endless succession of pie-fights that had characterized Wade's relationship with him from the day they met, when Tommy had attempted a shakedown for twenty bucks to buy model airplane glue. Now, after squandering Wade's day with her asinine prank, was she finally for once in their lives going to take his side? To encourage her unprecedented show of support, he gave her a tentative half-smile, admittedly a bit awkward in the context of his latest declaration. She pulled a hand off a hip, then pivoted abruptly toward him and poked him in the chest.

"Get the hell out of my house."

A man hasn't truly lived until he has been kicked out of a house he paid for by the woman he paid for it for, according to Allenby, who had hit the Trifecta: three times in holy matrimony joined, three houses (in his case *palaces*) paid for and booted out of. Wade hadn't paid for all of Brenda's shack, just the down payment and the mortgage since she had lost her job, but it still felt somehow validating to be issued his walking papers so emphatically.

"I won't be back," he said again. This time he was almost certain that he meant it. He tried in good faith to measure whether he had consciously manipulated his eviction. He had taken Brenda at her word that Tommy was no more, had reported dutifully to Stockton to lay to rest the opiated remains, and had listened to an imbecilic pitch when the promised pyre failed to materialize. What more could a man do? If incineration, dead or alive, wasn't in the cards, murder for hire was still a possibility. Wade figured he could probably find a hitman in this town for about what the airplane glue would have cost him. Or, hell, one of the local apprentices would probably do it *pro bono*, just for target practice.

It's over, Wade said again in his head, just to hear the sound of it, as he made what he fervently hoped would be his ultimate exit from his ex-wife's house, tribe, and life. *It's finally fucking over.*

Tommy pulled the door open behind him. Getting the last word in this family had never been easy.

"You know, bro, all we need is a couple thousand or so to get our church off the ground."

Wade abandoned verbiage and grabbed his crotch in a symbol so universal that even his idiot undead ex-brother-in-law could hardly fail to grasp its import.

"Check or cash, either will be fine. We'll be prayin' for you, Wade."

CHAPTER 19

I loved her against reason, against promise, against peace, against hope, against happiness, against all discouragement that could be.

—Pip, on his love for Estella, Great Expectations

Up until I was eleven I thought having a dad meant a man who came by every month and left twenty bucks.

—Bo Jackson

"I see you got your new tire. How was your visit with your ex?" Jackson asked, as he climbed into Wade's car for the return trip. "After the funeral, I mean."

How was Hiroshima after that cloud rolled by?

"Not bad," Wade said. "About what I expected. My ex-brother-in-law turned out to be only brain-dead, though."

"Oh, wow. They gonna keep him hooked up to some kind of a machine then?"

Wade envisioned a robotic Tommy attached to a crane that would deposit him periodically, face-down, on city streets or hospital floors to lick them clean. Finally a steady job he was suited for.

"Maybe," Wade said. He surveyed the terrain, making sure before pulling away from the curb that none of Stockton's brazen jaywalkers were about to cross not merely against the light but in the middle of traffic, and that no unlit, helmetless bicyclists were whizzing through the intersection in the wrong direction at Tour de France velocity, all but daring you to flatten them, turn them into roadkill to join the cat and dog carcasses decorating the city's thoroughfares amid the piles of poop that were beginning to proliferate, San Francisco style. "Maybe not. Around here there's a good chance a hit-and-run or a drive-by will finish him off pretty soon, anyway."

"What about your ex? She wants you back, right?"

Wade shook his head. "Happy to report that she threw me out and never wants to see my sorry ass again. Almost a direct quote." He reached to lower the volume on the radio.

"That the Giants you listenin' to? How they doin' tonight?"

Wade restored the volume level, and they heard Posey push a single to right field to drive in the game's first run.

"Smart hitter," Jackson said. "Don't try to pull the ball when they pitch him away."

"I guess Johnny Dawes could learn a thing or two from studying his at-bats."

"Anybody can learn from that dude. He be a manager someday, I'll bet."

"You might be right," Wade said. He was ready for Buster to take the reins right now. He was just hoping the *genius* currently managing the team would get his All-Star out from behind the plate before another crippling injury, or the cumulative abuse that the tools of ignorance entailed, cut short the Hall of Fame career of which he was capable. Rookie of the Year and then batting champ and MVP in his next full season, like Mays before him in New York, and with three rings so far, perhaps Posey had already qualified for that distinction, but Wade foresaw the same decline that had robbed the Reds' Johnny Bench of many productive seasons and God only knew how many home runs and RBIs. As to the question of managing someday or following Bench into the broadcast booth, Wade wasn't certain that someone who made the kind of money the Giants' catcher was earning would feel the need for gainful employment when his playing days were done, but he had a hunch the game was too deep in Posey's bones for him to give it up then. "Maybe you'll even get to play for him."

"That would be cool."

They listened in companionable silence as the game unfolded, the Giants playing their typical plodding station-to-station game on offense, and on defense catching everything hit on the ground. In deference to his passenger, Wade resisted the temptation to tune out as the inevitable inanities piled up. Sometimes, when he was alone, he twisted the knob so violently that he risked injury to both the equipment and himself. Once the game was over, of course, the real horrors began. If he bumped into a call-in show, Wade couldn't listen for more than a minute as the vainglorious program hosts interrupted and vied to exceed the moronity of their astoundingly ignorant callers. If television was a vast wasteland, radio was a cesspool at the wasteland's anus. Being stuck with the same announcers on either medium for the World Series was torture on the order of anything the shining lights at Abu Ghraib had come up with. If the Series reached the splendor of a seventh game, by the time you had endured the insufferable pomp of Joe Buck for the duration, you never wanted to hear another human voice as long as you lived.

Wade switched between innings to a news station and bumped immediately into something else you never wanted to hear—a bulletin indicating that four police officers had been killed while patrolling a Black Lives Matter protest on a college campus. Two days earlier, in a town nearby, an officer had fired six rounds into a mentally ill black man with his hands in the air. One bad cop could get a lot of good ones shot.

Jackson shook his head when confirmation came that today's shooter, also killed, was black. "Used to be, you heard about a shooting like that, you'd know it was some fucked up white boy or Asian dude, can't get no pussy. Black dudes and Mexicans be shootin' each other up all the time, nothin' to it, like goin' to breakfast, but you don't hardly ever hear 'bout them shootin' up a college."

Wade had often wondered when CSU could expect to join the ranks of the schools targeted by an assailant with a military grade weapon and the blessing of the local congressman who had stuck to his convictions and ignored a poll showing that 89% of his constituents favored a ban on the sale of such hardware. It seemed that there was no safe place left anywhere for anyone. In the city they had just left behind, a nutcase with multiple prior arrests had once strolled onto the grounds of an elementary school with an assault rifle (purchased, naturally, sans waiting period or background check) and killed or wounded thirty-five children and teachers before turning a pawnshop pistol on himself.

Not much to be done about it here and now except turn the radio off and change the subject. "Did you find that girl you were telling me about? Emma?"

"Gave her a call. She didn't call back. I think she's engaged to that geek from Pacific."

"Hard to beat out the pharmacists," Wade said.

"Hard to find one girl make you forget about all the rest, too. You hear about what Darryl Strawberry said, gettin' girls to do it with him, during games he was playin' in?"

Wade nodded. "Between innings, he says." He had wondered, when he read the story in the newspaper, what kind of a woman would pop out of her seat in the stands, allow herself to be conducted, in full view of thousands, into the clubhouse, let a ballplayer stick his dick in her for a minute or two, and then go back to her seat. What did she get out of it? And what did she say to her family or friends—or boyfriend—when she got back to her seat, or back home? Would she tell her grandkids someday?

How was he, grandma?
Fast. He was due to hit fourth.

"That's pretty fucked up," Jackson said. "I don't know about you, but I like to take my time with a girl, let her have some fun, too."

Wade nodded again. He didn't care to confess that he'd experienced more than a fair share of foreshortened sessions of his own, without the excuse of a pending turn in the batting order. His early humiliations, which he presumed typical, were thankfully behind him, although lasting as long as Angela could had sometimes proven beyond his capacities. He wondered if he would ever get the chance to keep up with her again.

Jackson jawed about Strawberry's exploits some more, then asked, "You ever had two girls at once?"

Only in my dreams. "I have enough trouble keeping one in my bed."

"I been with two a few times. Last time, the girls started arguin' 'bout who was gonna do what next, got into it with each other, and I had to break up the fight, right there in the bed. Stuck to one at a time after that."

Another gleesome threesome shot to hell. Was Wade the only one alive who hadn't tried it?

Jackson continued: "Magic Johnson wrote in his book that he went to bed with six women at one time."

"I've read that, too," Wade said, trying again to picture the geometry involved. "And Wilt Chamberlain claimed that he'd slept with *ten thousand* women."

"That's a lot of women."

"A nice round number," Wade agreed.

"Think it's true?"

Wade shrugged. "He averaged fifty points a game for a full season, led the league in assists another year, just to prove that he could do it, and took three different franchises to the finals. That's documented. I wouldn't exactly take him at his word on the other stuff, but I wouldn't put it past him either."

"Think he ever found one he liked more than the rest?"

"I don't know if he found her," Wade said, "but I'll bet he had damn good fun trying."

"I thought Cammie was the special one for me. Seems crazy, don't it?"

Wade shrugged again. What could a man married to Angela say about that? If *to be honest as this world goes is to be one man picked out of ten thousand,* what were the odds of finding a genuine woman? And why was Camellia Sanchez even in the conversation? What a man felt for a woman was completely irrational. Sinatra, who could have had just about any woman in the world, including Marilyn Monroe, before and after her marriage to DiMaggio, had chased across the globe after a wife who preferred hopping into bed with bullfighters. DiMaggio had never married again after the golden goddess had declined to stay home with Mr. Coffee instead of taking her chances on the casting couch. Hemingway had boasted that he'd had every woman he ever wanted, but had any of the four he'd married, or any of the many others in between, managed to keep that shotgun out of his mouth at the end? Wade's own father had deserted the most selfless soul who ever lived in favor of a shameless materialist, for whom *getting and spending* were as essential to the rhythm of her days as breathing or eating or telling her husbands what to do.

"Still can't believe she dumped me for Dawes. You know what that fool got under his license plate? *Four doors for mo' whores.* How's any woman get into a car with that shit wrote on it?"

Beats me, Wade stifled. "I don't know. Maybe she didn't get much guidance at home?"

"Cammie say her father used to come into her room, her sisters' too, and touch them, you know, down below. She don't remember nothin' more, she say, but still . . . somethin' like that could really mess you up."

More than a few women in Wade's classes had written of such experiences. One had written a research paper reporting that the incidence rate of incest in American families might be as high as 25%. Wade had also read that early experiences of the sort Cammie had reported often led to promiscuity. He debated whether to share that with Jackson, then contemplated another tack.

Apart from his half-hearted attempt to unite Allenby and Erica, in the matchmaking department Wade had little experience and less success. A few years ago, recalling his own struggles in getting to first base, he had taken pity on a world class nerd in one of his classes and suggested that the bright spark might make a friend or even score a date by volunteering to tutor one of his classmates, a very quiet girl who was having difficulty with the course. The project had backfired spectacularly when the offended coed (an Abstinence Only advocate, as it turned out) had sharply rebuffed the offer, and the would-be tutor had turned stalker, nearly getting himself expelled or arrested and Wade reprimanded or canned. It was a painful precedent and hard to ignore, but Wade decided to plow ahead anyway, *the triumph of hope over experience.*

"There's a girl I could introduce you to."

Jackson laughed at the offer: Wade as pimp. "You're not talkin' 'bout that big Mexican chick I met in your office, took your picture, are you?"

"I wasn't thinking of Norma, although she's a catcher, and she could probably help you with your fastball command."

Jackson laughed again. "Look like she swing from the other side, though."

Sometimes Wade wondered if he was the only man on the planet who could not instantly ascertain the sexual preference of everyone he met. He asked if Jackson had ever met Larashawndria Lewis.

"Never met her, but everybody know about Lara. She the best lookin' girl in the whole damn school. But she s'posed to got a boyfriend back home she don't cheat on."

"I'm pretty sure the boyfriend is history," Wade said. After her date with Planned Parenthood, Lara had sworn off romance and was concentrating on her classes and her sport. "Women's volleyball's in the fall. If you want to come to a game sometime, I'll introduce you."

"Maybe I'll do that. Black girls, though, I don't know, they all up in your business, tell you what to do, tell you what you thinkin' before you even thought it."

This sounded to Wade like a trait that applied equally to women of all races, but he would have to let Jackson decide about that. "Just meet her, see what you think, okay?"

"Guess I could check her out on Facebook, see if her status has changed."

"I think she shut down her social media accounts."

"Damn. Girl must be serious 'bout gettin' them grades up."

"Not a bad plan for someone else I can think of."

"I'm killin' it, Doc. Got a C+ on your last Hemingway quiz. Two points from a B. My good looks, you could've given 'em to me. You see that top Monica was wearin' last class?"

Wade nodded. Monica's tops were impossible to miss. He turned the radio back on to get his mind off them.

When Wade muted for a commercial, Jackson cleared this throat, and then spoke softly:

"Wasn't no girl I went to Stockton to see." He looked out the window, then back at Wade.

"You never said it was."

"I went to see—"

Wade hoped hard that it wasn't going to be the cap-thief from Ross's, out on parole and trolling for his new crew.

"—my so-called father. He showed up there, wanted to see me, make up, all that good shit."

Wade recalled Jackson's telling him earlier that he hadn't seen his father for almost ten years. "That had to be a tough conversation."

Jackson nodded. "Course it just a coincidence I might be 'bout to make me some big money from baseball."

"He wants to help you spend it?"

"Joker lookin' to *advise* me. Can't even advise his own self to keep a roof over his head, pay his bills."

"Doesn't sound as if he's changed much from when you knew him before."

"He ain't never gonna change."

Here was yet another opportunity for Wade to glimpse the rewards of the role that Angela had been so eager to foist upon him. He remembered his sister's bitterness when their father had divorced their mother. She hadn't spoken to him for five years and had never been close to him again even after Wade's sustained efforts to effect a reconciliation. His father had carried the wound to his grave. Allenby, too, had been alienated from his pampered daughters by divorce and recrimination. They still cashed his checks, but Wade wondered if his friend would ever feel like a real father to them again.

"Were you ever close to him?" Wade spasmed in his seat as soon as he spoke, recalling that Jackson had asked him the same thing about Tommy.

"He played some ball with me when I was little, pitched to me, played some catch, shit like that, but never for very long. A few minutes, if I was lucky. There was always some big business deal he had to get to or some chick he was seein' on the side, even when he was married to my mom. He's lucky she never shot his ass; she always had a gun, bein' in the military. I'm sure she was tempted many times. Wasn't no shortage of opportunities."

"Must have been pretty stressful to grow up like that."

Jackson shrugged. "About normal, I guess. Most of my friends I grew up with had the same deal. Raised by their mama or their grandma. Didn't see much of their fathers. Some of them livin' in another town, with another woman, some in prison, some in the rehab. I was real lucky my uncle took me in, took me to work with him, taught me all that stuff, made sure I knew how to behave. I might be in prison myself by now if he hadn't helped me out."

"You were with his family for five or six years, is that right?"

Jackson nodded. "He took me in when I was ten, died when I was sixteen. Heart attack. He was only forty-eight years old. Same age *his* father—my grandfather—died. Bad heart runs in my family, I guess. Plus he 'bout forty pounds overweight. Always told me to eat right, stay fit, but he didn't listen to his own preachin'."

Wade thought of Allenby's father, gone at almost the same early age, and next heard Angela in his ear, reminding him of his own borderline-high cholesterol count. Then another voice chimed in: *She's gone. Fuck the borderline. Eat whatever the hell you want. You'll probably never see her again anyway.*

"I know a good rib joint up ahead here on the highway. Sounds like we could both use some comfort food."

"Sounds good. My treat."

"On me," Wade said, "or we can just go dutch."

"Don't you never let nobody else pay for you?"

Pay your own way. It had been imbedded by Wade's parents into his moral code as indelibly as if a computer chip had been installed at birth to program him for life—or so he had thought. He'd had to modify the standard since Allenby and those first class air tickets had come along.

They wound up splitting the bill. Once back underway, they talked baseball and music and a bit of Hemingway until they reached Jackson's apartment. Sensing there was something more on Jackson's mind, Wade fished: "Your father have anything else to say, besides offering his financial advice?"

Jackson stared straight ahead for a long moment and then sighed. "He told me some new shit about my mom."

"Oh? What did he—"

"Turns out, they—the government—lied about the way she died."

"What do you mean?"

"She didn't die in combat in Iraq after all."

"Oh. How did she—"

"She killed herself so she wouldn't have to go back there."

"*Jesus.*"

"Somebody in her unit wrote to him, told him the real story. So he say anyway. Could all be more of his bullshit, I guess, but plenty of others have done it, ain't that right?"

Wade nodded. "Two to three hundred soldiers every year lately, quite a few of them women." He had read that women in the military were six times more likely than other women to commit suicide. He had no idea what else to say. He tried to imagine hearing that news about his own mother.

"That ain't all he told me."

And worse I may be yet. "What else did—"

"He say she never wanted to have me. Say I was supposed to be an abortion. He say he stop her, wouldn't let her get rid of me. You believe he tell me that shit *now?*"

Wade was still stumped for anything more to say.

"Man never tried to take care of me, never did nothin' to help her take care of me. She have to go in the Army to make a living. Now he tryin' to paint himself like the big hero, save my life."

Wade started to reach a hand out to Jackson's shoulder, but hesitated in mid-air as his passenger opened the door and started to get out. Then Jackson paused and said into the windshield, "I wish I had a father like you."

And I wish I had a son like you, Wade couldn't quite bring himself to reply. "Thanks," he said instead. "You wouldn't know how to change a tire, though."

Jackson didn't give him the laugh he was expecting. He turned and looked Wade almost in the eye now. "Lot of stuff more important than tires."

Wade shrugged. "Hard to get to Stockton—and back—without them. Thanks again for your help."

Jackson nodded. "Thanks for the ride, Doc. See you in class."

CHAPTER 20

What a beautiful day for a ball game. Let's play two!

> —Ernie Banks, Chicago Cubs, winner of The
> Presidential Medal of Freedom

Give my regards to the catcher.

> —Franklin D. Roosevelt, in reference to MLB
> catcher/OSS spy Moe Berg, who declined
> The Medal of Freedom for espionage relat-
> ing to Nazi efforts to build an atomic bomb

One of the bonuses of Wade's hybrid position was that he could now and then blow off a meeting and go to a ball game instead. On the pretext of keeping tabs on the athletes whose academic progress he was monitoring, he could spend an afternoon in the sunshine with peanuts and Cracker Jacks instead of stuck inside a conference room for an update on the latest life-saving break-through in MLA documentation format. With CSU's softball and baseball teams set to play on campus on the same day, a few hours apart, he decided to go all in.

The doubleheader had largely gone out of fashion in today's game, except for make-up games after rainouts or, in the amateur ranks, playoff elimination rounds. The toll on throwing arms caused pitchers and their coaches to hate them, but Wade still had fond memories of the custom. One day in his youth when his father had taken him to Candlestick, the second game had gone into extra innings. Attendance of twenty thousand or so had been announced, but by the time they finally made the return trip to the parking lot, they spotted his father's Ford sitting almost by itself. (Wade, ever the worrywart, had wondered when they parked how they'd ever find it again, amid a sea of similar vehicles, somehow doubting that a man who had navigated by the stars across enemy skies and brought his crew home safely through thirty missions could find his own car where he had left it.) They had wound up spending more than ten hours at the ballpark. Parking lot jitters aside, Wade had loved every minute of it. *Watch the way he carries himself*, his dad had said, the first time they saw #24 come out onto the field. *That's the best ballplayer in the world*. Mays had homered in the first game and made a catch for the ages in the second. In between, he had fouled a ball into the stands; Wade's father had snatched it, bare-handed, out of the sky, and then casually presented it to his son as if it were an Easter egg Wade had failed to unearth in the backyard hunt. Wade still had the ball. Years later, through a contact with someone in the Giants' front office, his father had arranged to have Mays sign it. It was one of the very few possessions to which Wade attached any importance.

As he took his seat in CSU's renovated softball park for Norma's game, Wade admired the improvements Allenby and his A.D. Marilyn Porter had made. Along with alumni leader Cal Logan they had spearheaded a fundraising drive to upgrade the campus's playing fields and locker rooms. One of the meeting rooms Wade had seen when he toured the facilities with Allenby two years ago was a Quonset hut dating to his father's military days. Allenby had made it clear from the outset that he wasn't sponsoring or encouraging others to sponsor an edifice complex to rival the Taj Mahal or JerryWorld. After soliciting bids from several contractors, he had negotiated an arrangement for two rival firms to work together. At his urging, a relatively new minority-owned firm that had submitted the lowest bid agreed to work with a more experienced contractor who had built stadia at other campuses. After working through a few inevitable glitches, together they had installed playable, modern all-weather synthetic turf fields, and comfortable, if far from plush, facilities for the athletes, with the option to expand the stands later. Allenby had flatly rejected more grandiose plans for current seating capacity: "Let's prove we can get two thousand out here to watch a game before we build for ten."

The president's caution was warranted. Most games on the CSU campus were lightly attended at the best of times. Wade guessed maybe three or four hundred were in the softball stands with him waiting for the first pitch to be thrown. Norma had recovered from her injury and was warming up the starting pitcher. Watching her surprising agility behind the plate, Wade was reminded that the best athlete he had grown up with, Carlie Richardson, had far outshone him and all the other guys in their class at every sport she turned a hand (or foot) to. Dodgeball, tetherball, kickball, soccer, as well as baseball and basketball— you name it, she dominated it. He had lost touch with her after high school and wondered now if she'd had the chance in the early days of Title IX to earn a scholarship with her talents. He hoped she hadn't turned out to be one of those women who had abandoned all physical activity except stuffing her face, like a certain someone he had promised himself never to think about again.

One of Wade's few disappointments with Obama (*Hyperion to a Satyr* compared to who might be on deck) had been his administration's failure to inspire a personal fitness movement akin to JFK's 50-mile hike fervor from the 1960's. Lean and fit himself, still playing competitive basketball as he hit his fifties, the President had been understandably too preoccupied with keeping nuclear weapons out of the hands of the insane leaders of North Korea, Iran, and the Republican Party to prioritize the obesity crisis, which he had largely delegated to his wife. Wade admired the First Lady's efforts to tackle exercise and nutrition issues, but still, looking around him every day, in town or on campus, he was appalled by the excesses that met his eye. Even a man who had tried to survive on cheeseburgers and pizza had to be alarmed by students at the cafeterias commonly lunching on a plate of *loaded fries* and a twenty-ounce soda packing enough sugar to poison half the populace of the Central Valley, often tendering in exchange for this nourishment a chit from Uncle Sam or one of his subsidiaries. In the meantime, high schools around the country had cut back on or even eliminated Physical Education, the most important class in the whole curriculum. What good did it do you to excel in Biology or Chemistry if you couldn't control your own consumption?

At CSU, as at other colleges and universities, so much emphasis had been placed on competitive programs that recreational classes had shrunk to a minimum. Athletic facilities were mainly devoted to the varsities, and even in the summers, the coaches ran clinics or camps there to supplement their own income and to cater to prospects for their teams. Good luck signing up for a badminton class if there was one section scheduled for a population of 20,000 students. There were intramural programs, such as the one Norma had thrived in, but a relatively small portion of the student body engaged in these. Allenby wasn't ready to deal with the blowback yet, but he had kicked around with Wade the idea of establishing a requirement at CSU for students to maintain enrollment every semester in a P.E. class and a community service class. All students would be required to do something to improve their fitness, and they wouldn't have to go to Mexico, as Norma had done, for their service projects; there were plenty of needs in the local neighborhoods. Allenby had a lot of good ideas, born of common sense. Implementing them in a culture that consecrated preservation of the status quo wasn't going to be easy.

Norma fired a strike down to second after the last warm-up pitch, and the game began. Wade fought off his annoyance with the *walk up* music blaring from the announcing booth as the first batter approached the plate; he had forgotten to bring his plugs, so he tore some napkins up and stuffed his ears. Indecorous, no doubt, but he wasn't about to risk any more hearing loss for the lyrical pearls forthcoming. At least, he noticed, he didn't have to worry about hiding an erection, as was common at one of Lara's volleyball games or various other events featuring female athletes in scanty, skin-tight garb. Either he was getting senile or the softball unis were distinctly anaphrodisiac. All those bouncing ponytails could probably be a turn-on if you let them, but Wade forced himself to concentrate on the game.

Both sides went down in order in the first two innings, the pitchers dominant, as usual in the women's sport. Wade was reminded that although in theory it seemed easier to hit the softball since it was so much bigger than a baseball, the shorter distance from mound to plate made the task actually more difficult. He remembered an exhibition in which Eddie Fegner had struck out Mays and Roberto Clemente, among other all-time greats, with his 104 mph fastball, so much in command that he needed only three defenders behind him: The King and His Court.

In the top of the third Norma made a nifty move from behind the plate to pick up a swinging bunt, the closest thing to a mighty blow Wade had so far seen, and throw the batter out. In the same frame she impressed Wade again by sprinting out of her squat to back up a throw from third base on a roller there; when the ball ticked off the first baseman's glove, Norma was right there to catch it in the air, preventing an advance to second base. Hitting in the eighth spot, with one out in the bottom of the third, she lined out to left field, the first solid contact a hitter on either side had made. In the sixth, with the game still scoreless, she advanced with a deft bunt the girl who had walked ahead of her to lead off, then hustled down the line and nearly beat the throw that retired her at first. The runner made it to third on the groundout that followed, and then came in to score on a single that the shortstop dived to knock down but could not pick up in time to get the out at first. The ball had never left the infield, yet CSU had the game's first run. The top of the seventh proved true the aphorism that every time you came to the ballpark you saw something new. With the tying run on third and two outs, the batter lined the ball sharply up the middle. The center fielder, playing at do-or-die depth, raced in, barehanded the ball on the first bounce, and fired it to first base, nipping the hitter by half a step for the game's final out. The audacity of the play reminded Wade of Mays' counseling young outfielders to charge balls on the ground rather than yield to fears of a bobble: *If you want to make money, don't play it safe.* He had seen this putout made from right field many times in softball, and a few times even in MLB, usually with the lead-footed pitcher blooping a fluke and then half-assing it to first—and Bo Jackson, he remembered, had once thrown a runner out at first from *left* field—but he had never seen the play made from center and had never seen a game end this way. Norma rushed out from behind the plate to greet her teammates, gripping the center fielder in a bear hug after similarly congratulating the pitcher of the shutout.

With a few minutes yet to go before the baseball game began, Wade walked down to the field to offer his own congratulations.

Norma spotted him almost immediately, disengaged from her teammates, and then headed over to the stands before turning back to greet him with two more of her fans in tow.

"Dr. Wade, this is my mom and my dad." She turned to her father, grinning as she pointed at Wade. "This is the teacher who almost flunked me in English."

"Thank you for help my daughter. Her English better now."

"Pretty good ballplayer, too," Wade said. "I hear she gets that from you."

Señor Rodriquez shrugged. "I try help her. I'm glad she get a chance to play here, for school."

"Norma tells me you never had that chance yourself."

Another shrug. "Quit school long time ago, go to work. Not so important now. This my wife. Her English not so good."

"Better than my Spanish, I'm sure," Wade said. He gave it a shot. "*Con much gusto,*" he said to Señora Rodriguez, sounding, he imagined, like someone fresh off the boat from Albania. She smiled tolerantly and put a calloused hand into his own, weathered mainly by the dishpan, then stepped back behind her husband.

"We kicked ass today, didn't we?" Norma said.

"Small balls," her father said, parental pride transcending language barriers. "You get good bunt down." *At last a man who understood the game. What would the Giants have to throw into the trade to get this guy in exchange for Bochy?*

"Yeah, but Wilma won the game for us with that throw from center," Norma said. "Have you ever seen that before, Dr. Wade?"

"No," he said. "And—"

"Neither have I," Head Coach Connie Estrada finished for him as she came up behind them. She thanked Wade for coming to the game and then spoke in Spanish with Norma's parents. Norma pulled Wade aside.

"What's going on with that case against you?"

"Nothing to report yet. The committee is still"—*counting its butt-hairs*—"considering the evidence, such as it is."

"Just remember: I'll be there to help if you need me."

Wade nodded his thanks.

"I really appreciate you coming today. I'm glad we didn't let you down. Sorry I couldn't hit a home run or anything for you."

"Maybe next time," Wade said. "See if you can point to the stands first, okay?"

Norma looked puzzled, the lore obviously lost on a generation far removed from the Bambino's exploits, real or apocryphal.

"Just kidding. It was an honor to meet your parents. They've got a lot to be proud of. And I don't mean just that nice bunt."

"I almost beat that out, did you see?"

"I saw," Wade said. "Good wheels. Nice game."

And on to the next. Juke Jackson had played a few innings in a road game earlier in the week, but this was his first game at home and his first start of the season. The team was hovering a few games above .500 and hoping he would give them a lift in the remaining conference schedule and playoff seeding. Wade looked around the stands, with a few more fans than at the women's game, and wondered if any in attendance were scouts. He wasn't exactly sure how you spotted them anymore, especially after *Moneyball*. Maybe that skinny East Indian guy with the laptop was working for Billy Beane.

Eduardo Alvarez had the CSU team playing hard and putting pressure on the defense with their speed at every opportunity. Several hit-and-runs kept them out of double plays early in the game; they scored single runs in the second and fourth on a sacrifice fly and an infield out, then added another to tie the game in the fifth after a stolen base, an errant pick-off throw, and a wild pitch. Jackson, obviously struggling to regain his timing, did not contribute to any of the early scores, whiffing in his first three at-bats, although in the third of these he raised some eyebrows with a four-hundred-foot foul ball. In center field he showcased his instincts and range, running down several balls in the gaps that initially had looked like extra base hits. In the top of the eighth, on a single to right-center that plated the go-ahead run for the visitors, he atoned for an earlier overthrow and helped to limit CSU's deficit with a perfect strike all the way on the fly to cut down the trail runner trying to score from second base. Allenby sat down next to Wade just in time to see it, after a day full of accreditation-related meetings and a physical examination squeezed in between them.

Wade filled him in on what he had missed, with emphasis on the loud foul.

"Doesn't do much good if you can't keep 'em fair," Allenby said. "Let's see what he does this inning."

In the bottom of the eighth CSU's leadoff hitter singled, and Alvarez put the hit-and-run on again. This time his counterpart was ahead of him, waiting for it; he called for a pitchout, and the runner was thrown out easily.

"Nothing works every time," Wade said. "I'm just glad Eduardo's willing to take some chances."

His rhythm possibly disrupted by the pitchout, the pitcher walked the second hitter on the next three pitches. Jackson stepped into the batter's box.

"Better take one here to see if the pitcher wants to walk him, too," Allenby said.

It was a strategy Wade generally endorsed, but it was hard to argue with the result when Alvarez started the runner again, the pitcher laid in a get-it-in-there fastball, and Jackson smacked it over the left field fence with plenty to spare. His first hit of the season: a home run to take the lead. Jackson, head down, ran around the bases quickly and joined his jubilant teammates in the dugout.

"I like to see that," Allenby said. "No showboating."

Wade nodded. "The other kid pitched a hell of a game until now. No reason to rub it in."

The opposing head coach came out to replace his ace, one batter too late. As Wade and Allenby waited for the reliever to warm up, Sherman Slate came over to join them in the stands.

"Quite a shot your quarterback just hit," Allenby said.

Slate nodded. "I'm just glad he's healed up so well."

The MLB draft would be taking place soon. Wade wondered how Slate was feeling about the prospect of losing his best player if the team that selected Jackson signed him and declined to let him keep playing football, as was all but certain, to protect its investment. "Hard to replace a talent like that."

"We've got another good QB who came in from JC as a spring transfer," Slate said. "Coach Barlow does a great job training passers in his program, and we've established a pretty good pipeline. We'll be okay if Juke doesn't come back." Slate looked at Allenby and smiled—if a bit wistfully, who could blame him? "As his football coach, it kills me to say this, but . . . if he were my son, I'd tell him to stick with baseball. Take the money and run."

Now Allenby nodded. "He could play this game for twenty years."

Or blow out his arm on his next pitch. Wade recalled Jackson's own risk assessment, as Alvarez moved him from center in the top of the ninth to close the game.

"Posey used to close sometimes for Florida State," Allenby remembered.

"Right," Wade said. "Their best hitter was also their best bet to finish the game. With that cannon of his, I bet he could still close now if the Giants gave him a chance."

Six fastballs, the last clocked at 99 miles per hour on CSU's sometimes-disputed radar gun, dispatched the first two hitters. The third managed to tick one foul before Jackson finished him and the game off with a killer curve ball that startled with the degree of its break.

"Tony Gwynn in his prime wouldn't have touched that one," Allenby said.

"I was thinking maybe not even Ty Cobb."

Jackson was back. Watching him celebrate with his teammates, Wade thought about the last time he had seen him on the field of play, carried off on a cart. Slate went down to the field to offer his congratulations and perhaps to say goodbye to this year's bowl aspirations.

Wade wasn't worrying about football yet. Two last-inning wins in one double-dip. How could a day get any better than that?

Allenby said, "The grievance committee came out with their ruling today. They dismissed Baynes' charges against both of us."

Wade pumped a fist. "That's great. Now you can get back to firing her unblack ass."

Allenby shook his head. "Don't plop that cherry on top just yet."

"Our Carlotta's not a gracious loser?"

"We may have to activate that background information you turned up on her after all."

"Oh?"

"She's taking her case to the Fourth Estate."

CHAPTER 21

It was not a military victory. It was a tragedy, and I had ordered it. I have been haunted by it for 32 years.

> —Bob Kerrey, in 2001, on his role in the massacre of civilians at Thanh Phong in the Mekong Delta in 1969

When our sorrows come, they come not single spies
But in battalions!

> —Claudius, *Hamlet*, IV.v

A few days later the local newspaper featured a front-page article by the same reporter who had questioned Allenby's military record when he first took on the presidency. Now she added more documentation about the details of his service and also picked up the thread of Carlotta Baynes' charges that he had discriminated against her both racially and sexually, with the added accusation that he had manipulated the campus grievance committee's findings in order to silence her complaints. The article also managed to insinuate that CSU under his leadership was about to see the sanctions incurred by the previous administration extended by the accrediting team that had recently concluded its visit.

When the announcement came the following day that Allenby had scheduled a press conference on campus, rumors instantly began to burn up the CSU email trail, much as out-of-control wildfires were burning up vast tracts of the state's leafier regions. The accrediting team had voted not merely to sanction the campus but to shutter it and sell the land it sat on to Tesla. The Board of Trustees had slashed the budget for next year, and even tenured faculty were getting pink slips. The baseball/football/field hockey/LGBTQ Studies/fill-in-the-blank program was being eliminated. Carlotta Baynes had been recruited by UCLA, and she was taking the entire Black Studies Department with her. Justin Bieber was enrolling at CSU in the fall, trying out for basketball, and majoring in Administration of Justice. Anita Hill had been replaced as commencement speaker by Sarah Palin, who was coming to stump for Trump and to tout his expertise in the management of universities. Angela Hardy was giving up her position at CSU and entering a monastery in Outer Mongolia to repent for her sins.

Wade figured that his private addition to the litany of speculative lunacies was about as likely to prove forthcoming as any of the others. His beleaguered friend hadn't said a word to tip him off, so he was as much in the dark as anyone else when he took his seat next to Erica Wiley in a buzzing auditorium. She met his quizzical look with one of her own.

"Nothing," she said. "I don't have a clue."

"Maybe he's decided this job is too small for him and he's going to run for POTUS. Considering the alternatives, that wouldn't be a bad idea at all."

"Hillary is going to do just fine," Erica said. "Give her a chance."

Erica had more faith in career politicians and in the sanity of the American electorate than Wade did. He remembered his Mencken—*No one in this world . . . has ever lost money by underestimating the intelligence of the great masses of the plain people.*

Nor has anyone ever lost public office thereby—and shuddered at the prospect of what lay ahead, then turned his attention back to matters more proximate.

"Did you see the protestors outside?" Students (and/or possibly others dispatched by Comrade Putin) carrying signs with variations of *Keep Our Black History Program* and *No More War Crimes at CSU* were milling in front of the auditorium.

Erica nodded. "I've never seen so much political activism on this campus before."

Wade's turn to nod. "I was trying to remember when I'd ever seen *any*."

CSU's scholars, over the years Wade had served them, had not proven the types galvanized to outrage by their country's penchant for bombing hospitals abroad, their state's predilection for funding prisons before schools, or their municipality's routine delivery of toxic drinking water. He nudged Erica. "The one time we saw students carrying picket signs around here was when the administration proposed to restrict the serving of alcohol at campus parties after that pledge broke his neck, remember? They rallied pretty impressively to beat down that gross miscarriage of justice. Some of the Greeks boycotted their classes for a month."

"I remember," she said. "I asked a couple of sorority girls in one of my electives if they wanted to help me out with a reading workshop at a local elementary school. They said they couldn't skip the *Save Our Toga Party* protest."

A few photos were snapped as Allenby came out to the podium. He didn't waste any time getting underway.

"I'm going to start today with some good news. The accrediting team that visited our campus has completed its preliminary report, and I'm pleased to tell everyone that, contrary to some reports you may have heard or read, the finding has been that CSU is making satisfactory progress—better than satisfactory in several categories—in fulfilling the team's previous recommendations. Pending final review, the probationary status previously assigned to our campus will be lifted at the end of this academic year."

A renewed buzz greeted the unexpected news.

"I am also pleased to report that the allegations against our athletic programs have been examined and declared meritless, with one related exception, which I'll elaborate on in a moment. But the overall assessment of our programs is positive, and our progress in improving graduation rates and representation of minorities in our coaching ranks and on some of our teams, notably baseball and softball, has been deemed worthy of approval. Colleges and universities should be leading the way forward, not lagging pitifully behind, in efforts to promote integration and equality of opportunity in all areas, and we can all be proud of the progress CSU has made in these programs."

Another round of buzz.

"The one negative exception I must note is that our African American Studies Department has been formally reprimanded for its failure to maintain appropriate levels of academic integrity, particularly in connection with our athletic progams. I will note here that our own internal review of this department yielded a similar result. While there is of course room at any university for a variety of grading philosophies, I hope we can all agree that we can't have teachers—professors—giving out A's and B's as if they grow on trees. Students have to earn them if they are going to mean anything, if the students are going to *learn* anything. I will also announce today that Professor Carlotta Baynes has submitted her resignation, effective immediately. In view of the extremes of impropriety cited, there has been some pressure to shut down this department, but my preference is to find new leadership and a new direction for it and to maintain its important role on our campus. With regard to the charges leveled against me personally and against several other CSU employees by Professor Baynes, I can announce that these have been withdrawn as a part of the termination agreement that she has signed."

Erica smiled at Wade. "Off the hook, then, both of you."

Wade nodded, wondering if that call from Nashville had come into play after all. "Why do I have the feeling there's another hook in the offing, though?"

"I have another announcement, relevant to the controversy that has resurfaced about my military record. This will no doubt come as a surprise to some of you, perhaps even a shock, but I have made a recommendation to our Board of Trustees to reestablish the ROTC program on this campus."

The buzz suddenly became much louder, and several catcalls punctuated it.

Allenby waited for calm and then continued: "I know there are many among you who see the university as a place for pursuit of peaceful goals, and I share the desire for that pursuit. However, the reality is that our country will always need to defend itself, and other countries around the world will need our help in defending themselves. Al Qaeda and ISIS and Boko Haram will not go away just because we want them to or tell them to, any more than Nazi Germany or Imperial Japan in the past could be defeated by mere wishes or words. They have to be eradicated, and we have to be prepared to do this ourselves. We can of course try to build alliances with other nations in hopes of uniting in defense of civilization, but ultimately we must count upon ourselves. To that end, we need college-educated officers who are trained to make good decisions—trained to make better decisions than the officers who led me into battle, and better decisions than I made myself on the battlefield."

Here it comes, Wade thought. He looked at Erica, who was pursing her lips.

"Those loud voices in our society pressing for more frequent and larger scale military involvement by our country need to be reminded that war should always be the last resort. If you go to war, there will be casualties. Innocent civilians will be killed. Sons and brothers and husbands—and now daughters and sisters and wives—will be asked, or ordered, to do terrible things. Most of us who served in Vietnam, like the soldiers who have done the actual fighting in every war before and after that one, had no idea what we were getting into until we got there. The politicians who sent us there were not the ones who had to deal with the terrors inflicted by a resourceful and relentless adversary, fighting on terrain he was intimately familiar with and we were not. Even if our mission and our methods were often muddled, and even if in the heat of battle we were not thinking of platitudes like 'serving our country,' that is in fact exactly what most of us were doing when we followed our orders and did our best to stay alive and to help our fellow soldiers to survive alongside us. I saw with my own eyes countless acts of heroism in which soldiers risked or forfeited their own lives to bring home their brothers. That some of these heroes came home to be insulted or spat upon, their service and their sacrifice reviled rather than honored, is an enduring legacy of shame that we must bear in mind as we strive now to do better by the heroes returning from the War on Terror."

Allenby paused, swallowed, took a deep breath, and went on. "It is also undeniably true that not all of all of us who served in Vietnam conducted ourselves heroically. I'm going to read to you now briefly from words spoken by John Kerry, currently our nation's Secretary of State, when he testified in the Senate about his own role in the war in Vietnam and about what he had heard from other Americans who had served there. This is what he said, about acts that occurred '*on a day-to-day basis, with full awareness of officers at all levels of command.*'

> They told stories that at times they had person-
> ally raped, cut off ears, cut off heads, taped wires
> from portable telephones to human genitals and
> turned up the power, cut off limbs, blown up
> bodies, randomly shot at civilians, razed vil-
> lages in fashion reminiscent of Genghis Khan,
> shot cattle and dogs for fun, poisoned food
> stocks, and generally ravaged the countryside of
> Vietnam in addition to the normal ravage of war.

In referencing these unspeakable atrocities, I also want to be sure to give credit to those who stood up against them. Some of you here today will remember the name Hugh Thompson, the pilot who refused to fire on civilians at My Lai and indeed even threatened to fire on his own troops if they continued with the massacre underway there. I hope there will be more emphasis placed on stories like his, even as we acknowledge our wrong-doings. He is not the only American who defied authority to do the right thing in Vietnam, and I am sure there are many others serving in the Middle East now who step up every day to do the right thing there. Those who follow their conscience to refuse indefensible orders and save civilians deserve to be honored every bit as much as the soldiers who carry their wounded comrades to safety under fire."

The impact of one man's moral choice under extreme duress was something Wade had thought about a lot. He had often invit-ed his students, as well, to consider this in their readings and their essays. In the cloister of the classroom, of course, there was little risk to declaring an opinion. Those *in the arena*, as Allenby had just reminded his audience, faced far more momentous decisions. Sometimes the choices, though, considering the consequences, seemed so obvious that Wade could not believe they had not been made. If Robert E. Lee had accepted Lincoln's offer of command of the Union troops, would the Civil War have been over in six months and a million casualties averted? If Bill Clinton had settled for watching some porn in the Oval Office, or Ralph Nader for admiring his adenoids in the mirror, would the nation and the world have been spared the subsequent absurdities of GWB, WMDs, and a trillion-dollar war? But Allenby wasn't talking about guys like that.

"You ask a lot if you send a soldier into battle with orders to kill in order to protect himself, his fellow soldiers, and his country—and then later call him a war criminal for following those very orders. You ask a lot if you ask him to accept this label."

Allenby paused again, gathered himself, and continued: "I would give anything I possess to be able to stand up here today and say that, like Hugh Thompson, I stood up against injustice and refused to follow orders that I knew were wrong. I did not. I followed orders, did as I was told. To acknowledge this in public, nearly fifty years later, is the hardest thing I have ever had to do. I believe I can honestly say that I have not generally shrunk from doing hard things in my life, but for far too long I have put off this acknowledgment of what we—of what *I*—did. I have shared this story with a few—a very few—friends over the years"—Allenby looked up from his script for a moment, and Wade wondered if his friend was trying to find his face, as he heard Erica muffle a sob next to him—"but as recent newspaper and television reports have indicated, I had not dealt with this matter with full disclosure. I am doing so now. I stand before you today to acknowledge that publicly and to accept the consequences. As a measure of my seriousness in acknowledging my culpability, I have decided to step down as president of CSU"—

"Oh, no!" Wade heard Erica gasp.

"—effective at the end of this semester. It has been my great honor to serve here at this campus, my alma mater. I hope to leave as part of the legacy of my presidency here, however brief, the prospect of helping other young men—and women—prepare to meet the terrible challenges of war better than I was prepared to meet them myself. I am proud of the progress that has been made in several areas on my watch, but, as the accrediting team has reminded us, we still have much work ahead of us. I regret that I will not be leading the continuing efforts for improvement, but I trust that everyone here today will carry on in earnest with those projects we have begun. Thank you, and that is the extent of my prepared remarks. I will now take your questions."

Allenby waited for the furor to subside. Wade had half-hoped his friend would sprint for the exit and spare himself further interrogation, but watched and listened in something verging on awe as Allenby patiently and thoroughly addressed the questions, however irrational or unfair, that peppered him. He picked the hostile reporter out of the crowd first, and, without apparent enmity, credited her for persisting with her investigation. He answered every question that came his way, then thanked his audience for asking them. Erica was in tears when the trial by ordeal finally ended. Wade watched Cenon Aquino march to the podium and shake Allenby's hand, then accompany him off the stage, no finer honor guard imaginable. Wade walked Erica back to her office, an arm around her waist to steady her, before heading over to the president's office to see if he could get past the secretaries and spend a few minutes with Allenby, who spotted him, put the phone down, and waved him in.

Maybe this is my last trip to this office. Wade sat down, looked around, and tried to figure out how to help. "Next time you schedule a press conference, why don't you wait until you have something to say?"

"Sorry I couldn't give you a heads-up. I didn't figure out what I was going to do until about 4:00 a.m."

"That's when I do some of my worst thinking, too. What the fuck are you doing, leaving CSU to fend for itself?

"CSU will be fine. I've given the BOT some suggestions about my successor. That accreditation report at least is an indication that we've begun to turn things around here."

Wade placed fuck-all faith in the report, including his own portion thereof, but nodded anyway. "You've accomplished a hell of a lot in a short—"

"Let's not get carried away. We've made a start. The truth is, as I said earlier, we've got a long way to go."

"I just can't believe you're not going to be here to—"

"It was something I'd promised myself I'd take a crack at, and I'm glad I did," Allenby said. "Looks like I may have to save my energy for something else. I may even be eligible for some of that medicinal cannabis you keep trying to prescribe for me, after all."

"What are you talking a—"

"There was something funky in my prostate exam."

Wade closed his eyes and sank back, wretched history about to repeat itself.

Allenby stood up, came over to Wade's chair, and put a hand on his shoulder, the halt comforting the hale. "If it's cancer, looks like they caught it early. It's all preliminary at this point anyway, but I'm exploring the treatment options and their side effects."

These Wade knew quite a bit about from his father's demise. He nodded again but didn't trust himself to speak yet.

"I may go with the European theory of watchful waiting."

Wade had urged that approach upon his father, to no avail. A cocksure surgeon had talked him into the operation, and his life had never been the same.

"Amazing, isn't it?" Allenby said, moving back behind his desk. "Half of the men in America don't even know what a prostate is until their own tries to kill them."

Wade nodded once more. Even with all of his own formal education, he hadn't known much himself about the ticking time-bomb within until his father's tumor had been discovered.

Allenby sat down and sighed. "The gland built to give you the purest form of pleasure possible is also programmed to kill you in the end."

"Intelligent design at its finest," Wade finally mumbled.

"Not just kill you, either," Allenby continued. "*We all owe God a death*, but it shouldn't have to come with a decade of wetting the bed or dragging around a limp dick."

Everything happens for a reason, right? Fuck.

Wade flashed to his shriveled father in a hospice bed at the very end, helpless son there trying to make small talk, complaining lamely about getting nowhere with Angela in their first go-round and seeing the stare in his father's eyes that said, *You think heartbreak is a bitch? Wait for cancer. Wait for chemo.* He wondered if Allenby would take Hemingway's approach rather than wait for a similar ending.

"Don't worry, I'm not going to blow my head off just yet. I've got some other shit to do first."

Wade went home pondering what else might be on a billionaire's bucket list, then turned inward and thought about what it was going to be like to lose him, how hard it was to lose all the people that you loved the most, those whose love in return defined your happiness and your life.

Angela's letter was waiting for him when he got there.

CHAPTER 22

There's a whole chapter on how to write an epistolary novel, but surely no one's done that since the eighteenth century?

—Hilary Swallow, letter to her husband Philip,
in David Lodge's *Changing Places*

The opioid epidemic is the canary in the coal mine with regards to our healthcare system.

—Anna Lembke, author of *Drug Dealer, MD*

Wade held the letter in his hands and stared at it for a long time, as if it might contain Anthrax or a new and improved form of Sarin. Why would Angela communicate with him this way instead of calling or emailing? Was news of a divorce filing in there, or would that come directly from an attorney's office? What was he going to do if she had decided to start a new life without him? How did you face the rest of your life without the one you were supposed to spend it with? He thought about how his mom had somehow coped with his dad's desertion after thirty years of marriage, half a lifetime together and then suddenly left to face the world without her one and only. Trapped in his own disappointments then, he knew he had never fully acknowledged the resilience she had displayed in forging a new life for herself without castigating Wade's father or even trying to change his mind. Was Wade capable of the same if this was Angela saying goodbye?

Other forms of communication had become so commonplace that he hardly ever got a real letter anymore. He thought about others he had received over the course of his life: the thin one from Stanford telling him he wasn't getting in; the fat one when he was accepted in the PhD program at Berkeley; the form from the Induction Board exempting him from military service (and sparing him the horrors Allenby had faced in Vietnam) because of a punctured eardrum. This one seemed equally portentous. As long as it was sealed, he was still married, still had hopes of resuming the life he had lost when Angela left . . . again. Once he stuck the bread knife under the seal or scissored a corner, would life as he had known and loved it vanish forever from his reach? As he stared at Angela's shaky script in the address lines, he heard her in his ear: *Don't be such a fucking chicken, Wade. Open the fucking letter. What's the worst that could happen?*

You knew you were in trouble when that question popped into your head.

Her shrink cured her and told her to go back to the man she really loves—Ronnie. Ronnie sold their tape to Adam & Eve, and they want Angela for a sequel: *The Dean Does Fourplay*. She fell in love with her shrink, and she's dumping me and marrying him. The shrink couldn't help her. She's dead. She stuck her head in the oven like Sylvia Plath and had this delivered posthumously, with a copy to Nicholas Sparks for his next crap novel.

Wade punched himself in the head and tore open the envelope.

Dear Wade,

I hope you can read this. I know how much you hated it when you had to decipher the hiero-glyphics in your students' in-class essays, so I'm sorry to add to your burdens. I have access to a computer but not to a printer right now, and I thought maybe a handwritten letter would be more personal anyway, even though I know this probably looks like I wrote it with my left foot or with a ballpoint in my asshole. I'm sitting up in bed, still pretty weak, after what I've been through here. My new doctor suggested that I send you this. So much to tell you, so hard to know where to start. I guess I'll start with the new doctor.

Almirah Khan is a godsend. She finally figured out what went wrong with the meds my previous doctors prescribed. I went through four different geniuses before her, and they all had a different theory about how to treat my depression. When my father died, on top of the stupid accident and the fucking tape, I just completely lost it. I wound up taking so many different kinds of psychotropics that my body just caved in. If the celebs who advertise weight loss products on TV ever really get serious about making a score, I can tell them exactly what cocktail to put on the market. I lost twenty pounds! I was down to eighty-five, if you can imagine that.

Mentally, I just shut down. I didn't want to eat anything, obviously. I didn't want to get out of bed, even though I couldn't sleep. I didn't want to talk to anybody, not even my mother when she came to see me. I was ready to give up. I just wanted to die. It was like that until about six weeks ago. Then my mother heard about Dr. Khan from a friend and prevailed on her to take a look at my file and then to take over the case. She got me off the fucking meds and back on a decent diet within a few weeks. I've gained ten pounds back and I'm feeling much, much better. I don't want to die any more.

I know you're worried about me and Ronnie. I can see you shaking your head and telling me that you're not, but I know you're lying. What I did with Ronnie and that tape was fucked up beyond belief, and what I did to you when I went back to him before was even worse. That's actually the worst thing I've ever done, hurting you like that. I know you won't want to hear this, but I got in touch with Ronnie and asked him to come to see me here in the hospital. I know I told you I never wanted to see him again, but I wanted him to see me, see what his threats had done to me. I actually thought there was something human in him that would come to the surface and cause him to feel some remorse. I thought he would feel so sorry for me, sorry for what he had done, seeing me lying here like the last survivor at Auschwitz, that he would give me the tape and promise not to threaten me with it anymore. Long story short, it didn't work. This time I mean it: I never want to see him again, Wade, and I promise you I never will.

This is getting to be a long letter. My brain has been scrambled, and I know I've rambled. The drugs I've taken will do that to you, but I'm getting better every day now. I don't know if there's still a job waiting for me at CSU, but when I feel a little stronger and able to travel sans barf bag in hand, I'd like to come home, in sackcloth and ashes if necessary, if you think you can ever forgive me. I'm still working on forgiving myself, and I can't promise that I'll get there any time soon, or maybe ever, but I know I don't want to spend the rest of my life without you. You're the one who makes me laugh, the one who gets my own warped sense of humor. I miss you so much—I can't even begin to tell you. I miss all the crazy conversations, the stupid movie lines, all the nutty stuff we did together. I even miss your stupid fucking Giants. Did you ever find anyone to assassinate Bochy?

If I ever had any doubt before, I know now that you're the one I love and the one I want to be with. I'm sorry for everything that I've done to hurt you. If you said you never wanted to see me again, I'd understand and accept your decision, as terrible as it would be for me, and let you get on with your life. Maybe Erica will come around if you stop pushing Allenby on her, and

you can try sleeping with your boss again. Good
luck with that if that's the way you decide to go.
Please let me know.

Love,
Angela

Wade spent a sleepless night drafting, editing, and reediting
his reply, then rose at dawn to transcribe the result of his deliberations and drop it in the mailbox.

Angela,

Nothing to forgive. Please come home.

Love,
Wade

CHAPTER 23

The only man who could have caught it *hit* it.

> —attributed variously, often to *San Francisco Chronicle* beat writer Bob Stevens, of Willie Mays' game-winning triple in the 1959 All-Star Game at Forbes Field in Pittsburgh

But the might-have-been is but boggy ground to build upon.

> —Herman Melville, *Billy Budd*

CSU's softball team, under Connie Estrada, won a post-season tournament game for the first time in ten years before a pair of tight losses ended their best season in fifteen. Norma got two RBIs in the victory, another in the elimination loss, and an offer of a full scholarship to extend her playing career for an additional year while she worked on a teaching credential or a master's degree. Wade figured he would be tapped for that letter of recommendation after all.

Eduardo Alvarez's baseball team had fared even better. When the top two seeds in the conference were upset in early playoff rounds, CSU came full circle from the previous season, playing for the championship again—only this time holding the home field advantage, as Allenby's renovations had resulted in hosting the tournament. After winning the first game of the final series, CSU needed to win once more to advance to the Regional Playoffs and a possible path to the College World Series. A win in the next game would avoid a doubleheader and save arms and innings for the next round—and, perhaps, down the road, for Omaha.

The home team took the field with confidence soaring. Eight runs in the top of the first altered the mood in both dugouts considerably. Needing the win to stay alive, the opposing coach had planned to trot out his top remaining ace, but after the huge early lead, he gambled and held him back, even after his preliminary warm-up, sending out a substitute who shut down CSU through the first five innings. Juke Jackson left runners on base in his first two at-bats before raising some eyebrows by legging out a single on what had appeared to be a routine groundout to shortstop in the sixth. In the seventh after three more runs were added to the deficit, Alvarez waved the white flag, pulling out his starters to save them for the second game. In order to preserve his bullpen, he sent a backup infielder with a backyard knuckleball out to pitch the final two innings, providing a measure of entertainment for the frustrated fans and a series of near-death experiences for the third-string catcher. The final score was 17-3, CSU's worst loss of the year. Somehow Alvarez was still smiling in the dugout, encouraging his starters to show their support for the scrubs to the bitter end, as if he knew something no one else did.

Allenby, his timing impeccable as ever, arrived to join Wade in the stands a few minutes after the opening debacle ended. He jerked his head at the scoreboard, still registering the result. "I trust you to manage one game without me, and this is what you come up with? That looks like a goddam football score."

"I know. Feels like we just got trampled by the Cornhuskers again. If it had been women's softball, they'd have invoked the mercy rule and called it off before the wounded were shot."

Wade winced at his own analogy even as it left his mouth. Allenby didn't need any more reminders, however innocuously intended, of what had ended his presidency. He either didn't notice or didn't bother to reprove Wade.

"Eduardo told me he's saving his freshest pitchers for the second game. I trust he didn't burn Juke in the first one."

"He was warming his buns on the bench when it ended," Wade said. "I wouldn't be surprised if he was taking a nap." *Baseball is boring,* he heard Angela and Erica tittering in harmony. Well, it certainly could be.

As the players rested briefly before the deciding game, Wade and Allenby bought hotdogs—the gourmand willing for once to set aside his standards and relish the guilty pleasure, rodent hairs and all—and caught up on what was going on in the majors, with the Giants and Dodgers neck-and-neck atop the NL West again, as in so many seasons past. Allenby, after his childhood in New York City's golden age, when the World Series left the boroughs only twice in eight years (for four games and zero wins by the Whiz Kids and the Indians), had spent his adolescence in L.A. during the Wills-Gilliam years. Mays and the Giants had first claim on his heart, but he didn't hate the Dodgers in the primal way that Wade felt a true believer was obliged to. Wade struggled to wrap his mind around the concept that someone could root for both teams, but, as usual, Allenby had found the perfect way to put the divided loyalties into perspective: "After your parents got divorced, you still loved both of them, right?"

Allenby rooted for players more than for teams. This was jolly convenient for him but somehow still felt like sacrilege to Wade.

"Look how much more pleasure you'll get out of the game," Allenby reminded him now, "if you don't bind your emotions to one franchise. You'll find someone to root for in the World Series every year."

"That's true," Wade had to admit, recalling how much he had enjoyed watching the Royals run to a title when they weren't facing his Giants. "Unless the Yankees are playing the Dodgers," he added. "Then I'd rather binge-watch *The Real Housewives of Benghazi.*"

"You probably do that anyway, since you're too cheap to pay for a porn channel."

Allenby mentioned a news report that Alex Rodriguez might be retiring from the Yankees at the end of the season and giving up his quest to break the home run record.

"Don't get me started on that," Wade said. "When he passed Mays on the list, I was hoping Brad Pitt would be there to greet him at home plate with the blade from *Inglourious Basterds* and carve an asterisk into his forehead."

Wade was still convinced that the home run breaking Babe Ruth's historic mark had been hit by the wrong man. He said now, as more than once before, "Put Aaron in a damn wind tunnel for most of his home games instead of those popgun parks in Milwaukee and Atlanta, then subtract sixty or so homers for two years of military service Willie did and Hank didn't, they probably come out about even. Can you imagine how many homers Mays would have hit if he played his home games where Aaron did?"

"America didn't love Hank the way we loved Willie," Allenby conceded. "But if you really want to play the *what if* game, just imagine if Mays had signed with the Dodgers instead of the Giants."

Wade stopped his hotdog halfway to his mouth. "Please, I'm trying to eat something here."

"Unthinkable, I know, but . . . *think* about it: if Willie signs with the Dodgers, joins that team with Robinson and Campanella and Newcombe, and then later Koufax, Drysdale, Wills, Gilliam, he goes to at least ten World Series: the three he took the Giants to—two of them were tied pennant races that went to playoffs with the Dodgers anyway—plus six the Dodgers went to during his career, not counting the Army years, and one more year when they tied with the Braves—*plus* however many more his being on that team might have led to."

As much as it hurt to think about it, it was a good point; Wade had to admit it. "*And* gets to hang out with Sinatra in Hollywood instead of having rocks tossed at his house in San Francisco."

Allenby continued: "Giants fans always remember that Marichal got hurt in the World Series in '62, pitched in only one game, and that cost them the championship. But they forget who else got hurt that year."

"Koufax." Wade had not forgotten. "You had to remind me, didn't you?"

Allenby shrugged. "You think that regular season ends in a tie if Sandy is himself in August and September?"

Wade nodded bitterly. "That was the only World Series Willie got to in San Francisco, and they didn't win."

Allenby shrugged again. "You worry too much about what Mays didn't do. You ought to be satisfied with what he *did*: I know I don't have to tell you."

Wade ran down the list: a pennant at twenty, a championship at twenty-three, 660 home runs, a batting title, league-leader in stolen bases four years in a row, two MVPs more than a decade apart, a dozen straight Gold Gloves dating from the honor's origin, fifteen wins in his last eighteen appearances in the All-Star Game back when it still meant something, when the AL barely acknowledged the existence of black players. Kept his team in the race pretty much year-in and year-out for twenty years. Made what is still the most iconic catch in the annals of a game going on a hundred and fifty years. And taught multiple generations, of every color, how to play the game with joy. Not a bad resumé.

"He's got nothing to apologize for," Allenby said, "and you can stop apologizing *for* him or wondering what could have been. Forget the *what ifs*. Celebrate what the man *did*, who he *is*, not what he might have done or been."

And thank God he didn't sign with the Dodgers. "Of course you're right," Wade said. "I just wish he had taken a crack at managing. He could have been the one to break that barrier, too. All that knowledge of the game, all that love for it, he could have passed so much more of himself on."

"I suspect he found his own ways to pass it on," Allenby said, "and not just to guys on the Giants. Remember Andruw Jones giving Willie credit for a big jump in his home runs after he spent some time with him?"

Some men spend their lives waiting for the Messiah; Wade had spent most of his waiting for the next Willie Mays. He remembered Andruw Jones, but he couldn't forget Bobby Bonds, George Foster, Garry Maddox, Gary Matthews, Chili Davis—the whole legion of fast, powerful outfielders the Giants had signed, drafted, and developed in Willie's image—and then lost in free agency or traded away, usually for next to nothing in return, just as they had traded him. Some hurts would never heal.

Fortunately, there was always another game to take your mind off them. The early innings of the second game set the stage for a tight, low-scoring contest. Alvarez had entrusted the season's most important game to a sophomore southpaw, one of the combo athletes who had joined the squad in April when the basketball season ended. He had pitched only in relief until now but had been steadily improving and had dominated in his most recent outings. He kept hitters off balance with his off-speed pitches and was able to escape the only trouble spots he ran into in the first six innings. With one out in the seventh, possibly tiring after a borderline 3-2 pitch was called a ball, he walked a second hitter and then left a curve out over the middle of the plate. The clean-up hitter launched it into deep right-center field. It appeared certain that two runs would score, perhaps all that would be needed on a day when CSU's bats had fallen silent. As Wade and Allenby jumped to their feet, Jackson turned his back to the crowd, sprinted into the gap, tracked the ball's flight over his shoulder, measured the distance to the fence, jumped at the last possible moment, twisted his torso, stretched out his gloved arm, and at the peak of his leap snared the ball in the very tip of the webbing, then pinballed off the padded chain links and flung the ball back to the infield, where the startled runners scrambled back to the bases they had left. It was the play of the season and one of the best Wade had ever seen, a companion piece to the supernatural touchdown pass Jackson had unleashed in Lincoln before injury had proven him human after all.

"Maybe he should stick to outfield," Wade said to Allenby, as CSU's lefty got the third out on an anticlimactic first-pitch come-backer. "That catch remind you of anyone?"

"Not a bad grab. Pretty good toss, too. Now he needs to do something with the stick." Allenby had glanced earlier at the scoresheet Wade had started in the first game before giving up in mid-rout. "He's left a lot of runs out there today."

CSU scored the game's first run in the bottom of the seventh, but yielded two in the top of the eighth. After CSU failed to score in its half of the inning, Alvarez moved Jackson in from center to pitch the ninth with a clean slate, to keep the score in reach.

Jackson had saved each of the tournament wins so far. In the previous day's win, he had secured the last five outs, four via strikeout. Along with his overpowering fastball and big curve, he was using more often now his slider, and it was proving almost impossible for college hitters to lay off or square up—just as he had said of Johnny Dawes last year.

"Even Ted Williams struggled to hit that pitch," Allenby point-ed out, as the first hitter in the inning flailed at the slider for strike two and then took another for strike three. "He said it was one of the main reasons he decided to retire."

Wade nodded, recalling in reverence the hitter with the high-est lifetime on-base percentage in history, the last man to hit .400. He wondered if anyone would ever do it again.

"Not just a great hitter, a great man," Allenby added. "Spoke up for Satchel Paige and and Josh Gibson at the Hall of Fame. A pretty bold move for a white man in 1966."

Mexican on his mother's side, Wade remembered. He was reminded of Allenby's tribute to Hugh Thompson. In a time and place where matters of race remained largely a national disgrace, it was good to remember those who stepped up to do the right thing when history beckoned. Wade thought of Leo Durocher, in the spring of 1947, when some of Jackie Robinson's teammates sought his trade before he ever set foot on an MLB field: *I don't care if the guy is yellow or black, or if he has stripes like a zebra. I'm the manager of this team and I say he plays.* And of shortstop Pee Wee Reese, putting his arm around Robinson's shoulders in full view of the hostile public when the first cascade of boos came down to greet him. And of Willie Mays' teammates in the minor leagues, who loved him so much that they snuck out of their hotel in the white part of town and into his in the *colored* section, just to keep him out of harm's way. All of them had played a part in creating the opportunity that stood before the young man on the mound now.

In Jackson's case the delivery of the slider came just a shade off his average fastball velocity. The only complication was that the slider was harder to control, and in two of the previous games he had walked runners into scoring position with it. He tried it again now on 3-2 to the second hitter, who managed to check his swing and take ball four on a pitch in the same spot that had just been called strike three. The next hitter punched a curve up the middle for a single, and then Jackson walked the following batter to load the bases on a fastball that looked unimpeachable to Wade, Allenby, and few thousand other fans in ballpark—but not to the only arbiter whose opinion mattered.

Wade groaned at the blown call. "They really need to hurry up and adopt the robot to call balls and strikes."

"Some say it takes the human element out of the game," Allenby said.

"Takes the witchcraft out of it, more likely. That *element* behind the plate might as well be using a Ouija board."

Alvarez sent the pitching coach out to see what Jackson had left in the tank with the season on the line. The infielders gathered briefly at the mound, then returned to their positions: in at first and third to cut-off a run at the plate, second baseman and shortstop at normal depth. Alvarez was gambling on the double play to get out of the inning on anything hit up the middle.

"This could be ugly," Wade said, recalling last year's walk-off loss. Another walk would add another run to CSU's deficit, a hit could add two, and a grooved fastball that turned into a grand slam would put the game effectively out of reach. Full circle indeed. "I hope it's not *déjà vu all over again.*"

"Have some faith, Yogi," Allenby said. "He's still throwing 97, 98."

Jackson got the first two strikes with his fastball and then missed twice with his curve. At 2-2 he needed to make his pitch, avoid going to 3-2 and leaving the outcome up to the fluctuant ump. Jackson breathed deeply, leaned in for the sign, and fired the slider again, low and away. The hitter, playing hero, tried to yank the ball over the wall, but tapped it weakly instead to shortstop. The sometime point guard who had succeeded Johnny Dawes fielded it nimbly and flipped it to second. The relay reached first just in time, the first baseman stretching to glove the ball a fraction before the hitter's foot smacked the bag. Double play. Inning over. Alvarez's gamble had paid off: still only one run down, one more chance to tie or win the game, with the top of the batting order coming up.

After the leadoff hitter grounded out to open the bottom of the ninth, the two hitter worked a walk. He immediately took an aggressive lead as Jackson stepped into the batter's box.

"You think Eduardo will send the runner?" Wade asked, as the pitcher snapped a throw over to first base.

"He's done it all year," Allenby said. "I don't see why he'd stop now."

The pitcher threw to first again, the play a little closer this time.

"He's got the pitcher worrying about that guy, anyway," Allenby added, "when he should be thinking about the one standing in the box."

"You'd hate to see him get picked off or thrown out here, though, with—"

Jackson ended Wade's worries by blasting a fastball deep into right-center, not far from where he had made his epic catch. True to form, Alvarez had again started the runner. With a head start, he got the green light from the third base coach and coasted for home with the tying run. When the ball hit the fence, it caromed directly to the center fielder, but Jackson, with the play in front of him, ignored the stop sign when he hit second base. He rounded the bag in full stride and raced toward third, where the strong relay throw was heading, right on target. Sliding adroitly away from the tag, Jackson beat the throw by a split second. Triple. He had hit the ball almost four hundred feet and been safe by perhaps half-an-inch.

Wade, who had held his breath until the safe call, expelled it noisily as Jackson called time, hopped to his feet, dusted himself off, and smiled broadly at his teammates roaring their approval.

"Looks like his leg is all the way back," Allenby said.

Wade breathed again and thought of Bo Jackson, when asked how he felt after the first time he had slid on his reconstructed hip: *I was fine. My surgeon fainted.*

"Good thing, too," Allenby added. "Long walk to the dugout if he gets thrown out there."

"Big play to get to third with one out, though." *That's what speed do.*

The clean-up hitter was walked intentionally to set up a double play. Alvarez immediately countered by inserting as a pinch runner one of his combo athletes, who stole second on the next pitch, the catcher not even risking a throw with Jackson's speed at third. The five hitter was walked to set up a force at home and put the game in the hands of the slumping six hitter, who had failed to reach base through the long afternoon and in the three previous games as well.

Jackson danced off third as if he had ideas of taking matters into his own hands. He bluffed down the line on the first two pitches, both swinging strikes, drawing on the second a throw from the catcher that nearly got away from the third baseman.

"*That* would have been a crazy way to win the game," Wade said. "Think he might try to steal home?"

"I wouldn't want to be that catcher if he decides to give it a shot."

One of the most dramatic plays in any sport, the steal of home plate had largely been excised from the modern game, except for the occasional delayed double-steal on the throw through to second base that had just been eschewed. Wade recalled how Billy Martin, head and shoulders above any other manager he had ever seen, had briefly brought the play back into vogue when he was managing in Minnesota, before the wonders he had worked with Oakland's bush league budget in the wild days of *Billy Ball*.

"Remember Rod Carew with Billy's Twins?" he said to Allenby.

Allenby nodded. "I was thinking of Jackie Robinson. That shot of him sliding under Berra's glove in the World Series."

"Wouldn't it be great to see that again?"

"They used to do it all the time in the Negro Leagues," Allenby said. "That's a big part of what we lost when those leagues folded."

Wade nodded, sharing a moment of regret with his friend. Neither had ever seen a game from the leagues that flourished before integration, where night baseball was conceived and born, and where thousands more than at many MLB games routinely roared for the locals or goaded the visitors. As much as baseball's role in desegregating America deserved to be celebrated, often overlooked or even forgotten was the concomitant death sentence for those historic organizations—not just the jobs of players and coaches and of the cast that surrounded and supported them, but the bravado of the whole culture that accompanied them. Allenby's uncle from Kansas City had followed the Monarchs in their heyday and had regaled him with tales of derring-do on the base paths: stolen bases galore, inside-the-park home runs, bunting for doubles, stretching singles into doubles or doubles into triples (as Jackson had done just now), even scoring from first on singles (as Lorenzo Cain had done against Toronto to get KC back into the World Series), gambits that for the most part had disappeared from today's game, along with the players fleet and fearless enough to pull them off.

"Maybe he'll go now," Wade said, watching Jackson shimmy down the line off third again. "Not much to lose, with two strikes already. This kid at the plate looks overmatched, anyway."

"Only one out," Allenby reminded him, as the hitter watched the second of a pair of teasers float well out of the strike zone. "Still a chance for the next guy to get him in if—"

Jackson suddenly exploded toward home. The trail runners took off behind him. Wade and Allenby leaped to their feet in unison again, as the pitcher, startled in mid-delivery, hurried the ball to the plate. The hitter squared and bunted the high fastball sharply toward first base, no thing of beauty but enough of a surprise to discombobulate the defense. The first baseman rushed in and gloved the ball, looked at home plate, too late with Jackson sprinting in, then reached to swipe-tag the bunter and turned to throw to second base to finish the double play—too late again. The tag had taken off the force at second, and the game was over when Jackson crossed the plate. Alvarez charged out of the dugout to lead the celebration. CSU had won its first-ever conference championship in baseball.

Wade was beaming, everything he believed about the game *bounded in a nutshell*. Good things happened when you put pressure on the defense. The fielder's only chance would have been to ignore the runner coming down the line right next to him and throw to second base first, to keep the double play in order.

"A two-strike suicide squeeze!" Wade said. "You gotta love that."

"Especially when it works." Allenby pointed down to the field, where Jackson was mobbed, tackled, and pummeled by his teammates. "I hope they don't cripple him again celebrating. That's not too far from felonious assault out there."

"I thought you were going to say *gang-rape in the gulag*." The rituals of a new generation were hard to fathom. "What ever happened to a handshake and a pat on the back?"

Allenby's cell phone rang. Wade figured it was somebody watching on TV, calling to congratulate him on qualifying for the Regionals, maybe even his buddy Obama, for whom he had raised big bucks, calling from the White House. It turned out to be much more important than that.

"My urologist," Allenby said, pocketing the phone. "He got the lab results back."

Wade held his breath again.

"The biopsy came back negative. The tumor is benign."

Wade's heart lifted. He fumbled for fresh words to express some measure of his gladness and relief, then fell back on an old standby: "I think that calls for a drink."

"I think you might be right."

Many rounds later, Allenby poured Wade into a taxi, paid the fare over his objections, and sent him home from the bar where they had celebrated. Somewhere between the third and fourth servings Wade had tried to tell him about Angela's letter. Wade couldn't remember, though, if he had made it clear that nothing was clear yet. Allenby, who didn't have cancer after all, wanted Wade to be happy, too. He wanted to know when Angela was coming home. He wasn't the only fucking one.

Wade remembered Jackson's reminder that the draft was on TV today and turned on ESPN to watch. The amateur selection process in baseball was an imperfect instrument, to say the least. Football and basketball had their share of spectacular misses, as the annals of the 49ers (Jim Druckenmiller, J.J. Stokes, A.J. Jenkins) and the Warriors (Cyril Baptiste, Ken Washburn, Todd Fuller) could certainly attest, but identifying elite talent in baseball was even more of a crapshoot. Mike Piazza had been drafted in the 62nd round, after 1389 other players, only as a favor owed to his father by Tommy LaSorda; he had become, alongside Manny Ramirez, one of the two most fearsome right-handed hitters of his era. Now he was on the way to Cooperstown. In 2009 the Giants had passed on Mike Trout in favor of a pitcher subsequently peddled to the Mets for a half-season of Carlos Beltran's services. Had San Francisco picked Trout, now viewed by many as the best player in the game, three recent championships might have become an unbroken string of six. Twenty other teams had made the same mistake, but it still rankled Wade. Trout, at least, had played his high school baseball on the distant coast. Even more galling were the cases when the Giants had missed Joe Morgan and Rickey Henderson right under their noses in Oakland. It didn't say much for the science of your methods when you couldn't find and draft the Hall of Famers in your own backyard. Wade wondered if the kid from Linden and Fresno State that the Yankees had signed would be the next great one who got away.

Jackson had been identified by some analysts as a possible late first or early second round pick, although there was speculation that concerns about his injury could push him farther down. Wade made it through the first round, without seeing him selected, before falling asleep. He was wakened when the phone rang: not the cell, just as well, he probably couldn't remember how to answer it anyway. He looked at the number but didn't recognize it. *Not Angela. Fuck. Not Brenda either, though. Thank God for—*

"I'm drafted, Doc."

Juke.

"Middle of the second round. It wasn't as high as we was hopin', but—"

The almost perfect ending to the almost perfect day. The only thing better would have been if Wade's wife had been there to hand him the phone and hear the news. *Unless . . .*

"Please don't tell me it was the Dodgers, or the damn—"

"Fuck the Dodgers, Doc. I'm going to be a Giant!"

CHAPTER 24

Look class, if I was capable of writing a book more than a handful of people wanted to read, do you think I'd be here teaching you?

—Mat Johnson, author of *Drop, Hunting in Harlem, Pym*, and *Loving Day*, in a tweet

Why couldn't my father be someone cool like Willie Mays?

—Barack Obama

The final exam for Wade's Hemingway class was scheduled a few days before CSU's baseball team was set to depart for the Regional Playoffs in Fort Worth. The Giants had invited Jackson to attend, on the day of the exam, a night game at AT&T Park. Jackson had in turn invited Wade and Allenby to come with him in lieu of the family members the Giants had offered to accommodate. Allenby had declined, fearing recent controversies might make his presence a distraction, but Wade was set to tag along.

When the exam ended, Wade distributed student evaluation forms and stepped out of the classroom according to protocol; Jackson emerged a few minutes later to deliver the packet with the completed forms to the dean's office. He jerked his head back at the classroom as he neared Wade standing outside it. "Monica still in there, ain't finished yet. Say she want to talk to you. You want me to wait, or—"

"Go ahead. One less eval form won't change the world."

"Look like she might got some good feedback for you."

Wade had just given back to his zaftig late-addition a term paper with a charitable D+ on it, wondering if her cup size hadn't unduly influenced his appraisal. He stepped back into the classroom.

"I was just finishing this up. Here you go."

She tried to hand the form to him, but he backed away, noticing that, as usual, she had missed a few buttons at the top of her blouse, exposing her forward assets. "I'm not supposed to see those," he said, "until after the grades have been submitted. I guess we'll have to toss that one, or—"

"Oh. You mean I did all that work for nothing?"

She frowned, then set the form down on a desk near the door, reached behind her for her massive purse, and began rooting around in it, Wade hoped not for a semiautomatic. Or maybe she had taken the Stanford anecdote he had shared with the class to heart and was about to extract a hammer and bash his brains in with it. It was one thing to bless Streleski in the abstract from afar but quite another to be on the flesh end of the umbrage. Wade glanced at the exit and measured the odds. What were the chances he could outrun a top-heavy twenty-two year-old in a tight skirt and three-inch heels?

Monica pulled a book out instead. Wade was startled to recognize his own handiwork.

A colleague had recently informed him that *The Sun Also Rises* was still selling a hundred thousand copies every year, mostly no doubt to students in courses like his. This was approximately ninety-nine thousand more than his own volume about the masterpiece's author had sold altogether.

"I just loved your book."

"I'm surprised you could track down a copy."

"I bought it on eBay for a dollar," she said. "Plus shipping, of course."

"Of course."

"Would you autograph it for me?"

Wade took the book from her. It appeared to be in pristine condition, its covers perhaps never cracked; he wondered if she had really read even a single syllable of it. Ah, well. If she hadn't, that would link her with just about every other book lover in the world, living or dead. He doubted, with Dickens, *if Robinson Crusoe could have read it though he had no other on his desolate island.* Wade opened to the virginal flyleaf. He never knew what to write when he signed a book for someone. He felt like a complete imposter, of course. Autographs were supposed to be from Willie Mays or Joe Montana, people who mattered, not from some no-name teacher/counselor at a twat college. Besides, whatever you scribbled on the spot was bound to be deemed inadequate afterward ("*That's* what he came up with? And he's supposed to be an author?"). The best you could hope for was that the autograph-seeker would help you out and tell you what to write. Maybe she wanted this for her grandfather, who had packed Hemingway's novels in his gear along with his C-rats through Korea or Vietnam.

"You can make it out to 'Monica, my all-time favorite student—and a fabulous lay.'"

Wade blinked. *Maybe it wasn't for grandpa after all.*

"Just kidding."

"Oh." He wondered if she was about to join the infamous legion who'd "do *anything* to pass this class."

Right. Except read directions, plan, proofread, or punctuate.

"I know I'm not your favorite student. I was a little rushed when I wrote that last paper."

I was typing it on my phone while I was giving my boyfriend a blowjob, and—

"I go to school full-time and also work full-time, and—"

My boss needed a blowjob, too.

"—sometimes it's hard to find time to—"

Put my panties back on before I come to your class.

"—do my best work."

"I understand," Wade said. "I worked my way through college, too."

"Yeah, but you're really smart, like a genius IQ or something. You got a PhD at Berkeley. I'm trying to get into Turkey Tech for a teaching credential. They're not too happy with my transcript."

Well, that beauty I just passed back should really improve your prospects.

Wade smiled noncommittally. "I hope you did better on the exam today than you did on the term paper."

"Oh, I'm sure I did. I studied my ass off yesterday."

Perfect time to start. Why waste January through most of May?

"When will you be finished grading the finals?"

Sometime after *I start, presumably.* "Would you like me to grade yours right now while you wait?"

This old chestnut almost never failed to drive them away.

"You mean, like right in front of me? Right now?"

Wade nodded, pulled a poison pen out of his pocket, and clicked to declare his readiness to deliver swift justice.

"Oh, I could never stand that kind of pressure."

Wade clicked the pen again and put it back in his pocket. "You might have to wait a few days for the results then." He almost let it go, but couldn't resist the addition: "Unless you'd care to grade your own exam."

She stared at him for a moment as if trying to divine whether the offer were genuine. Wade had put it out there a few times in the past, just to mess with grade grubbers who were pissing him off, but no one had ever called his bluff yet.

"Could I? Would you trust me to do that?"

Fuck. A first time for everything.

"Sure," Wade said. "The only catch is you'd have to grade the rest of the finals, too. That's only fair to the rest of the students, right? Can you have them back to me tomorrow?"

"Oh, okay, then I'll have to say no. I have to work tonight. I got a promotion, and I'm moving up to—"

A rim job for the—

"—assistant manager. I'll have to leave the grading to you. Please feel free to take your time. I'm sure you'll be more than fair."

Wade nodded, prying his eyes off the heaving cleavage on display.

"I'd really like to get to know you better, though. Maybe we could meet sometime, you know, for a drink or whatever."

"I don't think that would be a good idea. I'm married," Wade said, even though he hadn't felt very married for many months now. At least Angela's letter meant they weren't divorced yet.

"Oh, that's okay: I'm married, too." So much for the boyfriend Wade had invented and wasted a blowjob on. "I didn't say it had to be anything serious or permanent or anything like that."

Wade took a step back. Monica and her tits moved closer to take up the space. *Maybe the mountains* would *come to Mohammed.*

"Am I making you—"

Crazy? Angry? Horny? All of the above?

"—uncomfortable?"

"Not at all. It's just that—"

"Seriously, Dr. Wade, don't you think Hemingway would say *yes* if I asked *him* to meet me for a drink?"

Wade tried to consider the question fairly. "He'd be almost a hundred and twenty years old by now, but yeah, I have to admit, he'd probably be up for it. I'm sure he'd treat you to a Papa Doble or two."

"I bet that's not all he'd treat me to. But he'd be the one getting the real treat. I really am fabulous in bed."

"I'm sure you are," Wade said, and wished immediately that he hadn't.

She batted her eyes goofily, clutched the one-dollar volume to her D+ bosom, then leaned in quickly and, before he could move out of range, planted a smooch, which Wade's frantic pivot managed to divert from his lips to a cheek. She pressed something into his pocket as he turned away from her to expedite her exit by pulling the door open, only to find Juke Jackson about to step through it.

"Here," Monica said, on her way past Jackson out the doorway, scooping up and handing him the evaluation form she had tried to give to Wade. "You can add this to the other rave reviews."

Jackson watched her leave, then said, "That okay? Should I go back and turn this one in, too?"

Why not? Maybe she had told the dean how fabulous he was in . . . class.

Wade nodded, then shook his head. Girls like Monica could do that to you.

"Didn't want to break no rules, get you in trouble. Look like you got some lipstick on your face."

Wade reached for the spot where her lips had landed. He came away red-handed.

Jackson laughed. "You got more chicks than Wilt and Magic, Doc. Can't even leave you alone at work."

"She wants to pass this class."

"She gonna make it?"

"My grading policies are strictly confidential." *Shit, I sound like Carlotta Baynes.*

"I need to pass this class, too. Should I kiss the other cheek?"

Wade put his hand on his face again, this time with benefit of handkerchief. "Only if you wipe off your lipstick first."

Jackson accompanied Wade to his office. When he stuffed the hankie back into his pocket and fished for his key, Wade bumped into whatever Monica had slipped in there. He pulled out a crumpled note. Three phone numbers were written on it, each with a helpful annotation:

> This is my home number, if my husband answers, tell him you're my gynecologist and I'm due for a check-up. (JK, LOL)

> This is work, don't call me at this number.

> This is my cell, I'll have it on 24/7 until I hear from you.

> P.S. I'll do ANYTHING to pass this class.

Wade showed Jackson the note, took it back, tore it in half, tore the pieces again, and deposited them in his wastebasket, then rubbed his hands with a theatrical flourish. He debated whether to direct Jackson to do the same with the evaluation form he was still holding onto.

"Damn, Doc. You a better man than I am. She hot."

"I probably shouldn't have done that."

"You havin' second thoughts already?"

"I might need the evidence at my next sexual discrimination trial."

"I got you covered. I'll be your witness. You ready to go to San Fran? You probably safe there. Mostly gays, you know."

"I went to San Francisco State, remember?"

"Yeah, but that was back in the day." Jackson spotted the photo he had taken of Wade with Norma, on his desk. "Man, even the switch-hitters around here can't keep their hands off you."

"Another dream come true." And another option for his epitaph: *A man beloved of lesbians.*

"You ready to roll?"

"Born ready. I might need to grade some papers on the way. I tried to outsource them, but it didn't pan out."

"That's cool. I got one more final, some studyin' to do."

The Giants had offered to supply transportation, but fearing complications with the NCAA before the impending playoffs, Allenby had hired a limo and a driver instead to deliver Jackson and Wade to the ballpark in San Francisco. It was perhaps overprotection, but after what had happened to Bo Jackson for accepting the Tampa Bay Bucs' hospitality before his baseball eligibility at Auburn had expired, Allenby wasn't taking any chances. The driver picked them up on campus, as arranged, and they headed out. Wade couldn't quite fathom the distinction between which billionaires the NCAA's panjandrums would blame if they got a burr up their ass, but he didn't quibble with the perquisite of getting his finals marked while a professional dealt with the lunatics vying to annihilate them on the freeways. While Jackson studied, Wade graded for a steady hour before looking up into the traffic. Jackson laughed when Wade expressed his relief at being spared the complications that might have resulted from taking Aborto, as they bounced in cushioned luxury across the cavernous potholes of the Altamont Pass.

"Do you have any idea how much roadside service in the Bay Area costs? We'd probably blow through half of your signing bonus right there."

Jackson wouldn't be able to sign anything until CSU's season ended, but it was estimated that the Giants were going to pay him several million dollars just to put his name on a contract. This seemed like a good time to remind him about the lessons to be gleaned from the high finances of other athletes. Curt Schilling had recently filed for bankruptcy after earning multiple millions in his career and many millions more from endorsements and investments—before they had turned spectacularly sour. Kareem Abdul Jabbar's misadventures with his Arabian horses jumped out in Wade's memory, too, and he shared that cautionary tale with the multi-millionaire to be as well.

"Don't worry," Jackson said. "I wasn't sleepin' in that business class you made me take. It's all goin' into blue-chip stocks and DRIPs—"

"That's good to hear."

"—'cept for the fifty thou or so I blow when I take my CSU boys to Vegas after we win the College World Series. A couple thousand apiece to get 'em rollin', then they're on their own. That sound about right?"

"Perfect. Put a nickel in his busk kit for Pete Rose for me if you see him signing napkins at the craps table."

They hit gridlock for a bit on the last leg of the trip, but Wade found that getting stuck in traffic in a limo with someone else driving and an open bar at hand was considerably less distressing than his previous debacles behind the wheel in the City by the Bay. Eventually they made it to Willie Mays Plaza, and Wade nudged Jackson as they passed the eponymous statue, as always, one of the highlights of this trip.

When he was introduced to the general manager and a trio of other executives in a conference room inside the ballpark, Jackson followed the script he had roughed out with Wade, a preliminary draft for the press conference that would be held when he inked his contract: a blend of emphasis on the exalted tradition of the team he would be joining, credit to his CSU teammates and coaches, and commitment to finishing a degree. Listening nearby with approval, Wade saw Jackson abruptly stop and look over the heads of the officials in apparent surprise. Wade turned his head to follow Jackson's eyes to the back of the room. A tall, beefy black man in his late thirties or early forties had stepped into the room and was offering a smile and a thumbs up—to his *son*, Wade instantly knew.

Jackson looked back down, finished the sentence he had been in the middle of, and then turned to address the GM directly. "There's someone else here today I'd like to acknowledge."

Wade swiveled to see the prodigal father's smile widen. Good for him. The kid was going to let the past go and introduce—

"Dr. Malcolm Wade is my teacher and also my friend. I wouldn't be here today without his help. Big Giants fan, too. I wanted to introduce him to you all."

Wade shook hands all around, then tilted his head up in mid-hug to project into Jackson's ear. "Thank you. But you should introduce your father, too. He's here for you."

"He's here to cash in," Jackson whispered back.

"Give him a chance to do the right thing." Wade disengaged from Jackson's embrace and looked again to the back of the room. Jackson's father had disappeared.

Later they were escorted into the clubhouse to meet players from the current team—and a few others. There, waiting with an autographed bat and glove for Jackson, was the greatest all-around player who ever drew breath. Wade stood clear to give

Jackson private time with the legend, then gulped and almost fainted when Jackson waved him over to join them. Wade was still on cloud nine when they took their seats in the stands later.

"It's too bad the president couldn't come with us," Jackson said. "I owe him big-time, too."

"I can't wait to tell him who I shook hands with."

"I want you to have this bat and glove."

Even for Wade, who paid almost zero attention to material goods, this offer took his breath away. "I can't take these. He gave these to you. I've got a ball, anyway," he said, knowing even as he spoke the words, without ever having considered the matter for a single second before, to whom he would be bequeathing it.

"Take them," Jackson said. "I want you to have them. I'm sure he'll sign some more stuff for me if I ask him."

Wade called up instantly some of the many stories he had heard of his hero's legendary generosity: offering others, if not literally the shirt off his back, then anything they wanted out of his closet; giving the glove with which he'd made the most famous catch in history to a six-year-old (*You take good care of it, and it will take good care of you*); his plan to give the bat with which he had hit four home runs in one game in Milwaukee to the teammate who had recommended it, before it was pilfered from the visiting locker room. With no intention of keeping it, Wade reverently touched the grail Jackson handed to him, put it on, pounded his fist into the pocket, and was transported back to Little League days. Somewhere, stuffed away in a closet Angela hadn't raided yet, was the MacGregor USA model Wade's father had bought for him, with a stamped version of the same hallowed signature. He told Jackson now about showing it off to the neighborhood kids, how everyone wanted to borrow it and wear it when they played.

"You make some good catches with it?"

"If only." Wearing it hadn't helped Wade's defense any more than Air Jordans would have helped him to fly.

They watched the Giants beat the Marlins, who were missing Dee Gordon and Giancarlo Stanton, two players Wade would have paid to see. Afterward, as they were preparing to head home, the expensively tailored Giants' junior executive who had steered their earlier movements approached them again. "There's someone else who wants to talk to you."

Wade started to accompany Jackson back to the clubhouse, but the exec said, "He just wants to meet with Juke."

The disappearing father again, then. Wade looked at Jackson and guessed that he had made the same conjecture.

"You okay to chill in the limo for a few?"

Wade nodded and headed out to the car, carrying Jackson's gifts. For all the pride he had derived from acknowledgment of his role, he felt like an interloper, a man who had come between a father and his son. Why did he so often find himself in the wrong place at the wrong time? It should have been Jackson's father sharing this ride and this day with him. The driver let Wade into the back seat and then strode off for a bathroom break before the return trip. A few minutes later a tap on the tinted window interrupted Wade's self-flagellation. He wrestled with the controls, cursed technology, and then finally figured out how to lower the window.

Jackson's father stood beside the car, puffing on a cigarette. He threw it down as Wade looked out in surprise. If *he* was here, who the hell had his son been summoned to meet? Wade put a hand out the window and started to introduce himself.

"I know who you are," Jackson Senior said, ignoring the outstretched hand. "I heard the boy in there."

Wade nodded and tried to figure out what to say next. "Do you need a ride home?" He wasn't sure he was authorized to offer a detour to Stockton, but it was the first thing he could think of.

"I got my Benz," Jackson Senior said, with a vague nod toward the parking lot. A hundred feet away, his son reappeared, shaking hands with the young exec, and then turning to head toward them. Senior came closer to the car window, leaned in a bit, and pointed toward the artifacts on the back seat. "That shit there worth serious money. You need help makin' a deal, you give me a call."

He passed through the window a battered business card with an email address and phone number crossed out and two new phone numbers written in. "My home and my office on there. Call anytime."

As father headed toward son, the driver came back from his break. Jackson signaled that he would return to the limo shortly and then walked off a short distance from it with his father. They spoke briefly, parting with neither handshake nor hug.

"What did he want with you?" Jackson asked as soon as he had taken his seat next to Wade. "You didn't give him any money, did you?"

"Just wanted to share his business acumen." Wade showed him the altered card. Jackson glanced at it but didn't try to take it. "I offered him a chance to upgrade his ride."

"His ride? He drivin' his girlfriend's car."

"Who was it you had to go meet with in private?"

"Barry B. wanted to meet me."

"Holy shit, Batman."

"He coachin' for Miami now."

Wade nodded, wondering how long *that* would last.

"I think they want me to pitch here," Jackson said, "but he say if I go for outfield, he be glad to help me with my fieldin' and hittin'."

Wade decided to stick with the stats and set emotions aside. "He was the smartest hitter I've ever seen, or one-two with Joe Morgan anyway."

Jackson nodded. "What I heard. I only saw him at the end of his career. Too bad about the . . . other stuff."

Too bad he was such an asshole, too. Wade tried again to rise above and celebrate the moment. "If he wants to teach you, maybe that's another way for him to give something back to the game."

"He gave me his cell number, you believe that?"

Wade wasn't sure whether he believed it or not. He hadn't quite figured out Jackson's sense of humor yet, and no one had figured out Barry's. If in fact a phone number had been supplied, Wade wondered if a call placed to it might wake up George W. Bush in Texas, the new commissioner in New York, or the Grand Imperial Wizard in Bumfuck, Mississippi.

He also wondered what Jackson had said to his father. What could you say to a dad like that? *Thank you for not aborting me?*

Before long Jackson brought it up himself.

"He heard about my baby. Want to know when he gonna meet her."

Wade looked for the silver lining. "Maybe he wants to redeem himself, as a grandfather, for the way he—"

"He already got four other grandbabies, never done shit for none of 'em."

"What did you tell him, then?"

"Just told him I was gonna be a better father to her than he ever was to me."

"And what did he say to that?"

"Just laughed. Then he say, *Words is easy. It's more work than it look like, bein' a daddy.*"

Wade nodded. Out of his realm again, he said anyway, "He just might be right about that."

Jackson plugged in his headphones and picked up his text-book. Wade switched a reading lamp on and graded some more finals, learning that Zelda Fitzgerald was "the crazy nympho who dumped Hemingway for his best friend." Malcolm Cowley was "the British actor who played Frederic Henry in the first (very cheesy) film version of FAREWELL TO THE ARMY." When he came to Jackson's exam, Wade hesitated, then, noting that his co-passenger was still absorbed in his music and/or test prep, plunged in. Not too bad, he decided, when he reached the end. A solid C, which confirmed a passing grade for the course. He slid the exam over for a look, with the grade circled at the top. Jackson studied it, pushed the headphones back, and pursed his lips; for a moment Wade thought he was going to argue for a B.

"Thanks for showin' me this. I see what I messed up on. Look like I got the themes and shit down pretty good, though, don't it?"

Wade nodded.

"You're a good teacher, Doc."

Wade started to grade the exam from Monica, fabulous in bed, but decided to quit while he was ahead when he read that she was "rooting for the whale" in *The Old Man and the Sea*. Evidently she was counting on special consideration for ward-robe malfunctions and directory listings to get her through the class. He turned the lamp off and attempted to sleep, with the usual result. He tried one of his mostly useless tricks, counting his blessings: *I'm riding in a limo, not driving ass-deep in drug-crazed Bay Area road ragers, and if Juke and I get killed tonight, it won't be my fault. Juke passed my class, and I'm 'a good teacher,' or at least not complete shit at it. Allenby doesn't have cancer. Barry B. might not be such a creep after all. I SHOOK HANDS WITH WILLIE MAYS.* The only thing that could make this day better would be if Angela were waiting for him in his bed when he got home. Then, as usual when he lingered too long in Beldingsville, he slipped to the flip side: *What if Brenda's waiting in my bed?* He recalled a distant Thanksgiving, after their break-up, when she had ambushed him with a pop-in and then tried to woo him back by sharing her stash. They had nearly set the bed on fire, and not with lovemaking.

Wade gave up on sleep, set Monica aside, and picked up the exam from his graphic arts enthusiast, who had responded to a question inviting him to write an alternate ending to one of the novels by airlifting Robert Jordan from the grim final pages of *For Whom the Bell Tolls* to wall off the alien zombies invading Earth from the planet Trumpexico. Wade was glad again to be safe in the limo.

When they reached home, the driver first dropped off Jackson, who tried once more to press on Wade the bat and glove. Wade held firm in refusing them. He would need no new memorabilia to enshrine this day in his recall. Another man who had shaken hands with Willie Mays today, but not with his own father, shook with Wade and said goodnight. Wade gave the driver his address.

No one was waiting in his bed.

CHAPTER 25

It's a shame that the only thing a man can do for eight hours
a day is work. He can't eat for eight hours; he can't drink for
eight hours; he can't make love for eight hours. The only
thing a man can do for eight hours is work.

—William Faulkner

Be grateful for the life you have rather than regret the one
you don't.

—Edward Everett, in Joseph Schuster's *The
Might Have Been*

After turning in his semester grades, Wade stopped in at the
dean's office, formerly his wife's, now Erica's, to retrieve his student evaluation forms. He was startled to find there another old
familiar face.

"Don't ever retire," Clara Shelby said, by way of greeting.
"It bites. How many hours a day can you spend cleaning your
house anyway?"

Wade had never quite got straight on the difference between
the median and the mean, but in either case, he was pretty sure,

the honest answer for him was not far from zero. He nodded sympathetically anyway.

"I tried to keep busy," Clara continued, "but my ingrate relations tossed me out on the street. Good thing no Greyhound was comin' along, or they'd have thrown me right under it. Told me to put my teeth in, go back to work, and earn my keep. Plus they didn't want me teachin' the great-grandkids any more Alabama cuss words."

"It's great to have you back. We missed—"

"Of course you did. When Wiley got this job, she knew it was too big for her. Too big for anyone without me, really."

"You sound like someone the Republicans want to nominate."

"If you want to get your butt whipped, young man, keep talking that way."

Wade balled his fists, bobbed and weaved, made himself a little dizzy. Erica emerged from her office. "Look who's back," she said to Wade, beaming at Clara.

"I see," Wade said. "I guess she couldn't get along without us after all."

"I'm right here, you know. You don't have to talk about me in the third person, like I'm dead or fired or sent to the glue factory, like Gordo and Deadass." She studied Wade through her trifocals. "When's your crazy wife comin' back, anyway?"

"Good question," Wade said. "I wish I knew the—"

"Screw wishing," Clara said. "Get yourself on a plane and fetch her bony ass back where she belongs. If she knows I'm back to get all the work done, she'll probably hightail it back here anyway." She stood up from behind her desk. "I'm goin' to lunch. Want me to bring you two back anything?"

Just that same sweet politic disposition.

"No foolin' around in the office while I'm gone. You're probably horny as hell, your wife gone so long," she said to Wade, before turning to Erica, "and this one is as sexy as ever, but I don't want to have to spend my first week back here diggin' you two out of some goddam scandal." She shook a finger at them, Babu to Seinfeld, on her way out the door.

"How the hell did you pull *that* off?" Wade asked, as soon as Clara was out of earshot.

"About a month ago, I decided to give it another try. Nearly a whole academic year had passed, the paperwork was piling up on me, and I just thought maybe she might . . . miss us, half as much as—"

"Miss having us to boss around, you mean?"

"Apparently the kinfolk are less amenable to following orders."

"Well, anyway, congratulations. Quite a coup."

"I owe it to Arthur. He sent her a personal note to accompany mine. You might recall that when she left before, she took off so fast that we didn't even have time to arrange a farewell luncheon or a gift. Arthur had our notes delivered with her choice of a plane ticket to come back or a new car, to replace that jalopy she's been driving since the Reagan Administration—and she picked the ticket."

"Sharp as ever, I see. I'm glad you got past the—"

"It turns out I was wrong about her reason for leaving. It wasn't about me. It had to do with Angela."

"Angela? What the hell did *she* ever do?" *Other than star in the filthiest footage ever caught on tape.*

"Clara was upset that Angela didn't ask her to move up with her to this office, when she got the dean slot."

"Oh, crap. That was my fault, then," Wade said. "Angela asked me about it, and I told her I thought Clara was set for life in the English job."

"I guess we should just have asked her," Erica said. "In any case, I'm glad she told me, and I'm really glad she came back. She knows this place inside and out."

Wade nodded. "Where the bodies are buried. Probably even where the gold fillings were extracted and how much they came to."

"Exactly. She's going to be a big help. Especially if I keep this job, or—I don't suppose you *have* heard any more from Angela?"

"Just the letter I told you about. What about you? Have you had any indication at all of what she plans to do about CSU?"

"Nothing. Her leave of absence is officially open-ended, but we'll need to do something about her position soon, especially with Arthur . . . leaving us. If nothing else, we need to find out soon if she's planning to teach that Joyce-Faulkner course she put herself on the fall schedule for."

Wade had forgotten that Angela had arranged the class, and he guessed that she might have forgotten as well. "If she wants to come back, would you go back to being the English chair?"

Erica smiled. "There's a chance I might be moving in the other direction."

Wade was puzzled. "You mean—"

"The Board has asked me to consider stepping in as president."

"Holy—"

"That's pretty much what I said," Erica finished for him, deleting his expletive as was her way.

"What else did you say?"

"I haven't said *no* yet. Arthur has encouraged me to consider it. He promised to help out with the fundraising. He says the Cubs are heading for the World Series this year, and our country's finally going to have a woman calling the shots, so why not a woman on top at CSU, too? I guess he told them good things about my work as interim dean, and—"

"That's crazy!" Wade liked the Cubs' chances a lot better than the country's. "You'll vault right over the vice-presidents and—"

"In fairness, Arthur fired most of them."

"—go from department chair to president in less than—"

"Slow down, Wade. I haven't said *yes* yet, either. I'm still thinking it over. Clara would be a big help to me, of course, but it might actually depend to some extent on what Angela decides to do—and on what *you* decide to do."

"How's that?"

"Well, if I move up, and Angela comes back as dean, we'll still need a new English Department chair. One of the things I've learned this year is just how screwed up that department is. I could use your help in getting it straightened out. I know you turned down the chair before, but I was thinking maybe you'd reconsider under the circumstances, given the team we'd be putting together."

"You mean, as in I get to report to my wife and my best friend?"

"Thank you. I'm honored."

"But that sounds sort of like the deal I already have."

"*Had*," Erica said. "Arthur's leaving, remember? He thought maybe you'd be . . . more secure tucked into the English Department, where you have your degree, than continuing in the Athletic Department"—*given your history there* hung in the air between them, Erica too gracious to say what Wade knew she was thinking—"without his oversight. Those student evaluations from your Hemingway class looked pretty impressive, by the way."

She handed them over, and Wade thumbed through them indifferently. Allowing students to grade their teachers was sort of like putting the privates in charge of planning the invasion when they had barely been trained to clean the latrine.

According to his students, Wade was "cool, moody, awesome, boring, helpful, harsh on papers, too lenient on papers, easy to understand, hard to follow, in love with Hemingway, in love with the jock in the class, in love with the chick with the rack, in love with himself, humorous, blasphemous, too vocabularious, always available for extra help, unavailable whenever I went to his office" (for this Wade suspected Cartoon Man, who had once left a note on his office door indicating that he'd stopped by at 6:00 p.m. on a Friday to offer Wade first crack at the animated sequel to "The Snows of Kilimanjaro" he'd shot on his cell phone and hoped to substitute for a term paper), "sympathetic to my health problems, unsympathetic to my issues with getting to class on time and having to leave a little early once in a while—I work for a living!"

"About the usual mix," Wade said. "The ones who do well love you; the ones who struggle punish you for it. Some of them read a book like Mussolini."

Erica frowned. "You'll have to refresh my—"

"The first three pages, the last three, and three in the middle—all you need, according to *Il Duce. Der Führer* also gave the plan his seal of approval." *And, coming soon to the White House . . .*

"Nice company you've been keeping. But there are lots of good comments in there too."

"It's not all bad news," Wade conceded. He told her about Norma's reconnection with him this semester. "If they knew how much it means to us, do you think more students would come back to say *thank you* or just to let us know how they're doing?"

Erica shrugged. "Maybe not. Most people focus on themselves. It's natural; it's normal."

"All those hours we pour into their writing, into their lives, all that effort to connect, to motivate, to spark something in them—almost all of it goes unacknowledged."

"It's the way of the world, Wade. Look at all the soldiers who come home and can't get a job. After all they've been through in

Afghanistan or Iraq, do we care enough to make sure they can make a decent living here?"

Wade nodded. "Or even to make sure that they get the medical treatment that they need." He thought of Cenon, one of the *lucky* ones, who had survived his wounds and received the expert care required to rebuild his life. How many of his brethren were jobless or homeless or both, their PTSD untreated, their lives ruined by their sacrifice?

"Just appreciate the ones who do come back, knowing that you made a difference in their lives," Erica said. "There might be lots more like Norma that you've helped, some who don't even really understand what you were trying to do for them. I know you've enjoyed your role in counseling the athletes, but there are lots of other students who need your help with their reading and writing. If you came back full-time to English, you could help more of them."

"I'll think about it," Wade said, thinking again about the way his father had sabotaged his own life with his administrative path. Maybe, though, a department chair job would be less burdensome than the superintending responsibilities his father had taken on. He wondered what Angela would say about it. *If only she were fucking here to say anything.*

"What about you and Allenby?" he asked. Wade wondered how much she knew about their mutual friend's health scare.

Another shrug. "I've sent my traveling man packing. Now that there won't be any further workplace issues to complicate the relationship between Arthur and me, we'll see how it goes."

It also couldn't hurt any that Allenby's third wife was also officially off the active roster. Wade pictured briefly the prospect of his two best friends uniting: he had little faith in permanence of any kind, but it was at least a possibility to look forward to.

Maybe even somewhere to go for Thanksgiving if Angela never came home.

On his way out, Wade rapped his knuckles on the secretary's desk and then leaned back in through Erica's door. "You realize, of course, if you become the president, Clara will be running the whole school."

"Of course I will," Clara said, as she came in behind him, carrying aromatic bags. No one had ever said anything at CSU that didn't get back to her in ten minutes anyway. "And I'm gonna be too busy doin' it to put a Band-Aid on your boo-boos or pull your head out of your ass if you get it stuck in there again, so you'll just have to finally let your balls drop and look after yourself. Here's a hamburger. Your wife probably doesn't let you eat these, so take advantage of this while she's gone—and then get on a damn jet and go get her!"

Wade waved goodbye to Erica, saluted Clara, gobbled the burger, and then went to find Allenby, who was cleaning out his office but stopped to hear about Wade's evening with Jackson and the Giants. He sat down behind his desk and gestured Wade into a chair.

"If you happen to be looking for a new financial advisor, here's a candidate to consider." Wade reached into his pocket for the business card that had been pressed on him and proffered it.

Allenby set the specimen at arm's length on his desk, looking as if he wanted to reach for the bottle of hand sanitizer at its edge. "Jackson's father?"

"Biologically."

"I hope Juke won't throw too much of his money down that rathole."

"I wouldn't worry too much about that."

"He's already down fifty thousand."

Wade blinked. *The casino was a joke, right? And that was on the way* back *from—*

Allenby smiled. "He pledged the fifty thou to our Marcus Fund, as soon as he signs his contract." Allenby and Wade had started a scholarship fund in memory of Marcus Foster, after the CSU quarterback had been killed trying to break up a fight between a teammate and gang members. "Was that your idea?"

Wade shook his head. "He knew about Marcus, but I never told him about the scholarship."

Allenby nodded. "Kid's got a big heart. I hope his brain measures up, too. He's twenty years old, and he's looking at a bonus of several million bucks. Do you think the big money will screw him up?"

"I've been thinking about the same question. Hard to say how that kind of money will affect someone so young. Hemingway was offered a long-term deal in his twenties. He turned it down, thought it would mess up his future work. Then he worried about bills, off and on, for the rest of his life, like everybody else—well, *almost* everybody else."

Allenby smiled, deflecting the reference to his own success, as usual. "How is your next best seller coming, anyway?"

Wade thought of Jackson's father again; his own *writing career* was about as promising as Jackson Senior's international business prospects. Time for a reality check. "I sent it to your friend, the guy who published the last one. He more or less told me I should stick with literature and leave writing about sports to the sportswriters."

Allenby pursed his lips. "That's just one opinion. There are other publishers."

"It's not exactly the first rejection letter I've received."

Getting a book published, let alone a best seller, was like stepping into the batter's box with two outs in the ninth inning against Mariano Rivera. Oh, and by the way, the count is 0-2 because the poor fuck you're pinch-hitting for in mid-at-bat just fouled a ball off his groin on the way to the DL (dickless list). It was really hard to hit a home run. That damn cutter was more likely to saw the bat off in your hands and leave you grasping the handle, praying that no shards from it had punctured an artery, wishing you were safe in the dugout watching someone else attempt the impossible.

Wade had read that out of all the many thousands trying to wrest a living from writing books in the U.S., only a few hundred achieved a level of financial success that obviated the need for other employment. Most books sat on the shelf and were rarely read anyway. In the days when library books had check-out cards, Wade had often noted a gap of many months or even years between readers. Ten years after the publication of *The Sound and the Fury*, Faulkner's novels had been out of print, where they remained until the rescue mission by Malcolm Cowley (the scholar, not the thespian). Cowley's contemporary Clifton Fadiman had dismissed *Absalom, Absalom!* as *the last blow-up of what was once a remarkable, if minor, talent.* (Faulkner: *A few critics are worth reading. Not many.*) The only indisputable genius ever to emerge from American letters had resorted to hack work in Hollywood to feed his family. Many of the authors publishing fiction today supported themselves with a sinecure in an MFA program, profiting from luring others down the same path, which seemed not altogether unlike a Ponzi scheme: there couldn't be teaching jobs for *all* of them, could there? Unless you could get James Patterson to slip you the formula and stick his name on your cover as co-author, your chances of a big payday were even worse than the prospects of making it out of high school or college ball onto a farm team, never mind between the lines at Yankee Stadium.

"Maybe I should just stick with teaching. It's not such a bad way to make a living."

It seemed absurd to tout the contentments of academic life to someone like Allenby, who before his brief return to it had engaged the *real world* so fulsomely, had been to war and back, had beaten down racial barriers to build a corporation, and had created life-sustaining jobs and careers for others. But perhaps it was equally absurd to go through your life comparing yourself to guys like him, paragons whose greater gifts, ambition, and energy had made possible their accomplishments. Maybe there was finally a time to let go of the tension between trying to get better and accepting your limitations, being happy with who you were.

Wade thought about the ironically laconic epitaph Faulkner had suggested for himself: *He made the books and he died.* Yet another option for Wade's tombstone: *He graded the papers and he fell asleep.*

"Finally made your peace with it, huh?"

"You know what they say: *Those who can, do. Those who can't, teach. Those who can't teach, teach education classes. Those who can't do that, become administrators.*"

Allenby laughed. "And those who fail at administration . . . can go back to Vietnam."

Wade shot him a quizzical look. "What the hell are you talking about now?"

Allenby picked a letter off his desk and handed it to Wade. It was an agreement Allenby had signed to join a group of U.S. veterans who would be touring sites in Vietnam and providing assistance in rebuilding efforts there.

"You're really going back?"

Allenby nodded. "I've sent some money before, paid for a few other vets' trips, supported some schools and an orphanage, but I've never gone back myself before. Never could deal with what we—what *I*—did over there."

The other side had done unspeakable things, too, of course, Jane Fonda's endorsement notwithstanding. Wade thought about the nuns buried alive at Huế, the POWs like John McCain brutally tortured. He wondered if, for Allenby, forgiving the VC wouldn't be every bit as hard as forgiving himself.

"Anyway, I'm finally going to face it, stop trying to buy my way out of it."

"I'm sure the money you sent already helped a lot of people there."

Allenby shrugged. "I've been thinking a lot, since the . . . news I got, about the money I've made, and what it has bought or not bought. You know, all the money I made, it didn't buy me an extra day with my dad, a chance to say *thank you* for all those eighty-hour weeks he worked, tell him that I loved him, before he died. It didn't save any of my marriages, didn't make me a better father. Oh, I provided food and shelter and plenty more for all of the wives, both of my daughters, and the shithead stepson, too, you know that. I signed plenty of checks. Gave plenty of advice, nearly all of it unheeded."

Wade recalled the lost cause that had first thrown them together, his former student, the inherited son (back in rehab at last report) whom Allenby had tried to rescue from drugs, indigence, and precipitous marriage, along with the daughters who had rushed into ruinous unions of their own and were now raising their children alone—and on daddy's dime, of course.

"With daughters, it's hard," Allenby continued. "You look at every guy they bring home and you remember what you wanted to do with every girl you met when you were that age, and of course no guy is good enough. I told them to take their time, find the right guy, be smarter about marriage than I was. I guess it was—*I was*—a classic case of *Do as I say, not as I—*"

"You did all anyone could to help your family," Wade said. "You even helped me, treated me like family."

"Thank you for saying that. It's nice to be appreciated once in a while. I've got five grandchildren, and not one of them can pick up the phone or stick a note in the mail to say thank you for a birthday check or a tuition payment. All of them seem to need a new computer or a new car every year. The ten-year-old wants a pony now, if you can believe that. It's not that I can't afford it, you know that, too, and of course you don't do those things for the thanks you expect anyway, but it's just that they seem so . . . blasé about anything that anyone does for them. Why are they so worried about a new car or a computer or a fucking horse instead of how they're contributing to the fate of the planet? It's not the legacy I expected to leave."

"You're still creating your own legacy," Wade reminded him. "Your *Kilroy was here* won't be determined by your kids or your grandkids. Look what you've achieved just right here at CSU. You didn't fail."

"The BOT is holding up my ROTC plan, even though I told them I would fund it myself. Afraid of too many protests."

"Maybe you should get the campus Greeks involved," Wade said. "Combine it with their Naked Carwash Week."

"Good call. Get a few more of our fraternity and sorority leaders into uniform, our pols might be a little less reckless about sending them off to tangle with the Taliban."

Allenby thought there should be a law: no one who hadn't served in a war should be allowed to start one. By *served* he meant *fought*, not flew a desk or bunny hops in the backyard, but on the field of battle in unforgiving alien lands had seen and smelled and touched, perhaps even tasted, the blasted guts and brains and eyes and limbs, like Cenon Aquino's, that would never be whole again because of decisions made by the individual safe at the top of the chain of command. It made sense to Wade.

"Whatever happens with *that* proposal, you kept the accrediting team from shutting this place down, saved the baseball team, hired four great new coaches, got rid of redundant deans and veeps, a useless doofus top cop, *and* Carlotta Baynes—"

Allenby shook his head. "Looks like she'll get the last laugh after all. MSNBC just signed her to host her own talk show. I understand she's already made an appointment with a Hollywood dentist to get a new set of choppers for the gig. Get this: she invited me to come on as her first guest."

"No hard feelings, huh? Don't be surprised if she tries to give you a jump on the air."

"Whatever it takes to bump the ratings."

"Maybe she can interview the guy who wrote her dissertation, too."

"Maybe. You might be on her list, too. Have to do something about your clothes, though, if you go on TV."

Wade stuck a display finger under his chin and struck a pose. "Angela says this face was made for radio, anyway."

"Hard to argue with her there. When is she coming home?"

After their evening of wassail, Wade had told him again about the letter, but didn't have anything to add now. "Soon, I hope."

Allenby looked like he didn't know what to say about that either. "I hope so, too. I hope you two can work things out."

"Thanks." Wade stood to go and let him get back to packing. "I hope it goes okay for you . . . in Vietnam."

Allenby shrugged again and stood for a goodbye shake. "Can't be worse than the last time I was there."

Wade headed out, then paused in the doorway. "If I get back to Nebraska with our baseball team, I'll see if I can snag you a pair of those snazzy red pants."

"In that case I may just stay in Hanoi."

Wade walked home, pondering his prospects without Allenby at CSU and wondering if Erica could protect him half as well. At the threshold he stopped short when he saw his front door ajar. That likely meant one of two things: if he was lucky, a burglar was ransacking the house and lurking inside with a tire iron to beat him within an inch of his life; the alternative was that Brenda and Tommy had coked out, broken in, and waited within to bushwhack him with a Gatorade shower on the living room rug. *Pick your poison.* The only other possibility was—

The most beautiful face in the world suddenly appeared in the doorway, framed in shafts of golden sunlight. Bells rang and the angels sang from above.

"I'm home, Wade," Angela said. "Are you coming in, or are you just going to stand out there twiddling your dick?"

CHAPTER 26

Here's your happy ending.

—Thomas Fowler to Phuong, in Graham
Greene's *The Quiet American*

Thou wilt be condemned into everlasting redemption
for this.

—Dogberry, *Much Ado about Nothing*, IV.ii

Angela pulled the door wide open. Lightheaded, blinded by the sun, Wade lost his balance, stumbled, almost fell down, then swayed against her, nearly knocking her to the floor as well. He couldn't believe his blasted eyes. She was *so* pale, so thin—

"What the fuck are you doing, Wade?"

So Angela.

After all these months to prepare, he couldn't figure out what he wanted to say. He called in a ghostwriter: *"Of all the gin joints in all the towns in all the world, she had to walk into—"*

"*Casablanca*. Not cool, Wade. We disqualified that movie two years ago, remember? Too fucking easy."

"I guess I forgot" *what you look like, what you smell like, what your voice sounds like, and WHAT THE HELL HAPPENED TO YOU?*

"Could you please stop looking at me like I just climbed out of my fucking casket?"

"Sorry." Wade realized he was crying and reached up to wipe his eyes with a sleeve. Angela started crying, too. "It's just so great to see you again," he finally said. "I can't believe you're actually here. I thought you were a burglar. I was going to kick your ass with some of those karate moves you taught me." Wade essayed a brief demo and nearly wound up on the floor again.

"Sorry to disappoint you, Elvis. Still coming up short, I see. Are you ever going to kiss me?"

Wade hopped to and put his arms around her. He tried to be gentle but felt like he was embracing a wounded bird.

She stepped back. "Those psychotropics nearly did me in. I didn't want you to see me again until I got back to a hundred pounds, but . . . I couldn't stay away any longer."

"I'm glad. I think there's some champagne in the fridge. Let me—"

"I'm an alcoholic, Wade. I can't drink anymore."

"Of course, of course. That was stupid of me." Wade almost reached up to smack himself in the forehead. "I'll . . . quit, too, then. Today." He said it before he had even thought about it, but he knew he meant it, knew he could do it, if it meant she was really back, if it meant she would stay. "How about a sasparilla instead?"

"Sounds great."

"Too bad. We don't have any."

"Asshole."

"I'll see if there's some apple juice that hasn't fermented yet."

"Fuck the apple juice. Just sit down and put your arms around me again."

They sat down on the couch, Angela almost in his lap, Wade remembering a thousand other occasions in the same perfect place.

"I opened some windows. It smells like monkeys have been fucking in here. Did Brenda and Tommy move in after all?"

"Tommy died," Wade said, "but he came back as the Holy Crap. I thought I was doing pretty well with the housekeeping."

Angela ran a finger along a lamp stand and then under his nose.

"I flunked dusting," Wade admitted. "But I've had the maid in every—"

"What have you been doing about food? I didn't see much fit for human consumption in the kitchen. You've lost weight, too, haven't you?"

"I've been on the popcorn diet. My wife's been out of"— *her mind*—"town. Thank God for the microwave. Man's true best friend."

"Figures. Lazy fuck. Thanks for your letter, by the way," Angela said. "You must have stayed up all night working on that."

Wade shrugged. "I was up anyway. You know me and sleep."

"I can tell you the name of every pill in the world that won't help."

"You should have let me come and—"

She shushed him with the dusty digit. "I should've done a million things differently, Wade. In your letter you said you could forgive me."

"I took my cue from Dith Pran."

"*The Killing Fields*," she said automatically. "Did you mean it?"

"Tell me again about Ronnie."

"Later, okay? First, tell *me*: what the fuck happened to your head?"

After years of alternately trying to ignore or disguise his diminishing crop, at his last haircut Wade had decided to take Allenby's advice and go for broke. In the barber's chair, trying not to talk himself out of it, he had closed his eyes and envisioned

Michael Jordan, so heroic in every aspect that he could dispense with his locks and still look like a god. When the shearing was over, he had opened up and wondered how heroic MJ's aspect would be when Wade blocked his shot and knocked him off his donkey.

"What the hell were you thinking? Did you lose another bet?"

"All I'm at liberty to say is that there was a jackass involved."

"Tell me something I don't already—"

"No way of knowing until I gave it a shot. Some guys have skulls that actually look good shaved clean."

"Don't try to tell me other people *like* it on you."

"One of the girls in my Hemingway class said I looked like Ben Kingsley in some gangster flick."

"I thought you were going to say in *Gandhi*."

"It doesn't get any sexier than that."

"How did Hemingway go over, anyway? I forgot you were trying to be a teacher again."

"Not bad. Had some fun, didn't have to flunk too many. Juke Jackson took the class."

"You're shitting me. Isn't that sort of like . . . Benjy's year at Harvard?"

"He's not Benjy, Ange. He did okay. Kept up with the reading and made some progress with his writing."

"Sorry. That was a dumb thing to say. I liked him when—"

"I introduced him to Lara Lewis." Rather than waiting for volleyball season, Wade had plunged in and arranged a coffee date, which had led to an evening out.

"Still playing matchmaker, eh?"

Wade shrugged again. "Seemed like they had a lot in common."

"Hell yeah, they have a lot common. *Perfect* genes. Can you imagine what a beautiful—"

"*It seems to me I've heard that song be—*"

Angela cuffed his Sinatra impersonation to a halt.

"They've had two dates," Wade said. "Let's give them time to grow up and graduate and start their lives before we send out another birth announcement." He figured if he was going to make the commitment he had been contemplating, this was as good a chance as any. "I know you've probably been too . . . busy to think about this, but I've been thinking some more about that . . . project you mentioned."

"*Project*? You mean *baby*?" Angela shook her head. "I don't think any adoption agency in the world would clear me after what my poor brain and body have been through. Not to mention a certain public embarrassment."

"Are you kidding? They give babies to people who have been in prison or on drugs for years. They gave a baby to Madonna, for Christ's sake. Who could be more publicly embarrassing than that?"

She sighed. "I guess I should tell you about Ronnie now."

"Okay." Wade braced himself. "I can't believe you let him come to see you, but you wouldn't let *me*—"

"Oh, Christ, Wade. It was about the fucking tape. I was trying to get it back. That's all there was to it."

"You said he wouldn't—"

"He wouldn't give it to me. So I decided to called his bluff."

"Good for you."

"Yeah, great for me—great for *us*—except . . . he wasn't bluffing."

"What do you mean?"

"When I said *public embarrassment*, I wasn't talking just about my DUI."

"Oh."

"Ronnie uploaded it yesterday. There were eight thousand hits in the first fifteen minutes. It's up to a hundred thousand already."

Wade loosened his grip on her shoulders and swallowed hard. He had always supported in principle, had never really even questioned, the right to distribute adult pornography, just as he had always supported the legalization of prostitution—but principle all of a sudden didn't seem quite so persuasive when your wife was the featured attraction.

"What did Ronnie say to you when he was there, anyway?"

Angela pulled away from him, put her head down, and then looked up again. "You really want to know?"

"That's why I came home today."

"*I* came home, asshole."

"So what did he say?"

"I'm lying there in the bed, all eighty-five pounds of me, barely still in the world; he leans over the bedside and whispers in my ear, *When you get out of this place, come and see me. I'll fuck you so hard your sister will come too.*"

"Must've been quite a turn-on."

"I think he heard it in a movie."

"*Diner,*" Wade said. "It's a variation."

"Where's your famous cell phone, anyway?"

Wade didn't ask why she wanted to know. He went into the bedroom, found it, and brought it back to her.

"It's real, then. Will wonders never cease."

"I got it for you. For your calls"—*that never came*—"I mean," Wade said. "I don't really know how to use it."

"You should get a first-grader to show you." Head bowed again, Angela clutched the mobile, studied her emaciated wrists and forearms, and then spoke without looking up. "So, do you want to watch it?"

Wade didn't have to ask what *it* meant. "I'd rather watch Comanches tear out my intestines," he said. "And barbecue them after. Thanks for the offer, though."

"You might learn something, you know."

Wade laughed in spite of himself. "I'll wait for a hands-on lesson. When you're feeling better."

Angela handed back his phone. "I'm really tired, Wade. That flight totally kicked my ass. I need to take a nap."

She went to lie down. Wade followed her into the bedroom, tossed a blanket over her toes, and kissed her chastely on the forehead.

"Is that the best you can do?"

"When you feeling better," he said again, "I'll show you some tips I picked up in Carlotta's office. Did I mention she's going to have her own TV show?"

Angela yawned. "I bet she'll want to interview me."

"You can go on right after Allenby."

Another yawn. "Sometime I'll tell you about when she hit on me in the Ladies.'"

"Better save it for the show."

She closed her eyes. "No peeking at my tat while I'm napping."

Wade tried for soprano but came out more like strangled cat: "*Keep your filthy paws off my silky drawers.*"

She opened one eye. "Can of corn: *Grease*, Stockard Channing's character."

Wade nodded. "Rizzo. Two points out of three. Welcome home."

Angela went to sleep. Wade called Erica to let her know who was back. He decided he should also give her a heads-up about the latest Internet sensation.

"Way out in front of that, Wade. Clara already told me all about it. The whole campus knows by now. The whole world, really: there've been something like three hundred thousand hits."

Wade sighed. "Good news travels fast. We haven't figured out how we're going to handle it yet, or even talked about her role at CSU."

"I'm just glad she's back and feeling better. This too shall pass. Give her a couple of days, and then we'll make a plan."

"Okay."

Unflappable, as usual, Erica made him feel better, as always.

"The other good news is enrollment in her Joyce/Faulkner class went up 300%."

"I can't imagine why."

Wade let Angela sleep for a couple of hours and then phoned Juke Jackson without waking her. Another hour later he was at their door with a bundle in his arms. Wade told him to ring the bell again and then stepped outside behind him to hide. Jackson had to ring twice more before Angela appeared, brushing hair and sleep out of her eyes. It was love at first sight.

"Who the fuck is there?"

Wade popped out from behind Jackson to perform the introductions.

"Oh, my God! This is the most beautiful baby I've ever seen."

Women always thought babies were beautiful. Wade had never been moved to such pronouncements himself, but even he could tell that this child was something special.

"So, this is sort of a try-out, if you're up for it. Juke is going to leave Arabella here with us for a few days, if you agree. I can call my sister, see if she's free to come help us out, if—"

"Shut up, Wade. I get this beautiful girl all to myself for a few days."

Okay, how do you feel about the next twenty years?

"I got the baby stuff in the car," Jackson said. "You never believe how much stuff you need, take care of a baby."

Wade was about to find out. He walked out to the car with Jackson while Angela took Arabella inside, cooing, without apparent irony or other rhetorical remove, in a way that Wade would never have imagined possible. Jackson handed off two big bags and carried the crib in himself, then went to put a finger into Arabella's tiny hand as she snuggled in Angela's arms. On the way back out, he had some instructions for Wade.

"Cammie's sister say make sure nobody in the house smokin' while the baby in there. Not even weed."

Wade nodded. "I guess it might be time to give that up, too." *Great, just when it's finally about to become legal. What the fuck am I going to have left?* "Thank you for giving this a shot."

"I should be the one thankin' you, Doc."

"We haven't done anything yet," Wade said. "It's up to the women, in the end."

Jackson nodded. "Always up to the women."

"You want to bring Cammie by tomorrow, see what she thinks?"

"Lara prob'ly kill me if she know I'm gonna see Cammie again. Won't need no gun neither—just shoot me down with that death-ray she got in her eyeballs."

"Maybe you can give me Cammie's number, then, and her sister's, and I'll invite them both over to meet Angela and see the house, give them the grand tour."

"Bad idea, Doc. Them sisters hate each other. Cammie hate her whole family, really. Blame 'em for how she mess everything up. She only give the baby to her sister cuz her father say she have to. You bring them two together, they liable to beat each other's ass right in front of the baby. Trust me, you don't want to get in the middle of that."

"Okay, well, maybe separate visits then, or blindfolds and handcuffs. We'll figure something out."

"Don't matter to me if Cammie's family don't have too much to do with this. You and your wife decide you want to raise Arabella, Cammie might let you have her just to piss her sister off."

Okay, if that's the play, I guess we'll have to cross Big Sis off the babysitter list.

"You two raise her, she be a professor like you, or a doctor or a lawyer, somethin' important like that."

"We may be getting a little ahead of ourselves," Wade said. *With daughters, it's hard,* Allenby had said. The smartest guy in the world, and look what happened to *his* kids. A girl Wade tried to raise could wind up pregnant at fourteen, by some prince like Tommy, then face-down in a gutter five years later, with track marks all over her arms. He fought off the shadow of a self-fulfilling prophecy and forced himself to focus on a more uplifting outcome—and a practical consideration: "If she makes it into medical school, I'm not sure I'll still be around to foot the bill. You and the Giants might have pay for it."

"You got a deal, Doc. Who knows, maybe my little girl will even run for President some day. Get rid of guns and wars and shit like that."

"She's got my vote," Wade said. "As long as she doesn't get rid of baseball and football, too."

"I guess I'm good without football." Jackson flexed his mended leg before stepping back behind the wheel of his car.

Wade nodded, hypocrite again: he knew he'd be glued to the tube come September to see what Harbaugh could pull off at Michigan this year and how the 49ers would fare again without him. It might not be pretty, but, like a train wreck, it would still be hard not to watch. By then, of course, there might be *Sesame Street* and *Captain Underpants* to contend with for control of the household entertainment.

"Good luck in Texas." As soon as he saw Angela, Wade had realized he would have to pass on accompanying the team to the Regionals. He was sure she would tell him it was okay for him to go, but he knew even more certainly that he wasn't going anywhere, now that she was back. CSU's historic season would go forth without him. He could live with it. He put his hand through the car window and gave Jackson's shoulder a squeeze. "I'll be watching every inning on TV."

"We'll try to take care of business."

"We'll try to take care of your daughter."

Jackson drove home to pack for a crack at the College World Series. Wade went back into his house to find Angela feeding Arabella from a bottle. Still cooing. Would this get old?

"Do you want to hold her?"

Did he? Wade wasn't sure.

"Sure," he said, reaching to accept the bundle. It was another of those offers you really weren't allowed to decline. How hard could it be, though? Eighteen years or so ago he must at some point have held his niece when she was a baby. He had a distinct memory of getting spit up on: Gerber's mixed carrots and Wade's Budweiser. (He had recklessly supplied a surreptitious sip before it came spewing back to hit him in the lip, their dirty little secret not merely revealed but transmitted in Technicolor and 3-D.) Some things were hard to forget.

The alarm went off almost immediately now.

"You can't hold a baby like she's a hand grenade, Wade."

"Oh. Sorry. I didn't realize I was—"

"Better give her back."

After Arabella had been put down for a nap, Wade brought Angela up to speed on family background.

"Oh, great," she said. "Add incest victim to promiscuous drug user in the genetic make-up you're offering me."

"Don't forget *drop out*," Wade reminded his alcoholic, porn-slut wife. "Cammie had to go back for a GED. But that's only half of the picture. This baby's got Juke Jackson on the other side. Half-black, half-Mexican, with white parents—what could be more All American than that?"

Angela nodded, appearing to concede the point. "Unless I dumped you for an Asian guy or a Navaho."

"Always an option." At least she hadn't said an Asian *and* a Navaho.

"What about my job, though?"

"Erica's tired of doing double duty at all the meetings. She really wants you to come back and be dean again." He told her about the presidency that Erica might or might not want.

"How about you? What do you want?"

"I really want you to come back, too. But I don't care if you go back to being dean. In fact"—he paused, took a deep breath, *what the fuck*, next to the baby this was nothing, and let it fly—"if she keeps the dean job or moves up, either way, Erica offered me the department chair, which would be a little more money for us. If you wanted to quit your job and stay home full-time so you could . . . bond with the baby or whatever, I'd be—"

"Are you out of your fucking mind?"

"Probably."

"You'd be going to meetings all day, and I'd be staying home with—"

"The most beautiful baby you've ever—"

"—an infant who can't even speak, let alone identify an objective correlative. We'd be ready to kill each other in a week."

"I'll bet we could last a month. You don't have to decide today."

He sat down next to her and leaned in for a kiss. She pulled back.

"Chairman Mal. Now I've heard everything. What about your book?"

"The publishing industry isn't exactly breathing down my neck to bring out the next *Fifty Shades*. I could put that on the back burner for a while."

"It can keep company there with mine, then."

"Okay by me. Or you can write your ass off while you're staying home and taking care of the—"

"Dickhead. Only a man could come up with *that* plan. That's how babies drown in the toilet or get snuffed in the fridge."

"Okay, no bookmaking for a while then."

"We don't have to worry about money in the meantime. My dad bought Amazon at $200 per a few years ago. He left it all to me—to *us*, I mean."

How many shares? Wade wondered but managed to suppress.

"What was really hard was not using some of it to pay off Ronnie. I just didn't believe I could trust him to keep his word."

Wade nodded. Dealing with Ronnie was sort of like dealing with the ayatollahs and their nukes: *Trust but verify* just wasn't going to cut it. At some point you had to step back and let Mossad blow up a few suspicious types with plutonium under their fingernails.

"I just hope he doesn't show up here," Angela added.

"I'm still shopping for a shooter to take out Tommy; I'm sure someone in the guild has a two-for-one special going this month."

"Don't forget Einstein," Angela said. "Anyway, there's plenty of money, in case you have cold feet about those meetings, or if you just want to take it easy for a while."

It had taken Wade forty years in the work force to find a full-time job he didn't despise, and he wasn't sure he was willing to give it up just yet, but this was another reminder that, as Allenby had persuaded him (and as Juke Jackson had already figured out), investing could yield some gratifying returns. Amazon was trading around $800 per share now. However warranted the hue and cry about the one percent and corruption on Wall Street, average Americans had every opportunity to increase their own wealth if they just paid attention to individual stocks or put some money into a vanilla fund like the Vanguard 500 every month instead of blowing whole paychecks on crap they didn't need, like cable TV packages with a thousand channels they never watched.

Angela rested her head on the couch and eyed the Samsung. "I've completely lost track of the Giants. Are they playing today?"

Oops. Even lacking a hardcore option, Wade had a pretty pricy cable bill himself. Certain allowances had to made.

"They beat the Dodgers in L.A." Wade had flipped through the victory on the DVR while Angela was sleeping. "Posey won the game with a sacrifice fly."

The Giants' telegenic superstar was Angela's favorite player. Wade imagined she'd be just about as happy to see him again as she was to see her husband—maybe more. Much better teeth and hair. Wade touched his scalp and wondered if anything was going to grow back up there.

"Good for him. So are we in first place?"

"Three games up now. Kershaw snapped Buster's hitting streak, though."

"Too bad," she said, with a stagy cluck and a sorrow-struck shake of her head, *followed hard upon* by a beatific smile that would have done no shame to Mother Teresa at the top of her game. "But, you know, Wade, everything happens for a—"

"Fuck you, Angela."

"I knew you'd say that." She grinned wickedly now, all the way back in spirit if not yet in flesh, then nestled closer on the couch and nuzzled Wade's ear. "Maybe he'll start a new one tomorrow."

Wade kissed her gently and put his arm again around her slender shoulders, hoping he wasn't holding on too tight. "Maybe he will."

QUESTIONS FOR DISCUSSION

1. How would you describe the relationship between Wade and Juke Jackson? What brings them together in spite of their differences, and what do they contribute to each other's lives?

2. What was your reaction to scenes involving Juke's interaction with municipal and campus police? Can you compare any personal experiences with law enforcement officers? How has the Black Lives Matter movement affected your views of law enforcement?

3. How did you respond to the characterization of Angela in this novel? How did the revelations about her history affect you? Does the "double standard" for men and women enter into your own feelings about her? How did you respond when Wade told her there was "nothing to forgive?" Do you think she will be able to forgive herself? Explore the theme of forgiveness in the novel and in your life.

4. What does this book have to say about fatherhood? Comment on the development of this theme through its part in the lives of Allenby, Jackson Sr., Trip (Lara's boyfriend), Juke, and Wade.

5. What does this book have to say about contemporary university education? How did you respond to the description of Wade's feelings about teaching and his interaction with students or former students? Have you ever had a teacher like Carlotta Baynes? How did you feel about her defense of her grading practices? What impact did Wade's revelation from his student days about helping another student too

much have on your feelings about him and about academic integrity issues? Have you ever given or received more help on an assignment than you should have?

6. What do the scenes involving Camellia, Erica, Lara, Norma, Monica, and Clara contribute to the novel? Have you met someone whose behavior compares with the behavior of one or more of these characters?

7. Allenby tells Wade, "It's never *over* with an ex." Do you agree or disagree? What was the impact of Wade's visit to Brenda and Tommy? How did you react to Wade's comments about "unconditional love?"

8. How did you respond to the description of Stockton in this novel? Compare your own response if you have lived or visited there.

9. What impact did Allenby's statements at the press conference have on you? What do you think was the most important thing that he said? What do you think about his plan to bring ROTC (Reserved Officers Training Corps) back to the CSU campus? How can you relate the impact on him of his experiences in Vietnam to what you have learned about others' experiences in or after war?

10. This novel pays tribute to the role that black baseball players had in the integration of the U.S. What examples can you think of, past or present, of athletes who served or serve as positive or negative role models and/or took or take important or controversial political stances? Hall of Fame basketball player turned commentator Charles Barkley has famously said that athletes shouldn't be expected to be role models; he says that children's role models should be their parents,

teachers, and civic leaders. Do you agree or disagree with him? Relate your response to the novel.

11. The novel raises the issue of the traumatic injuries often suffered by football players, suggesting that baseball is a more feasible career path, especially for African Americans, who fill a disproportionately high percentage of positions on college football and NFL teams. What impact did Jackson's football experience have on you, and how do you account for your own interest or lack thereof in football? Compare this with your interest in other sports and explain your preferences.

12. How did you respond to the decisions about their pregnancies made by Lara and Camellia, and to Wade's role in resolving each of those situations? What you would have done in either case? Consider this exchange of dialog: Wade asks, "Don't you think the world is confusing enough for a kid without adding pigmentation issues into the mix? Shouldn't black babies be raised by black parents?" Angela replies, "Don't be an idiot. Babies need food, shelter, clothing—and love—not coloring lessons." Who wins this rhetorical exchange? One early reader of the novel said that her jaw dropped at the very notion that Wade and Angela might make better parents for Arabella than her birth mother would. What do you think about that?

13. What were your most and least favorite scenes in the novel? Who were your most and least favorite characters?

14. Which character, scene, or theme from this novel has the most direct relevance to your life? Why?

15. Compare this novel with another book you have read or a film you have seen.

AN INTERVIEW WITH
THE AUTHOR

1. Your previous novels dealt with college basketball and college football. College baseball has a considerably lower profile. Why turn to that topic now?

Baseball was my first love. It some ways it remains the sport closest to my heart. The role it played in the integration of our country has always held special interest for me. Having grown up watching and worshiping Willie Mays, I've always especially admired the verve that black players brought to the game, and I've been appalled by the decline in their numbers at the MLB level and by the failure of our colleges and universities to provide opportunities for them. As Allenby says in the novel, and as Professor Richard Lapchick has often and eloquently reminded us, our institutions of higher education ought to be leading the way in promoting opportunities for minority student-athletes and coaches in all sports. A specific problem I wanted to highlight is that universities are making it harder rather than easier for student-athletes to develop their talents in baseball by limiting them to one sport, which is especially unfortunate because the risk of disabling injury is so much greater in football. Everyone remembers what happened to Bo Jackson. Consider also what Antwan Randall El, suffering from memory loss at age thirty-six, said in 2016: "I love the game of football, but right now I could still be playing baseball."

I also wanted to call attention in this book, as in my previous ones, to universities' exploitation of black student-athletes. Too many college presidents and head coaches are playing the corporate raider game, building their own careers and salaries on the backs of student-athletes. As Professor Boyce Watkins said, "universities make it very clear that their number one priority is to make money, not to educate athletes. What they do is they educate white kids with money earned by black kids on the basketball court and the football field. It's really a transfer of wealth due to the labor of what you might call indentured servants."

2. You dedicated your first book in part to Mays, featured him prominently in your second, and he's all over this one. What gives?

There's a contemporary historian at USC, Daniel Durbin, conducting interviews of the living black players who followed Jackie Robinson into Major League Baseball, from 1947 to 1971. One of the recurring themes of his conversations with these men is the astounding greatness of Willie Mays. These guys, who played with and against him and saw first-hand what he did day after day when he took the field, are still in awe of him almost half a century later. Curt Flood and a few others criticized Mays for not being more active in Civil Rights, but I'd make the argument that the example he set for Americans of all colors by the way he conducted himself was an important part of that movement. Barack Obama acknowledged this when he presented Mays with the Presidential Medal of Freedom. Progress comes in many forms. As James Hirsch reported in his bio of Mays, Stan Musial, aboard a train bound for a distant All-Star game, sits down at a table where Mays and his friends are playing cards and says he wants to join them. "But we're all black," Willie points out. "So what?" says Musial. "Deal me in." Small acts like that break down prejudice and get passed on to others every day. When Musial died, Mays said of him, "I never heard anyone say a bad word about him."

I think Rob Manfred, the Commissioner of Major League Baseball, spoke for millions when he said, after coming to the 2016 All-Star game, "this trip to San Francisco's now officially worthwhile. I just got to spend five minutes with Willie Mays." I also was lucky enough to spend a few minutes with him, and the conversation remains one of the highlights of my life. Other than my dad and an uncle, Mays is the man—not just the ballplayer, but the man—I grew up most wanting to be. He's the reason I've never had a cigarette in my mouth, including the kind that Malcolm Wade partakes of from time to time.

3. Wade is the protagonist of your previous two novels as well as this one. How much of this character is autobiographical?

Most of Wade's scenes are just stuff I made up. The truth is he has a lot more fun than I do—and gets in a lot more trouble.

4. Juke Jackson joins Marvin Walker and Marcus Foster from your previous books as another African American student-athlete with whom Wade bonds. Are these characters based on real students you have known?

All of them are inventions or amalgams. In one of the first college classes that I taught, there was a kid recruited to play football who couldn't read, as I discovered when I asked him to participate in a read-aloud session in class. A few years later on the same campus a basketball recruit from Harlem was falsely accused of a serious crime. Several faculty members who knew him well, including Bob Williams, later head coach at UC Davis and UC Santa Barbara, produced exculpatory evidence, but the police investigating the case, the D.A. prosecuting it, and the judge presiding over it weren't interested in what we discovered. The judge actually kicked me out of the courtroom when I revealed specifically relevant crimes committed by members of the family accusing our student. That trial was the most dramatic experience I've had in an otherwise sheltered career. I could hardly eat or sleep: during the two weeks of testimony I lost ten pounds. As we were sitting in the courtroom (after my ban expired) waiting for the verdict, my heart was pounding so hard I thought I was going to have a heart attack. Fortunately, and remarkably, this young man kept his composure through the whole ordeal, and his own voluntary testimony proved to be the key to his exoneration. After the "Not guilty" verdict was announced, one of the white women on the jury approached us, gave him a hug, and said, "You get on with your life, young man." We lost touch and then, twenty years later, he tracked me down in the Writing Lab at Delta College, put his arms around me, and said, "I love you." He let me know that he had served in the Gulf War, earned a law degree, and thrived in a career finding homes for disabled orphans. While inventing many details of the characters, I've had that young man in my heart and mind while writing about Marvin, Marcus, and Juke.

Also, after writing about the tragedy of black-on-black crime in *Desperation Passes*, I wanted to acknowledge in *Where Triples Go to Die* the recurring problems that too many black Americans continue to face with improper police enforcement. When I visited a class taught by a colleague, Julie Artesi, and brought up the issue of Driving While Black, I mentioned that in fifty years as a licensed driver, I've been pulled over by officers a total of four times. A young African American male in the class said that he had once been pulled over four times in one *day*. That revelation formed part of the backstory that went into Juke Jackson's character. While my own experiences with law enforcement officers have usually been positive, and respect for the dangerous work they do remains my prevailing response, I wanted to show my awareness that this isn't the case for everyone.

5. Apart from race and baseball, you focus in this novel, as in your others, on sex, and you're not shy about using explicit language. Has that caused any issues for you?

Many of my readers so far have been students, some of them basically captured at gunpoint, and a few of them, especially those from devoutly religious backgrounds, are offended by the language in my novels. I tell them I decided a long time ago that I wanted to write in what Ben Jonson called "the words that men do use." I'm trying to confront issues of race and sex honestly and in accurate contemporary vernacular, mindful even in my own obscurity of my debt to giants like Edward Albee and Philip Roth for liberating the language of modern drama and fiction from previous constraints. Anyone who reads much contemporary literature will regularly see far more detailed sexual descriptions than anything I have written. I'm most often trying to use the abundant humiliations of carnal pursuit to make readers laugh rather than to turn them on. I've also tried to be clear in repudiating inappropriate sexual behavior of all kinds, another continuing major issue on college campuses that I'm trying to call attention to. I keep hoping my books will be banned in Boston or Stockton or some other place equally relevant to the literary scene, because I could sure use the publicity, but so far, no such luck.

6. You don't pull any punches in your description of Stockton. Are you anticipating any blowback from that?

I was attacked a block from my home in Stockton, and a colleague at Delta College had a shotgun pointed in his face a few blocks from the campus, so I have no illusions about the dangers of this city. On the other hand, I love lots of things about living and teaching here, and you won't find a better example of the melting pot anywhere in America. People of every color and ethnic origin are working hard to improve their lives here. Instead of blow-back, I'm hoping for progress. Columnist Michael Fitzgerald and Assemblywoman Susan Eggman, among others, have repeatedly raised the issue of the need for a California State University in Stockton, and I'm hoping this book will contribute in its own small way to advancing that cause, so that "the least literate city in America" can get the resources it needs and deserves to address its deficiencies.

7. Your books, including *Where Triples Go to Die*, are full of literary allusions—to Shakespeare, Milton, Samuel Johnson, Byron, Dickens, Mencken, Hemingway, and Faulkner, to name just a few. Any concern that these will go over the heads of readers who think they have picked up a book about baseball?

It's true that all of those figures are cited, but so are Ernie Banks, Leo Durocher, Joe Morgan, Chris Rock, Richard Pryor, and lots of others not associated with literary masterpieces. There's a wonderful line in Richard Rush's film version of *Stunt Man*, mag-nificently delivered by Peter O'Toole as the madcap director Eli Cross, in lecturing his screenwriter: "If you've anything to say, it's best to slip it in while they're all laughing and crying and jerking off over the sex and violence." As in my previous books, with the epigraphs and other quotations I've tried to honor some of the authors and athletes who have inspired me—and to slip a few memorable lines in between the sex, the violence, and the sports.

8. You mentioned *Stunt Man*, and it's clear that movies in general have had a big impact on your characters. In *Where Triples Go to Die*, there's even a recurring bit of business involving identifying memorable movie lines. What do you say when confronted with the conventional bias that movies are seldom as satisfying as books?

Hemingway, like many other writers, often spoke dismissively of movies. On one such occasion, the director Howard Hawks replied by betting him that he could take the worst book Hemingway ever wrote and make a great movie out of it. Hemingway took him up on the challenge, and one way or another they agreed on *To Have and Have Not* as the least estimable of Hemingway's available works. Here's my favorite part of the story: Hawks then hired, among others, William Faulkner to work on the screenplay, thus enlisting the services of the one contemporary author whom Hemingway sometimes regarded as a worthy rival. The resulting movie, featuring Bogart and Bacall, bears little resemblance to Hemingway's novel, but it's an all-time classic, still eminently watchable today.

It's true that lots of terrible movies get made, and I suppose it's even true that *most* of the movies that get made are terrible, especially now that comic books seem to have become the primary source material, but it's still a thrill when you find a gem that moves you. A great movie, with the advantages of soundtrack and cinematography, including visual flashbacks, can be every bit as satisfying as a great novel. The connection that Wade and Angela have over movies that have meant something to them is part of what holds them together, however tenuously, in spite of the forces pulling them apart.

9. President Obama appears in several of your epigraphs. It seems fair to assume that he has earned your admiration. How much of the characterization of Allenby is based on Obama?

I was raised by bedrock Eisenhower Republicans, and I still have abiding respect for the core values they instilled: work hard, pull your weight, serve your community, treat others with respect until they give you a reason not to, and don't start a fight you can't finish or a war you can't win. I think Obama embodies those values, too, along with all of the progressive ideals he has stood for. I think he's a noble man who did a remarkable job of leading our country in the face of almost inconceivable intransigence from the contemporary crackpot version of the GOP. And of course I was delighted to see him honor Willie Mays—who was also, by the way, just as a little model of the bi-partisanship we ought to be courting, the favorite player of George W. Bush (among millions of others) as well.

Allenby shares Obama's intelligence, integrity, and common sense, and the theme of emerging leadership opportunities for black Americans—or lack thereof—is certainly an important part of the novel. I got a bit of valid criticism from Tama Brisbane, the poet laureate of Stockton, for making Allenby too much of a "magical negro" in my previous book, so I tried in this one to include more details about what he sees as his own failures.

10. What's your next book going to be about? Have we seen the last of Malcolm Wade?

Well, at last glimpse Wade was swearing off booze and pot and taking a crack at raising a kid. Short of having him hit by a train, I can't think of a more climactic kiss-off for his character arc.

Whatever comes next, I can promise you that it won't be about Wade and the college hockey squad.

What I'd really like to work on now is getting a book of students' writing published. My colleagues Will Agopsowicz and Bob Bini, continuing a project begun by Jane Dominik, have provided a splendid role model with the literary magazine *Delta Winds*. The ways that our students have found to meet the many challenges that life puts in their path—certainly far more than I ever faced—are truly humbling and inspiring. To share their writing with a wider audience would be the most rewarding work I can envision.

AN ELEGY FOR ROBERTO

I cried when Roberto died.
I actually cried.
It had been a long time between tears,
Years, perhaps, since my last,
And I'd thought my time for tears had passed,
That after Kennedy and King and Kennedy again,
After Watts and Huế and My Lai,
There was nothing left to make me cry.
I was all of twenty-two and what was there
That death could do
That it hadn't done a billion times before?
I'd thought, you see, that no man's death
Could diminish me any more.

I thought I'd never cry again,
But when I heard the New Year's news,
I cried for Clemente then
And cried for all who must endure
The ineffable agony of living in this world,
Where a man of courage and compassion
Reaches out his hand
To his afflicted fellow man
And for the taking of this trouble *dies*
As flies to wanton boys.
(Oh God, so now he's a tragic hero, eh?)
Yes. He is no prince, perhaps, in the usual sense,
But then Hamlet never hit three-fifty
That I know of,
Managua matters just as much as rotten Denmark,
And I shall not look upon his like again.

Remember:
That crazy man
Crashing the wall and catching the ball
That could not be caught;
Lashing the pitch a foot outside and over his eyes
Over the fence and out of the lot;
Throwing out by fifteen feet the rook so rash
He thought he'd flash from first to third
Before he got The Word:
"Don't run on The Great One, son,
Unless you like the pay
In Triple-fuckin'-A."
That was Roberto.
He is gone now,
And there is only the pallid consolation
That while all that lives must die,
A man may die in many ways,
Disease, decrepitude may drag out his days,
But Roberto died, as he lived,
In reckless questing crashing style;
We'll remember him thus,
At the top of his bent,
At the peak of his powers,
As that proud man would want to be
Remembered.

And perhaps whenever these memories move us,
At any time, in any town,
Anywhere in the world,
When we see another man
Taking the ball off the right field wall
And making the play perfectly,

Or when we hear of another man who loves his life

Yet loses it, for the sake of something higher,

Then that will be Roberto's resurrection.

And the ghost of the Great One will walk the land,

Not for forty lousy days, but always,

In sunshine and in thunder,

On Opening Day and when the earth bursts asunder

In its wantonest way,

Roberto will be there

Redeeming our race

With the gift of his grace,

Forever, *usque ad finem*,

As long as the game goes on.

—January 1973, revised July 2017

Author's note: Roberto Clemente led the Pittsburgh Pirates to two World Series titles, in 1960 and 1971. In 1972, he got his 3000th hit in the final game of his career. In December of that year, he died in a plane crash in an attempt to bring supplies to the victims of an earthquake in Managua, Nicaragua, and to keep the supplies out of the hands of the corrupt regime of Anastasio Somoza. In 1973 Clemente became the first Latin American player elected to Major League Baseball's Hall of Fame, and he remains the only player for whom the Hall's five-year post-playing career waiting period was waived. The first winner of baseball's Humanitarian of the Year Award, posthumously named in Clemente's honor, was the San Francisco Giants' Willie Mays.

ACKNOWLEDGMENTS

Publication of this book was made possible by a grant from The Human Fund. I thank George Costanza for directing my attention to this unique (*very* unique, as my students would say) organization.

I am grateful to Sean Jones and the staff at Inkwater Press, especially Michael Ebert for his inspired work on this book's design. I also thank my previous publishers, Dr. Robert Katz at Willowgate Press, and Paula Sheil and Robert Reinarts at Tuleburg Press (with extra thanks to Diane Smith and her crew at Tokay Press and to Michael Oliva for his outstanding cover art). I would not have written this book without their help in getting my others into print. I thank Elinor Fox for reviewing my manuscript and for giving me honest criticism of my previous books that I hope has helped me to improve on them with this one, and Patrick Wall for his generous and meticulous list of corrections.

I owe thanks for help with the research for this book to Cathie Moss at the Negro Leagues Baseball Museum in Kansas City and to Professor Richard Lapchick, Director of the Institute for Diversity and Ethics in Sport at the University of Central Florida and author of the annual (and indispensable) *Racial and Gender Report Cards.*

I am indebted to the reviewers who have deemed my fiction worthy of their attention, especially James A. Cox in *Midwest Book Review*, Molly Culbertson in *Manhattan Book Review*, Candace Andrews in *inside english*, Tony Sauro in *The Record*, Howard Lachtman in *The Current*, and Jack Saunders at Delta College.

My friend Anna Villegas, the best writer I know, has been a continual source of encouragement and inspiration. To any readers who have not yet dipped into them, I recommend her three novels (*All We Know of Heaven,* and, with Lynne Hugo, *Swimming Lessons* and *Baby's Breath*) and many splendid short stories.

I have benefited from many enlightening conversations with former Willamette University second baseman Jeff Topping, previously a full professor at Mississippi State and now my esteemed colleague, and with fellow aficionados Joe Gonzales (the best colleague, boss, and friend a man could hope for), Matt Wetstein, and Sam Hatch. Pat Doyle, formerly head coach at Delta College and also of Team USA in the Baseball World Cup, was the source of the anecdote about Ted Williams and the slider.

I have taken some liberties with football and baseball schedules. Nebraska did not play in August in 2015, and the first game on its schedule in early September that year was actually a competitive one, which the Cornhuskers lost, to BYU. The next week South Alabama visited Lincoln and paid the price: 48-9. The Major League Baseball draft normally occurs during the Super Regional round of the college playoffs, so I have (wishfully) speeded up the timetable for Juke Jackson and God's own team. I invented, in service to one of the novel's strands and in homage to two of the current generation's greats, the game in which Clayton Kershaw ended Buster Posey's hitting streak. A check of the records will show that the Giants were indeed looking down on the Dodgers and the rest of the NL West in the spring and early summer of 2016 before a precipitous post All-Star Game plunge and a bullpen meltdown in the playoffs put an end to their run of even-year magic.

I am honored that some of my colleagues have elected to share my books with their students, including Julie Artesi, Ginger Holden, Eric MacDonald, Matt Marconi, Pamela Pan, Zachary Prince, Rebel Rickansrud, Paula Sheil, James Van Dyke, and Kevin Walcott, with results that have been generally positive (although not exclusively—no author not named Patterson can claim to please everyone). I hope I have not left anyone out and will gladly stand corrected if I have.

I thank collectively the many other colleagues, students, and friends who have taken the time to read my books and to send me their thoughts, especially those who have posted reviews of their own on Amazon.com. I am blessed with a lot of very literate and generous friends. I thank also my teammates on the Woodside Plaza Merchants and B&D Sports for contributing to the trove of baseball memories tapped within these pages.

Finally, I thank my always first and best reader Joan Bailey, not only for her eagle-eyed editing but also for a lifetime of laughter and love.

A NOTE ABOUT THE AUTHOR

Phil Hutcheon grew up in Redwood City, California, where his youth baseball teammates included Dick Sharon, later of the Detroit Tigers and San Diego Padres. With his father he attended games at Seals Stadium and Candlestick Park in San Francisco during the heyday of Willie Mays. He earned a bachelor's degree from University of the Pacific and a PhD from Rice University. He teaches composition and film at Delta College. He has also taught at Pacific and at Menlo College. *Where Triples Go to Die* is his third novel. He can be contacted at phutcheon@deltacollege.edu or at inkwaterpress.com.

CPSIA information can be obtained
at www.ICGtesting.com
Printed in the USA
FSHW020719211218
54616FS

9 781629 015149